Globalization and Change in Higher Education

Beverly Barrett

Globalization and Change in Higher Education

The Political Economy of Policy
Reform in Europe

For Cullum,
Best regards and thank you
for contributing to this piece!

palgrave
macmillan

Beverly Barrett

Beverly Barrett
University of Houston
Houston, TX
USA

ISBN 978-3-319-52367-5   ISBN 978-3-319-52368-2   (eBook)
DOI 10.1007/978-3-319-52368-2

Library of Congress Control Number: 2017937466

Cover image: © Igor Sorokin/Alamy Stock Vector
Design inspired by architecture of Bologna, Italy

Printed on acid-free paper

This Palgrave Macmillan imprint is published by Springer Nature
The registered company is Springer International Publishing AG
The registered company address is: Gewerbestrasse 11, 6330 Cham, Switzerland

To my parents, who have fostered a love of learning

FOREWORD

The combined impact of globalization, technology, and demographics is changing the landscape of higher education worldwide. Europe is not an exception: The internationalization of higher education and its institutions has continued to accelerate since the Bologna Process was launched nearly two decades ago.

In this context of transformation, Beverly Barrett's book shows how much governance and the political economy influence higher education policies. There is increasing value placed on quality higher education attainment, namely, for its teaching of individual competencies in an increasingly competitive and technological world.

The key explanation for the policy reforms in higher education considered in this book is the political economy at multiple levels of governance. There is an emphasis on countries in the European Union (EU) that are part of the European Higher Education Area (EHEA). Complementarily, the Europe 2020 objectives for higher education provide a benchmark that values attainment, specifically for EU member countries.

Since the Bologna Process launch nearly 20 years ago to create the EHEA, the European Commission has a been a partner alongside the participating countries, providing support for education initiatives in the region and globally. During the years that I served in the Directorate-General for Education and Culture, we witnessed the role of education becoming even more central in our societies and economies.

Unprecedented in scope, this twenty-first century initiative recognizes education as central to cohesion, and as a solution to overcome the financial crisis. The countries participating in the EHEA have pursued their interests while incorporating European qualifications agreed upon at the conferences of education ministers that take place every several years.

From the case studies in this book, we learn lessons from Portugal and Spain's experiences in policy implementation. Portugal served as a member of the Pathfinder group of countries, between 2012 and 2015, for national recognition of academic degrees in the EHEA. Spain reformed its education system at the national level to integrate into Europe, while its 17 autonomous communities maintain prerogatives that provide for variations in educational features across the country.

As the EU has enlarged over recent decades, the harmonization of higher education across its member countries and in the broader region of Europe has become increasingly relevant to regional integration. The EHEA has provided a model for a regional qualifications framework in higher education. Similarly, countries in Asia and Latin America are following this model to establish regional qualifications frameworks.

The recent history of higher education policy reform in Europe provides a foundation for continuing to work together in additional functional areas across the region. Dr. Barrett's book provides a thoughtful, comprehensive analysis of the historical developments that brought about the changes in higher education we are witnessing today.

Xavier Prats-Monné
European Commission, Director General
Directorate-General for Health and Food Safety, 2015–
Director General, Directorate-General for Education
and Culture, 2014–2015
Deputy Director, General Directorate-General
for Education and Culture, 2010–2014

PREFACE

Globalization and technological advances have been hallmarks of geopolitical and economic change since the end of the Cold War. Since the beginning of the 1990s they have had a significant influence on the trajectory of national economies, individual opportunity, and higher education systems worldwide.

The expansion of the European Union (EU) has been a part of this wave of globalization. At the end of the Cold War, there were 12 EU member states; today there are 28. The region of Europe experienced political, economic, and social change as the EU enlarged eastward. The project to establish the Economic and Monetary Union (EMU), among select countries within the EU, introduced the common currency, the euro, in 1999. This temporally intersected with the initial meeting of European education ministers to launch the Bologna Process on June 19, 1999. The objective was to establish the European Higher Education Area (EHEA) by 2010.

The Bologna Process and EHEA were instrumental in unifying European countries to work toward a common framework for higher education. At the time, there were more than a dozen candidate countries to accede to the EU, all eager to participate in this unprecedented initiative in the regional integration of higher education. On the heels of Europe's establishment of a common market—known as the Single Market—as an economic partnership in 1992, the Bologna Process and

EHEA formulated qualifications for recognizing academic degrees across participating countries to create a unifying higher education system.

Despite these steps toward Europeanization, the outcome of the recent United Kingdom (UK) referendum (June 23, 2016) on whether to exit or remain in the EU—which became known as Brexit—demonstrated the desire of the majority of UK voters to exit. This has been interpreted by some as a rejection of globalization, but whatever the underlying sentiment of the UK populous, the old adage attributed to the Greek philosopher Heraclitus rings true: Change is the only constant.

Nevertheless, globalization—defined as the interconnectedness of economic, political, cultural, and technological activity—continues. The ideas of a cohesive Europe and the institutions to enable recognition of academic qualifications, constructed by the Bologna Process, reflect a sociocultural European identity and the aim for a dynamic, growing economy in the twenty-first century. These geopolitical changes have been especially powerful in the decades following World War II, which divided Europe politically. The challenge is for each country and its citizens to define their economy's and culture's relationship to globalization in our time.

This book provides explanations for change in a political economy context, where the interests of sovereign states and economic markets intersect. It complements research on regional integration in Europe that has expanded from economic and political cooperation post-World War II into newer policy areas, including education in recent decades. In the twenty-first century, higher education institutions have increasingly played dual roles—as recipients of policy change from Europeanization and as agents of policy change in the knowledge economy that is characteristic of the twenty-first century. Some of the findings described in this book are the importance of consistency in political leadership, the structure of government, and dedicated funding for achieving higher education policy reform, as well as the significant relationship between gross domestic product (GDP) per capita and higher education attainment in the countries in the EU.

The process of Europeanization, as well as globalization and intergovernmentalism, has been a catalyst for higher education policy reform. Previous experiences provided me with observations of European cultural and social life. Bringing together my educational and professional experiences, I have attempted to assess the political, economic, and social contexts shaping higher education reform in the region of Europe.

Any errors and inconsistencies in this book are my own. As a student in Madrid, Spain, and in Bologna, Italy—as well as on a professional assignment in Helsinki, Finland—I learned about the transformation of countries in Europe. This led me to focus my doctoral research on political economy within the European Union Center of Excellence in Miami, Florida. Specifically, the Iberian countries have been compelling as case studies, given the political governance and socioeconomic changes that they experienced in the decades prior to joining the EU simultaneously in 1986.

My research findings on the European experience in higher education reform are instructive for other world regions. The interdisciplinary approach of my research in the social sciences helps to explain institutional change in economics and political science as well as to understand organizational change management in business.

This book is intended for students and researchers of globalization, international economics, and higher education policy. Further, it is hoped that all readers with an interest in international relations, regional integration, and institutional change will find this book informative and insightful.

Houston, USA   Beverly Barrett

The original version of the book was revised: For detailed information please see Erratum. The erratum to the book is available at https://doi.org/10.1007/978-3-319-52368-2_11

ACKNOWLEDGEMENTS

This book would not have been possible without the guidance and input from many people. The editors, Kathy O'Brien Adjemian and Teri Duncan Canal, were instrumental. Thank you to the entire publishing team at Palgrave Macmillan in London, especially Laura Aldridge and Eleanor Christie. Thank you to my doctoral fellowship professors at the University of Miami in International Studies, including Bruce Bagley, Roger Kanet, Laura Gomez-Mera, Nick Myers, Ruth Reitan, Joaquín Roy, and Bill Smith. Thanks also to Markus Thiel at Florida International University, who served on my dissertation committee with professors Kanet, Gomez-Mera, and Roy (Jean Monnet Professor at the European Union Center of Excellence) at the University of Miami.

The opportunity to attend the April 2012 European Higher Education Area (EHEA) Ministerial Conference in Bucharest, Romania, is much appreciated. In the months following, interviews with members of the Bologna Follow-Up Group provided insights into the progress of the policy reforms. In Spain, Rafael Bonete Perales generously provided knowledge about governance at the university level and at the national level. In Portugal, Maria de Lurdes Correia Fernandes, Vice Rector of the Universidade do Porto, kindly shared updates on the policy implementation process. Xavier Prats-Monné and Adam Tyson, both with the European Commission in Brussels, have been invaluable sources of knowledge. As former Director-General for Education and Culture and former Head of Higher Education and Erasmus, respectively, they have shared the requisite facts and updates regarding advances in higher education policy. Many thanks to officers in the Directorate General for Education and Culture, especially Krzysztof Kania, Patricia Pérez-Gómez, and Valerie Anderlin, who provided fundamental background and guidance on the higher education policy in Europe.

I sincerely thank each person who served as a primary source of research in qualitative interviews and correspondence. In Portugal, Alberto Amaral leading the *Agência de Avaliação e Acreditação do Ensino Superior* (A3ES), together with his fellow research scholars at the *Centro de Investigação de Políticas de Ensino Superior* (CIPES, Centre for Research in Higher Education Policy), provided valued insights and essential points to understand the Bologna Process reforms and their implementation at multiple levels of governance. Dr. Amaral's reviews, detailed explanations, and reference materials were very beneficial. A special thank you to Carmen Matilla Vicente, formerly at the Ministry of Education in Madrid, for serving as an insightful source of information about policy reform and the internationalization of higher education in Spain. Thank you to Rafael Llavori de Micheo at *Agencia Nacional de Evaluación de la Calidad y Acreditación* (ANECA) in Madrid and to József Temesi at Cornivus University's Center for International Higher Education Studies in Budapest for providing foundational facts and information to improve the quality of my research.

I thank the scholarly reviewers for generously taking the time to review and to comment on my doctoral dissertation project, on which this book is based, and in particular the qualitative case-study chapters comparing Portugal and Spain. These scholars include Carlos Eduardo Pacheco Amaral at the Universidade dos Açores, Manuel Cienfuegos at the Universitat Pompeu Fabra in Barcelona, Manuel Porto at the Universidade de Coimbra, and Luis Ritto at the International School of Protocol and Diplomacy in Brussels.

While I conducted research in Europe, friends living there were especially generous in welcoming and teaching me more about their countries through their eyes. Thank you to Afonso Januário and Diana Soller in Lisbon and, in Madrid, to Maria Fabregas de Cassinello and Marta Arespacochaga as well as their families. In memory I acknowledge Elizabeth McNeill-Leicester, a dear friend of Edith Colvard Crutcher, who inspired me with her stories of public service and friendships during her international career, which she chronicled in her many books. Many friends and colleagues provided encouragement in the research process, especially Cullen Geiselman, Laura Morgan Horton, Bernardo Goarmon, Jane Holston, Tracy Yonghong Liu, Alessandra Macri, Vanessa Meintjes, Rita Men, Tony Payan, Caroline Seureau Jinks, Sylva Talpová Žáková, Diana Urelius, and Rimi Zakaria. Utpal Dholakia, Anna Mikulska, Marwa Shalaby, and Ching-Hsing Wang kindly made recommendations and reviewed my quantitative analysis research, for which I am grateful. I hope to continue on an unending quest for learning, like Micky Wolfson, from whom I have learned about European culture and history, which has fascinated and enriched me. There are many others to whom I am grateful for the guidance they provided and the knowledge they shared about international education.

Contents

MEMBERS OF THE EUROPEAN HIGHER EDUCATION AREA

Country (EU member since)	Bologna process signatory
Albania	2003
Andorra	2003
Armenia	2005
Austria (1995)	1999
Azerbaijan	2005
Belgium (1952)	1999
Belarus	2015
Bosnia and Herzegovina	2003
Bulgaria (2007)	1999
Croatia (2013)	2001
Cyprus (2004)	2001
Czech Republic (2004)	1999
Denmark (1973)	1999
Estonia (2004)	1999
Finland (1995)	1999
France (1952)	1999
Georgia	2005
Germany (W. Germany 1952)	1999
Greece (1981)	1999
Hungary (2004)	1999
Iceland	1999
Ireland (1973)	1999
Italy (1952)	1999
Kazakhstan	2010
Latvia (2004)	1999
Liechtenstein	2001

(continued)

(continued)

Country (EU member since)	Bologna process signatory
Lithuania (2004)	1999
Luxembourg (1952)	1999
Macedonia	2003
Malta (2004)	1999
Moldova	2005
Montenegro	2007
Netherlands (1952)	1999
Norway	1999
Poland (2004)	1999
Portugal (1986)	1999
Romania (2007)	1999
Russia	2003
Serbia	2003
Slovakia (2004)	1999
Slovenia (2004)	1999
Spain (1986)	1999
Sweden (1995)	1999
Switzerland	1999
Turkey	2001
Ukraine	2005
United Kingdom (1973)	1999
Vatican City	2003

ABBREVIATIONS

AC	*Comunidad autónoma,* autonomous community (Spain)
ACF	Advocacy Coalition Framework
ANECA	*Agencia Nacional de Evaluación de la Calidad y Acreditación* National Agency for Quality Assessment and Accreditation (Spain)
ARWU	Academic Ranking of World Universities (Shanghai Jiao Tong University)
A3ES	*Agência de Avaliação e Acreditação do Ensino Superior* National Agency of Assessment and Accredition of Higher Education (Portugal)
ASEAN	Association of Southeast Asian Nations
BFUG	Bologna Follow-Up Group
CET	*Cursos de Especialização Tecnológica* Technological Specialization Courses (academic certification, Portugal)
CIP	Competitiveness and Innovation Framework Programme
CRUE	*Conferencia de Rectores de las Universidades Españolas* Conference of Rectors of Spanish Universities
CSIC	*Consejo Superior de Investigaciones Científicas* Advisory Council of Scientific Research (Spain)
DGEAC	Directorate General for Education and Culture (European Commission)
DGES	*Direção-Geral do Ensino Superior* Director General for Higher Education (Portugal)
DS	Diploma Supplement
EC	European Community
ECB	European Central Bank

ECSC	European Coal and Steel Community
ECTS	European Credit Transfer and Accumulation System
ECVET	European Credit System for Vocational Education and Training
EEC	European Economic Community
EES	European Employment Strategy
EFSF	European Financial Stability Facility
EFSM	European Financial Stability Mechanism
EHEA	European Higher Education Area
EMU	Economic and Monetary Union (of the European Union)
ENQA	European Association for Quality Assurance
EQAR	European Quality Assurance Register (for Higher Education)
EQF	European Qualifications Framework
ERA	European Research Area
ESG	European Standards and Guidelines (for Quality Assurance)
EU	European Union
FCT	*Fundação para a Ciência e a Tecnologia*
	Foundation for Science and Technology (Portugal)
FDI	Foreign Direct Investment
FHEQ	Framework for Higher Education Qualifications (Portugal)
GDP	Gross Domestic Product
GDP PC	Gross Domestic Product Per Capita
HEI	Higher Education Institution
IMF	International Monetary Fund
IPE	International Political Economy
ISCED	International Standard Classification of Education
LOU	*Ley Orgánica de Universidades*
	Act on Universities (Spain)
LOMLOU	*Ley Orgánica de Modificación de la Ley Orgánica de Universidades*
	Act Modifying the Act on Universities (Spain)
LRU	*Ley de Reforma Universitaria*
	University Reform Act (Spain)
MECES	*El Marco Español de Cualificaciones para la Educación Superior*
	Spanish Qualifications Framework for Higher Education (EHEA)
MECU	*El Marco Español de Cualificaciones*
	Spanish Qualifications Framework (Spain)
MercoSur	*Mercado Común del Sur*
	Common Market of the South (South America)
MFF	Multiannual Financial Framework (seven-year European Union budget)
NQF	National Qualifications Framework
OECD	Organisation for Economic Co-operation and Development
OMC	Open Method of Coordination

PALOP	*Países Africanos de Língua Oficial Portuguesa*
	African Countries with Official Portuguese Language
PISA	Programme for International Student Assessment
R&D	Research and Development
RUCT	*Registro de Universidades, Centros, y Títulos*
	Registry of Universities, Higher Education Centers, and Academic Degrees (Spain)
SMEs	Small and Medium-Size Enterprises
TEC	Treaty Establishing the European Community
TeSP	*Cursos Técnicos Superiores Profissionais*
	Advanced Professional Technical Courses (Portugal)
TFEU	Treaty on the Functioning of the European Union

LIST OF FIGURES

LIST OF TABLES

CHAPTER 1

Background on Higher Education Policy in Europe

By 2020 we are determined to achieve an EHEA where our common goals are implemented in all member countries to ensure trust in each other's higher education systems; where automatic recognition of qualifications has become a reality so that students and graduates can move easily throughout it; where higher education is contributing effectively to build inclusive societies, founded on democratic values and human rights; and where educational opportunities provide the competences and skills required for European citizenship, innovation and employment.
Yerevan Communiqué (excerpt), May 15, 2015

When 29 countries initially signed the Bologna Declaration in Bologna, Italy, on June 19, 1999, the idea was to complement the common market (called the Single Market in Europe since 1992) defined by four freedoms: goods, services, labor, and capital. The ultimate recognition of academic credits and degrees, together with the mobility of students and graduates, are the central priorities for the European Higher Education Area (EHEA).[1] The European Research Area (ERA) was introduced soon after with the European Commission's proposal in 2000 to the European Council, the European Parliament, the European Economic and Social Committee, and the European Committee of the Regions. The Erasmus international education program initiated by the European Commission in 1986 is a precedent to the Bologna Process, and its success inspired the idea for a broad regional educational integration scheme (Neave 2003a: 33; 2003b). The confidence in the effectiveness of the Erasmus program led policymakers to

© The Author(s) 2017
B. Barrett, *Globalization and Change in Higher Education*,
DOI 10.1007/978-3-319-52368-2_1

take the regional integration initiative a step further, beyond a student's limited period of study outside of the home country, to make academic degrees compatible across countries. This purpose remains steadfast to that of the European project: to create an ever closer union of Member States, with the "Europe of Knowledge" concept as the impetus for the Bologna Process (European Commission 1997).

THE BOLOGNA PROCESS'S ROLE IN "A EUROPE OF KNOWLEDGE"

In 1999, the Bologna Process began to advance the idea of a regional approach to higher education reforms and to meet the demands of the "knowledge economy" going into the twenty-first century. A knowledge economy emphasizes the value of education to cultivate an economy that is dominated by the service industry, technology and innovation, and investment in human capital (Powell and Snellman 2004).

As an effort to modernize the centuries-old university institutions in Europe, the launch of the Bologna Process followed the 1997 report of the European Commission "Towards a Europe of Knowledge." This report highlighted the challenges facing the European higher education systems (many of the most historic in the world, steeped in deep traditions) and the region to compete in the new global economy, which places a premium on information in a services-driven knowledge-based society. Soon after the Bologna Process launch, the European Commission, in 2000, presented the concept of the ERA and in 2007 established an ERA Board in the Commission Decision 2008/111 EC.[2]

The model to advance research and innovation took some inspiration from the United States, where there are academic partnerships with the business and the industry sectors to spur investment in research and development (R&D) (Mazza et al. 2008:9). Although these partnerships may be a valuable source of institutional revenue, there is criticism that financial investors, rather than academic autonomy, may drive the academic research agenda (Cantwell and Kauppinen 2014). The middle-ground perspective is that the industry–academia relationship is a partnership and that both institutions may jointly determine the direction of research that combines external financing and talent in the form of knowledge. In the Bologna Process, education and training to produce innovation and competitiveness among graduates are valued as requisites to build the knowledge economy.

There are various political, economic, and social factors that determine the implementation of the Bologna Process at the national level. Countries have pursued this non-binding, voluntary, soft policy in partnership with the European Commission, which provides guidance. As a broad commitment of economically and politically diverse countries, the requirements for the Bologna Process reforms are inclusive enough to be relevant to participating countries, from Andorra to Russia. In the multi-level governance of higher education in Europe, the national-level policy reform requires new legislation, and the institutional level of implementation takes additional time that varies across countries.

INFLUENCES OF GLOBALIZATION AND EUROPEANIZATION

Since the beginning of this millennium, new institutions and ideas have led to policy reform, changing the higher education landscape for nearly a quarter of the world's nations. Over the past two decades, the governance of higher education in Europe has taken place on multiple levels—institutional, national, and increasingly international. Especially because of advances in technology, the pressures of globalization are affecting these institutions at increasing speed. In response, higher education institutions in Europe continue to evolve within the framework that underpins the Bologna Process, the largest regional integration scheme in higher education policy, launched shortly before the dawn of the twenty-first century. Since then, the constructs of institutions and ideas reflect the momentum, even through the years of the global financial crisis encountered toward the end of the first decade (2007–2009). Institutions at the supranational level of the European Union (EU) influence the implementation of policies at the national level. The ideas emanating from the top-down process of Europeanization have not been exclusive to the 28 Member States in the EU but have extended beyond to include 48 countries, in total, that are participating in the Bologna Process. These ideas were born at the University of the Sorbonne in Paris on May 25, 1998, among the ministers of education of France, Germany, Italy, and the United Kingdom (UK). Their concept initially garnered institutional commitments from 29 countries, with the release of the Bologna Declaration taking place the following year in 1999. This landmark meeting at the end of the millennium paved the way for the institutions and ideas that would create the European Higher Education Area (EHEA).

The Bologna Declaration, creating the Bologna Process, is significant on multiple fronts. First, the site of the creation of this written commitment was in Bologna, the oldest university in the Western world, dating from 1088. The gathering of ministers of education in this historic location embraced the depth of history to envision a far-reaching future based on the ideas of the "knowledge economy" that would define the twenty-first century. The European Commission, the policy-making body of the EU, had issued a directive in 1997 acknowledging a "Europe of Knowledge" The Bologna Process set in motion the initiative to construct the EHEA by 2010, when the Ministerial Conference would take place in Budapest and Vienna. The initiative would create an institution to serve human purposes (North 1990, 2005; Scott 2014). That is to increase the attainment and the quality of higher education in the region of Europe, and, in turn, to strengthen the region with a sociocultural European identity and to support economic growth through employability of graduates (European Commission 2011).

The Bologna Process, which was launched in a period of economic growth in Europe, has been a relative success in regional educational integration. However, because of the subsequent state of the global political economy, challenges exist in the larger context, namely the high level of competition for employment that graduates face and competition with technology. The changes that have taken place in the political economy have impacted higher education policies. Adding to ongoing concerns about employment nationally and employability of graduates, the euro zone countries experienced a double-dip recession in 2009 and 2012.[3] The inclusion of countries in the broader region serves as a balancing mechanism to keep the Bologna Process initiative anchored and the momentum moving forward, even when there have been concerns about the future of the EU and the euro zone. On June 23, 2016, the UK popular referendum favored (by a thin margin) leaving the EU, an outcome now known as Brexit. Even with this political uncertainty about the EU, the EHEA continues with the 48 members. The US and UK educational systems—their three-tier degree structure (bachelor, master, and doctorate)—are models for reform. Institutionalizing the complementary degree structure is part of the Bologna Process reforms.

After the Bologna Process created the EHEA in 2010, the countries reaffirmed their commitments to higher education reform at the Bucharest Ministerial Conference in Romania in April 2012. This took place despite recessionary economic circumstances, including sovereign debt crises in the euro zone in the intervening two years. The Yerevan

Ministerial Conference in Armenia in June 2015 was the first ministerial meeting held outside of the EU, demonstrating the Bologna Process commitment to all participating countries in the region of Europe. This book explains the factors relating to the political economy, embedded in institutions and ideas, that influence the national-level policy reform and implementation of Bologna Process objectives. The power of institutions (Keohane and Nye 2012; Moravscik 1998; Simmons et al. 2006) and the diffusion of ideas (Börzel and Risse 2012; Katzenstein 2005; Risse 2007) explain this regional integration trend, which is unparalleled in the number of participating countries. Neoliberal institutions in international cooperation that promote social cohesion contribute to a robust regional political economy (Schmidt and Thatcher 2013). These institutions are the foundation for, and drivers of, the Bologna Process. Responding to threats to international security, in recent years the European Commission has declared education to be very important as a means of preventing radical extremism that can lead to terrorism, underscoring its crucial role in political, economic, and social stability (European Commission 2014, 2016).

Especially since the global financial crisis starting in 2007, there have been voices seeking to reverse trends in regional integration in Europe. The supranational design of the EU, with liberal democratic member states, provides for adaptation to excessive crises (Lefkofridi and Schmitter 2015). The design's flexibility takes into account preferences by the state and societal stakeholders in confronting resistance to change in policy areas such as economic and labor integration (as well as ongoing efforts for cooperation in higher education) in the post-financial-crisis context. The Greek sovereign debt crisis, which began in 2010, has heightened uncertainty about economic commitments and political associations within Europe and from external stakeholders (Matthijs and Blyth 2015). Additionally, Brexit has led policymakers into unchartered territory as the UK negotiates its exit from the Lisbon Treaty currently governing the EU, formally referred to as the Treaty on the Functioning of the European Union (TFEU).

CONTENT AND ORGANIZATION OF THE BOOK

Chapter 2 defines the Bologna Process and the national-level policy reform for the implementation of the degree structure criteria in the EHEA. In addition, it introduces the theoretical frameworks—policy coordination and institutional change—together with the policy processes of liberal intergovernmentalism and Europeanization. The theoretical frameworks are the basis for developing the research question about higher education attainment and regional integration. This research uses a mixed methodological approach with complementary qualitative and quantitative analyses to address the research question.

Chapter 3, on institutional change in higher education policy and the regional integration of education, presents a historical perspective for understanding liberal intergovernmentalism and Europeanization as it relates to higher education. Europeanization is a top-down process in which the states are recipients of supranational policy influences (Schmidt 2009b), while the states cooperate side-by-side in the process of intergovernmentalism (Moravcsik 1998). This chapter takes a historical institutional approach to understanding trends in regional integration and higher education policy convergence, alongside interacting process of intergovernmentalism and Europeanization (Bickerton et al. 2015; Pierson 2004). It explains that the Bologna Process, as international cooperation in higher education, is part of a path-dependent process of regional integration that began in the post-World War II era (Pierson 1996, 2000). Insights into the higher education dimension in regional integration are viewed from the dominant theoretical explanations provided by literature on international political economy, institutionalism, intergovernmentalism, and Europeanization.

Chapter 4 explains the dual roles of higher education institutions. They are recipients of policy change influenced from the European level. Additionally, they are agents of policy change in the knowledge-based economy that is more important in the twenty-first century.

Chapter 5 discusses opportunities and challenges for policy reform, approaching the topic from a perspective of historical institutionalism that lends to rational analysis. Statistical regression analysis uses panel data for cross-national statistical analysis of the select 26 EU countries between the years 2000 and 2014. This research method is useful to identify variables in the political economy that may facilitate implementation of the Bologna Process and Europe 2020 objectives.

Chapters 6–9 take a closer look at two case-study countries in the Iberian Peninsula. The process of higher education reforms and policy implementation is compared between the centralized government of Portugal and the decentralized government of Spain. There is evidence of intergovernmental and Europeanization processes that are considered in the two countries in depth. The five points of comparison in the qualitative analysis are national governance background, political economy context, and higher education governance (in Chaps. 6 and 7), the role of stakeholders in the policy process, and the modernization of higher education institutions through research and innovation (in Chaps. 8 and 9). In the qualitative case studies, Portugal is presented as pursuing intergovernmentalism and Spain as responding to Europeanization in implementing the Bologna Process. The analysis of these case-study countries reveals economic and political successes and challenges for policy reforms as part of the Bologna Process.

Chapter 8 reflects on the policy reform to implement the Bologna Process criteria, how this complements the Europe 2020 economic growth strategy, and how it may be a globalmodel for regional integration in higher education. This chapter summarizes conclusions and provides insights into the three explanatory dynamics within the political economy that influence the implementation of reforms in higher education in Europe: globalization, intergovernmentalism, and Europeanization. Analysis of regionalism in higher education policy compares the reforms in Europe to the progress of similar undertakings in other world regional groups such as North America, Latin America, Asia, and Africa. There is an emphasis on the unique ties between Portugal and Spain to Ibero-American countries. These countries in Latin America, with a colonial heritage, are modeling some of the reforms being implemented in Europe. Reflecting the trajectory of the Bologna Process over the first decade-and-a-half, perspective is provided on the near-term commitments in the second decade toward the year 2020 and beyond. Participating countries have achieved policy coordination to converge upon some objectives, as the Bologna Process operates in its second decade and the EHEA has delivered considerable progress on reforms. There remain challenges in achieving the objectives of automatic recognition of academic degrees and mobility of students, as countries vary in outcomes in these areas.

NOTES

1. The European Credit and Transfer and Accumulation System (ECTS) was introduced as part of the Bologna Process. It has become the European standard for measuring higher education credits across countries.
2. European Commission. 2013. European Research Area. Available from: http://ec.europa.eu/research/era/understanding/what/what_is_era_en.htm.
3. As of the year 2017, 19 of the 28 countries in the European Union use the euro common currency.

REFERENCES

Bickerton, C. J., Hodson, D., & Puetter, U. (2015). *The new intergovernmentalism: States and supranational actors in a post-Maastricht era.* Oxford: Oxford University Press.

Börzel, T. A., & Risse, T. (2012). From Europeanisation to diffusion: Introduction. *West European Politics, 35*(1), 1–19.

Cantwell, B., & Kauppinen, I. (Eds.). (2014). *Academic capitalism in the age of globalization.* Baltimore: Johns Hopkins University Press.

European Commission. (1997). Towards a Europe of Knowledge. COM(97) 563 final. Communication from the Commission to the Council, the European Parliament, the Economic and Social Committee and the Committee of the Regions. November 12,1997.

European Commission. (2011, September 20). *Supporting growth and jobs—an agenda for the modernisation of Europe's higher education systems.* Communication from the Commission to the European Parliament, the Council, the European Economic and Social Committee and the Committee of the Regions. COM (2011) 567 final.

European Commission. (2014, January 15). *Preventing radicalisation to terrorism and violent extremism: Strengthening the EU's response.* Communication from the Commission to the European Parliament, the European Council, the European Economic and Social Committee and the Committee of the Regions. COM (2013) 941 final.

European Commission. (2016, June 14). *Supporting the prevention of radicalisation leading to violent extremism.* Communication from the Commission to the European Parliament, the European Council, the European Economic and Social Committee and the Committee of the Regions. COM (2016) 379 final.

Katzenstein, P. J. (2005). *World of regions.* Ithaca: Cornell University Press.

Keohane, R. O., & Nye, J. (2012). *Power and interdependence* (4th ed.). Boston: Longman Classics in Political Science.

Lefkofridi, Z., & Schmitter, P. C. (2015). Transcending or descending? European integration in times of crisis. *European Political Science Review, 7,* 3–22.

Matthijs, M., & Blyth, M. (Eds.). (2015). *The future of the euro.* Oxford: Oxford University Press.

Mazza, C., Quattrone, P., & Riccaboni, A. (Eds.). (2008). *European universities in transition: Issues, models, and cases.* Northampton: Edward Elgar.

Moravcsik, A. (1998). *The choice for Europe: Social purpose and state power from Messina to Maastricht.* Ithaca: Cornell University Press.

Neave, G. (2003a). On the return from Babylon: A long voyage around history, ideology and systems change. In J. File & L. Geodegebuure (Eds.),

Reflections on higher education in the Czech Republic, Hungary, Poland and Slovenia. Twente: CHEPS (Csenter for Higher Education Policy Studies).

Neave, G. (2003b). The Bologna declaration: Some of the historic dilemmas posed by the reconstruction of the community in Europe's systems of higher education. *Educational Policy, 17*, 141–164.

North, D. C. (1990). *Institutions, institutional change, and economic performance*. Cambridge: Cambridge University Press.

North, D. C. (2005). *Understanding the process of economic change*. Princeton: Princeton University Press.

Pierson, P. (1996). The path to European integration: A historical institutionalist analysis. *Comparative Political Studies, 29*(2), 123–163.

Pierson, P. (2000). Increasing returns, path dependence and the study of politics. *American Political Science Review, 94*, 2.

Pierson, P. (2004). *Politics in time: History, analysis, and social analysis*. Princeton: Princeton University Press.

Powell, W. W., & Snellman, K. (2004). The knowledge economy. *Annual Review of Sociology, 30*, 199–220.

Risse, T. (2007). Social constructivism meets globalization. In A. Held & D. McGrew (Eds.), *Globalization theory: Approaches and controversies* (pp. 126–147). Cambridge: Polity Press.

Schmidt, V. A. (2009a). Re-envisioning the European Union: Identity, democracy, economy. *Journal of Common Market Studies, 47*, 17–42.

Schmidt, V. A. (2009b). "The EU and its member states: From bottom up to top down." In D. Phinnemore & A. Warleigh-Lack (Eds.), *Reflections on European integration: 50 years of the Treaty of Rome* (pp. 194–211). London: Palgrave Macmillan.

Schmidt, V. A., & Thatcher, M. (Eds.). (2013). *Resilient liberalism in Europe's political economy*. Cambridge: Cambridge University Press.

Scott, W. R. (2014). *Institutions and organizations: Ideas, interests, and identities* (4th ed.). Los Angeles, CA: Sage.

Simmons, B. A., Dobbin, F., & Garrett, G. (2006). The institutional diffusion of liberalism. *International Organization, 60*(4), 781–810.

CHAPTER 2

Institutions and Ideas: The Political, Economic, and Social Context for the Bologna Process

A Europe of Knowledge is now widely recognised as an irreplaceable factor for social and human growth and as an indispensable component to consolidate and enrich the European citizenship, capable of giving its citizens the necessary competencies to face the challenges of the new millennium, together with an awareness of shared values and belonging to a common social and cultural space.
The Bologna Declaration (excerpt), June 19, 1999

Although there have been some doubts about aspects of European regional integration, particularly regarding the monetary union, the cooperation in higher education has continued to progress with increasing membership since the inception of the Bologna Process. Within a theoretical framework of institutions and ideas, this book considers the European Union (EU) countries and the case studies of Portugal and Spain. The independent variable is the political economy context acting upon the dependent variable of policy reform and higher education attainment. In light of the Bologna Process, the Europe 2020 economic strategy provides targets for higher education attainment in the EU Member States, along with an average target for all 28 countries. The Iberian countries, Portugal and Spain, have had similar political and economic experiences since ending authoritarian rule in the 1970s. This similar political context is useful methodologically to control variables as much as possible to focus on the independent and dependent variables of analysis. These countries, despite having similar political backgrounds,

© The Author(s) 2017
B. Barrett, *Globalization and Change in Higher Education*,
DOI 10.1007/978-3-319-52368-2_2

have diverged on the timing of implementing the criteria of the Bologna Process, given that reform has been more rapid in Portugal in some circumstances. With similar backgrounds of having ended authoritarian rule approximately a decade prior to joining the EU in 1986, Portugal and Spain implemented the credit and degree system components of the National Qualifications Framework in 2007.

The Lisbon Recognition Convention has been adopted nationally as part of policy reforms undertaken in the Bologna Process to create the European Higher Education Area (EHEA) (Rauhvargers et al. 2009:122).[1] There are three defining aspects of domestic politics:

1. Structure of government (unitary vs. (quasi-)federal)
2. Leadership consistency providing support for the reforms
3. Funding for education or wealth (measured by GDP per capita)

Each is important for policy change and cooperation at the international and European and institutional levels in the multi-level context. "It is important to acknowledge that a European common space for higher education can continue to exist and play a positive role in the future even though the European integration process might be stalled or even in some ways reversed" (Bologna Process Researchers' Conference 2014). The relative success of the Bologna Process may be compared to more challenging initiatives for regional integration in Europe, such as the Economic and Monetary Union (EMU). The euro, as the common currency of the EMU, was introduced as a physical currency in 2002, three years after the Bologna Process launch. Approximately one decade into the Bologna Process, the global recession in 2008 was marked by an asset loss worldwide of more than a trillion U.S. dollars when the financial markets spiraled downward. The economic crisis in Europe heightened in early 2010 when Greece revealed its troubles with sovereign debt. Nevertheless, the Bologna Process continued to progress steadily into its second decade. In recent years, there have been a rising number of domestic political voices resisting the initiatives of EU, particularly in response to economic uncertainty, which has intensified with increasing globalization.

This book identifies significant influences of the political economy as they relate to the implementation of the Bologna Process objectives for policy convergence. This is done by evaluating the political economy context as it influences higher education policy reform at the national level. The Lisbon Strategy, initiated in 2000, and the Europe 2020 economic growth strategy, initiated in 2010, are led by the European Commission. These initiatives have had a co-constitutive relationship in concert with the Bologna Process, which has provided the impetus for the international policy coordination in higher education that is achieved with the Open Method of Coordination (OMC).

The policy reform in the Bologna Process varies across countries, depending on various political economy contexts and stakeholder influences. This book's focus is on the reform of the EHEA credit and degree structure at the national level, as well as higher education attainment. Most participating countries had achieved the credit and degree structure criteria by the 2015 EHEA Ministerial Conference in Yerevan, Armenia. National quality assurance criteria and international degree recognition criteria are also central to policy reform in the Bologna Process. The institution of quality assurance agencies in each of the 48 countries builds trust among all participants in the EHEA (Amaral 2013; Llavori de Micheo 2013). The Bologna Process is an intergovernmental policy initiative. This liberal intergovernmental, state-led cooperation provides states with the power to determine the direction of the policy (Moravcsik 1998; Bickerton et al. 2015). Although the Bologna Process originated with the four countries that were signatories to the Sorbonne Declaration, outside of the European Commission, the European Commission became a partner during the development of the Lisbon Strategy and the OMC in the early 2000s (Gornitzka 2007; Keeling 2006).

The stated intentions for the Bologna Process were to be updated in the communiqués following the EHEA Ministerial meetings, initially every two years until 2012. The EHEA education ministers currently meet every three years. The agenda includes international recognition of academic degrees, enhanced educational quality, mobility of students, and student-centered learning. While some communiqués stated the intention for greater employability of graduates that in turn will strengthen the European economy, the latest communiqué from Yerevan emphasized the student dimensions. The cumulative intentions can be summarized as supporting economic competitiveness for the participant countries and for the region of Europe as an entity, and to support social cohesion (EHEA 2015). Alongside the economic growth in the common market and neighboring countries, international policy coordination in higher education aims to bring about cultural and social cohesion across countries, affirming the idea of a unified Europe. All of the Bologna Process countries are signatories to the European Cultural Convention of the Council of Europe from 1954. The membership of the countries in the Bologna Process and the Council of Europe overlap. However, members of the Bologna Process such as Israel, Kazakhstan, and Belarus are not members of the Council of Europe. The Principalities of Monaco and San Marino are members of the Council of Europe but are not members of the Bologna Process.

INTERACTION OF EDUCATIONAL REFORMS AND THE POLITICAL ECONOMY

The Bologna Process is a key element to anchor new democracies in the practical implementation of broad, stakeholder-driven civic governance. Especially in Central and Eastern Europe, higher education institutions have played a key role in providing a refuge for people with policy views that challenge those of the state (Tyson 2013). This effort to build the EHEA is an example of the social construction of the idea of Europe (Christiansen et al. 2001; Lavdas 2006; Nokkola 2007).

There are three processes in the political economy that influence the Bologna Process. Global economic pressures act on national economic concerns and preferences of societal interest groups, which drive their engagement in the political economy. Domestic politics influence negotiations at the international level (Keohane and Milner 1996; Milner 1997; Putnam 1988). These negotiations and bargaining are part of intergovernmental cooperation (Moravcsik 1998; Moravcsik and Schimmelfennig 2009). The norms transmitted from the EU socially construct preferences and impact the national level of domestic institutions through the process of Europeanization (Börzel and Risse 2000, 2012; Risse 2009; Schmidt 2009). These three processes are explanatory variables of the international political economy, which are traced throughout this book (Fig. 2.1)

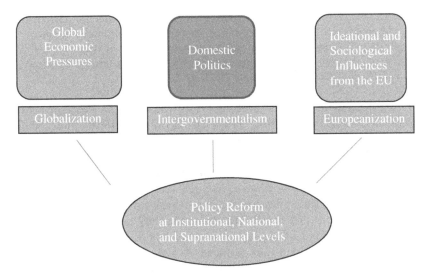

Fig. 2.1 International Political Economy Influences on Policy Reform

FOCUS ON DEGREE STRUCTURE CRITERIA AND EVOLUTION OF BOLOGNA PROCESS ACTION LINES

The focus of the research done to write this book, particularly for the qualitative case studies of Portugal and Spain, is the national-level institutional changes needed to implement the degree structure criteria of the Bologna Process. The second important focus is quality assurance, which is still in progress as countries continue to design their policies for national accreditation agencies. Each EHEA country has at least one quality assurance agency that is part of the European Quality Assurance Register (EQAR) and complies with the European Standards and Guidelines (ESG). The third important focus, and the ultimate objective of the Bologna Process, is international automatic recognition of academic qualifications across participating countries. This is challenging because of differences in educational quality across countries and institutions within countries. The participating countries affirmed their commitment to automatic recognition at the EHEA Ministerial Conference in April 2012:

> We are determined to remove outstanding obstacles hindering effective and proper recognition and are willing to work together towards the *automatic recognition* [emphasis mine] of comparable academic degrees, building on the tools of the Bologna framework, as a long-term goal of the EHEA. (Bucharest Communiqué 2012: 4)[2]

It is not possible to assess each aspect of the Bologna Process and its implementation in this book. The focus is on the reforms in academic degree structure and higher education attainment as part of Europe 2020. The political economy context provides explanations as it facilitates or impedes convergence on the original policy criteria of the Bologna Process. The qualitative research focuses on the criteria of the degree system action lines for the three tiers (or cycles) of degrees—bachelor, master, and doctorate—and the NQF, which defines the qualification content of degrees. Countries in the EU have two NQFs: a national/EU qualifications framework and an EHEA qualifications framework. At the national level, policy implementation takes place when the primary sources of legislative documents are created. However, this is not a linear process from the national level to the institutional level of governance. Following the introduction of reforms and criteria for higher education institutions, the national and institutional timing of policy implementation has varied across and within countries. It is important to distinguish among policy formulation, implementation, and reformulation (Cerych and Sabatier 1986).

The criteria for the implementation of the Bologna Process have evolved over time. During 2006, before the London EHEA Ministerial Conference, a set of 10 Bologna Process policy objectives was established (Reinalda and Kulesza 2006: 9). The central tenets of recognition of academic degrees and mobility of students are achieved through the policy implementation of these objectives and action lines across participating countries (Reinalda and Kulesza 2006: 9).[3]

Bologna Process Policy Objectives or Action Lines (2006)

1. Adoption of a system of easily readable and comparable degrees
2. Adoption of a system essentially based on two cycles (undergraduate and graduate)
3. Establishment of a system of credits (ECTS—European Credit and Transfer System)

4. Promotion of mobility by overcoming obstacles
5. Promotion of European cooperation in quality assurance
6. Promotion of European dimensions in higher education
7. Lifelong learning
8. Involvement of students
9. Promoting the attractiveness and competitiveness of the European Higher Education Area (EHEA) to other parts of the world
10. Doctoral studies and the synergy between the European Higher Education Area and the European Research Area

The action lines of the Bologna Process have evolved at the EHEA Ministerial Conferences since 1999. The later action lines follow the earlier action lines in implementation. The ten action lines have been defined over time in Bologna (1999), Prague (2001), Berlin (2003), and Bergen (2005) before the London (2007) ministerial meeting. Later ministerial meetings have taken place in Leuven and Louvain-la-Neuve (2009), Budapest and Vienna (2010), and Bucharest (2012). In 2012, by the time of the EHEA Ministerial Conference in Bucharest, the previous 10 action lines had been refined to focus on key areas. The stocktaking indexes for 2005, 2007, and 2009, created to identify progress on these issue areas, were not continued as a format for periodic country reports. There were concerns about the consistency between the national and institutional levels of reporting in the stocktaking reports. The Bologna Process administrative tasks of national reporting on stocktaking have been criticized for not accurately reflecting institutional realities (Veiga and Amaral 2009a). The EHEA rotates the location of the Secretariat to be in the city where the next Ministerial Conference is scheduled to take place. In 2018, the EHEA Ministerial Conference in Paris takes the education ministers back to the city where the idea was created on May 25, 1998, with the Sorbonne Declaration.

At the EHEA Ministerial Conferences in Bucharest and Yerevan (in April 2012 and May 2015 respectively), the criteria and corresponding policy objectives aimed to commit the participating countries to the Bologna Process through 2020 and beyond. These policy areas were assessed in context within *The European Higher Education Area: Bologna Process Implementation Reports* presented in Bucharest (2012) and in Yerevan (2015) at the conferences of education ministers (Eurydice 2012 and 2015).

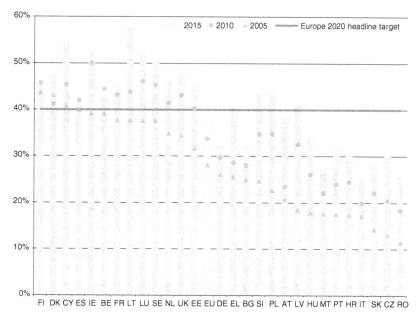

Fig. 2.2 European Commission. 2015. "Higher Education Attainment, 2005–2015". Directorate-General of Education and Culture. Education and Training Monitor. Page 48. *Source* Eurostat (EU-LFS, 2005–2015). Online data code edta_lfse_03. *Note:* The indicator covers the share of the population aged 30–34 years having successfully completed higher education (ISCED5–8); break in time series in 2005 for DE, ES, MT, and SE; in 2010 for BG, DE, HR, NL, PL, RO, and UK. The data on higher educational attainment 2005–2010 for AT should not be compared with data from 2015, since under ISCED 1997 the qualification acquired upon successful completion of higher technical and vocational colleagues is reported in ISCED level 4, not in ISCED level 5 as in ISCED 2011 implemented from 2014

Bologna Process Refined Criteria and Objectives (2012)

1. Degree system
2. Quality assurance
3. Social dimension
4. Effective outcomes and employability
5. Lifelong learning
6. Mobility and internationalization

7. Student-centered learning
8. Recognition

These relatively abbreviated criteria that have evolved aim to appeal to a broader audience and emphasize the key aspects of higher education as they relate to both social cohesion and human capital development for maximizing the growth potential of the economy. These criteria complement the European Commission's economic growth strategy, established in March 2010 and called Europe 2020. Building upon themes from the Lisbon Strategy in the first decade of the twenty-first century, the economic growth strategy of Europe 2020 addresses the global context of slowed growth in developed countries and focuses on the five key areas of (1) education, (2) employment, (3) innovation, (4) social inclusion, and (5) climate/energy sustainability. Higher education attainment is measured as part of the Europe 2020 economic growth strategy (Fig. 2.2). These five key areas of the economic growth strategy are interdependent and are supported by the component of attainment in higher education to advance the overarching goals of a "smart, sustainable, and inclusive Europe."

Theoretical and Historical Foundations: Regional Integration and Institutional Change

The theoretical foundations that guided my research for this book are drawn from previous work in international political economy, on theories of policy coordination that consider both domestic politics and international relations (Keohane and Milner 1996; Milner 1992, 1997), and on theories of historical institutionalism and institutional change (Hall 2010; North 1990, 2005; Olsen 2009a, 2010; Pierson 2004). Within the purview of policy coordination and institutional change, there exist even further subsets of analysis. Policy coordination or policy convergence takes into account competitive pressures from globalization (Rodrik 2011; Rosamond 2002; Spring 2009), domestic political pressures (Putman 1988), and institutional design together with credible commitments of actors at various levels of governance (Maassen and Olsen 2007; Moravcsik 1998; Rodrik 2000).

Institutional theory, which is the basis for institutional design and change, may be viewed in historical, rational, and sociological perspectives (Hall and Taylor 1996; Peters 2012). Historical institutionalism is valuable for process tracing and the contextual understanding of regional integration and the European project in particular (Pierson 1996, 2004). Rational institutionalism and sociological institutionalism are used to explain, respectively, the preferences of state actors and the influence of the supranational entity of the EU. This analysis of institutions is referenced in the theory promulgated by Andrew Moravcsik in *The Choice for Europe* (1998), a seminal project that advanced the centrality of states in leading policy decisions through rational self-interest in a liberal intergovernmental approach. The state-driven policy positions were challenged by theorists who argued that the EU is primarily a supranational entity (Keohane and Hoffmann 1991). Moravcsik's position, built upon previous decades of literature on regional integration theory that determined integration, stemmed from functional dynamics of cooperation in particular issue areas, such as the production of coal and steel or synchronizations of telecommunications and postal services (Mitrany 1943). This phenomenon in a neo-functional perspective identified spill-over effects from particular functional areas of cooperation into ever more broad areas of political cooperation (Haas 1964). The liberal intergovernmental policy process is descriptive of the Bologna Process, and it is enlivened in the Bologna Declaration.

> We hereby undertake to attain these objectives – within the framework of our institutional competencies and taking full respect of the diversity of cultures, languages, national education systems and of University autonomy – to consolidate the European area of higher education. To that end, we will pursue the ways of *intergovernmental* [emphasis mine] co-operation, together with those of non-governmental European organisations with competence on higher education. (Bologna Declaration 1999)[4]

Theories of policy coordination are found in research on the international political economy (Keohane and Milner 1996; Milner 1997). The important role of institutions in this process calls for analysis through a variety of institutional perspectives that contribute to political economy explanations. Recognizing that International Political Economy and International Relations theory literature most frequently present the historical, rational, and sociological perspectives of institutionalisms, these three types of institutionalisms are the most relevant to this research. Historical and sociological institutional perspectives place the Bologna Process in a chronological context of regional integration in Europe, driven by social leaders and their interests. Rational institutionalism explains the preferences of states that seek to maximize their benefits and utility in political power and economic influence. Current interpretations of these institutionalisms build upon the previous regional integration literature, which is discussed in Chap. 3 (Haas 1964; Keohane and Hoffmann 1991; Mitrany 1943; Pierson 1996).

The liberal intergovernmental theory advanced by Moravcsik is important to interpreting the Bologna Process as a Member State-driven initiative supported by the supranational framework of the EU. By committing to the tenets of the Bologna Process, the Member States have de facto endorsed its objective to create a European higher education area, enhance economic competitiveness, and strengthen Europe as a regional power in the world. From the beginning, the Bologna Process was related to the cornerstones of European Commission education policy, such as learning mobility and recognition of qualifications across countries (Kania 2012). This shows that the normative power of the EU extends beyond the 28 Member States, given that 48 sovereign states are participating in the Bologna Process. Sociological institutionalism explains the contextual power of the EU in the region and the institutional constraints to policy implementation that exist across various levels of governance. This is connected to social constructivist notions of the EU as a power that establishes norms, creates institutions, and provides regional identity. The preferences of the state and the influences of the EU interact in the "policy space" between national power and supranational governance. The policy diffusion of European ideas has driven the policy reforms through the top-down process of Europeanization acting on the national level (Berry and Berry 2014; Börzel and Risse 2000, 2012). In this work, historical institutionalism is important as a synthesis between rational and sociological institutionalisms (Hall and Taylor 1996). The qualitative case-study comparisons of Portugal and Spain show that, ultimately, rational motives to pursue internationalization were important for the policy implementation at the national level, through the 2007 laws to establish the requisite NQFs.

The European Union's motto "unity in diversity" is at the heart of the Bologna Process's impetus for policy coordination. The objective is for higher education to complement the mobility of labor, capital, goods, and services in the Single Market. The European project for regional economic integration began with economic and political cooperation in the European Coal and Steel Community (ECSC), as a result of the Treaty of Paris in 1951. Following this post-World War II agreement, the six original countries of France, Germany, Italy, and the Benelux (Belgium, Luxembourg, and the Netherlands) continued their cooperation from the ECSC to create the European Community with the Treaty of Rome in 1957. In the more than half a century since then, the cooperation has intensified among the original members and has broadened to include additional member states in the region. The Treaty of Maastricht signed February 7, 1992, stated in Chap. 3, Article 126:

> The Community shall contribute to the development of quality education by encouraging co-operation between Member States and, if necessary, by supporting and supplementing their action, while fully respecting the responsibility of the Member States for the content of teaching and the organization of education systems and their cultural and linguistic diversity.

The Treaty of Lisbon, signed December 13, 2007, went further to define the European Union's extent of engagement with education policy[5]:

1. The Union shall contribute to the development of quality education by encouraging cooperation between Member States and, if necessary, by supporting and supplementing their action, while fully respecting the responsibility of the Member States for the content of teaching and the organisation of education systems and their cultural and linguistic diversity (The Lisbon Treaty 2009 Title XII, Article 165).
2. Union action shall be aimed at:
   —encouraging mobility of students and teachers, by encouraging inter alia, the academic recognition of diplomas and periods of study (Title XII, Article 165).

The regional integration that began in the mid-twentieth century expanded into the policy space of education through the formal treaties that had economic and political foundations before becoming manifest in the Bologna Process at the end of the century. Policy initiatives occasionally find resistance to change at the levels of governance of the state and in the sub-regions, such as in federal systems of government (Börzel 2000; Lijphart 1999). In recent years, resistance to the Bologna Process has been present at the levels of state and of higher education institutions due to some skepticism of these stakeholders toward the EU. Concerning institutional changes in the EU, two decades ago Robert Keohane and Stanley Hoffmann identified the realist political sources of decision-making at the commencement of the Treaty of Maastricht (Keohane and Hoffmann 1991). With the signing of the Treaty of

Maastricht in 1992, the European Community became the European Union. More than two decades of liberal intergovernmental cooperation has ensued since that important step in regional integration. Moravcsik built upon these ideas with his argument that liberal intergovernmentalism is a rational motivation that has a tripartite explanation of integration: "economic interest, relative power, and credible commitment" (Moravcsik 1998: 4). Translated into the context of this research, the tripartite explanation provided by Moravcsik corresponds to the three central dynamics that influence policy coordination in higher education. These central political economy processes, which serve as explanatory variables for the implementation of the Bologna Process, are combined with Moravcsik's tripartite explanation in the following synthesis of ideas:

1. Globalization: Given *competitive economic pressures* and globalization, states continue to pursue their economic interests.
2. Intergovernmentalism: *Domestic politics* at the level of the state continue to drive decision-making in an intergovernmental context of relative power.
3. Europeanization: *Norm-setting leadership for the region* stemming from the supranational European Union is the context in which credible commitments are made.

These compromises in the negotiating states' "grand bargain" described by Moravcsik (1998) come into play between two levels: domestic politics and international diplomacy (Putnam 1988). This two-level negotiating is typical among national ministers of education in the ministerial forums of the Bologna Process.

A MIXED METHODOLOGICAL APPROACH

A mixed methodological approach uses complementary qualitative and quantitative methods to carry out empirical research (Goertz and Mahoney 2012). The quantitative cross-national data analysis used in writing this book considers 26 EU countries among the 48 countries undertaking higher education policy reform.[6] The qualitative case studies, Chaps. 6–9, compare the processes of the policy implementation for degree structure criteria at the national level in Portugal and Spain. The qualitative case studies present the Iberian countries, Portugal and Spain, in historical institutional perspective from the pivotal time period of adoption of new democratic constitutions in the mid-1970s.

The quality assurance and automatic recognition criteria components of the Bologna Process continue in the implementation process, and this is of interest for future research. Given institutional change as part of democratic politics in the EHEA countries, this research reveals the strengths and weaknesses of change in the relationship between the political economy context and outcomes in policy reform. Qualitative research in case studies utilizes process tracing for historical and cultural analysis of institutions and policy-making decisions over time and to research the similar case-study countries to determine historical influences on policy and diverging outcomes not explainable by quantitative analysis alone (George and Bennett 2005: 253).

Research Questions on Policy Reform
The primary research question is addressed qualitatively and quantitatively:

- What are political and economic explanations for achieving the criteria for higher education reform, and higher education attainment, for countries in the Bologna Process?
  Research Question 1 (RQ1)

The secondary research questions are addressed qualitatively and are opportunities for further research:

- What is the relationship of globalization, measured by regional integration in the economy by the extent of international trade, to policy implementation?
- What is the relationship of stakeholders'—academic, public, and private—commitments to policy reform on policy outcomes?

This mixed-methods project uses historical institutional analysis for qualitative case-study research and empirical analysis for quantitative research. This qualitative approach in historical institutional perspective is essential to interpret the intergovernmental and Europeanization influences that impact the policy reform within countries. Advancing this analysis, social constructivism is useful to explain how the Bologna Process originated as transnational policy discourse and developed into the material manifestation of policy adoptions and institutional changes (Nokkola 2007, 2012). Further, the European economic space and objectives for

Multilevel Analysis
Higher Education Policy at Three Levels

Analysis of Interest

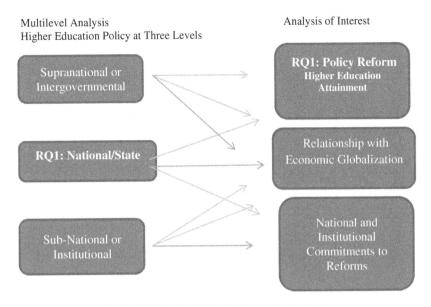

Fig. 2.3 Research Analysis Embedded within Institutional Structure

competitiveness can be explained by social constructivism (Rosamond 2002). A quantitative empirical approach complements the institutional perspectives and uses statistical analysis to measure the relationship of economic indicators to the education policy outcome of higher education attainment. The term "higher education" is used for higher education throughout this book. The higher education attainment benchmark comes from Europe 2020, the European Commission's economic growth strategy.[7] This relationship of the political economy context within countries to higher education outcomes is useful to consider when qualitatively evaluating the processes of institutional change. Regression methods explain the influences of independent variables—per capita GDP, R&D as percentage of GDP, economic integration through trade, employment, and government spending on education—on the dependent variable of higher education attainment. The quantitative analysis assesses higher education attainment as the dependent variable over time, from the start of the Bologna Process in 2000 until 2014. The 26 countries are assessed together, and Portugal and Spain are assessed uniquely to provide a closer look at variables in these case-study countries (Fig. 2.3).

Rationale for the Case Studies Selection

The purpose of presenting the case studies is to provide understanding that becomes generalizable and relevant to others countries experiencing these policy reforms. Chapters 6 and 7 on Portugal and Chaps. 8 and 9 on Spain provide qualitative case-study analysis to compare policy implementation at the national level in the two countries of the Iberian Peninsula. Five points of comparison in qualitative analysis provide the historical institutional framework to assess similarities and differences in higher education governance and administration:

Chapters 6 and 7:

1. National governance background
2. Political economy context.
3. Higher education governance

Chapters 8 and 9:

4. Role of stakeholders in policy process
5. Modernization of higher education institutions

The research offers a unique perspective by identifying trends in the political economy as they relate to outcomes in higher education policy across regions of the EU and specifically in Portugal and Spain. These countries are understood as most similar cases applying John Stuart Mill's "method of difference."[8] There is an important diverging explanatory or independent variable, which is the structure of government, alongside other similar independent variables (Bennett 2004: 31; George and Bennett 2005: 50). The difference in the dependent variable of interest, which is higher education attainment, highlights Portugal's heightened pace in increasing higher education attainment and in moving forward with the EHEA reforms.

The structure of government is a definitive factor in the political economy contexts of these two case-study countries. The structure of government influences domestic policy decisions and international cooperation with the EU and neighborhood countries in the Bologna Process. Portugal has a unitary government, while there is a quasi-federal or devolved government of 17 autonomous regions in Spain. This raises the possibility that an explanation for policy reform divergence may be found in government structure. The research design, using the method of difference, identifies the diverging independent variable in the political economy that explains the distinct dependent variable. The shared independent variable between these two cases is the broader governance context of being transition countries after authoritarian rule, before acceding to the EEC/EU simultaneously in 1986. Another shared variable of interest is the NQF degree structure, established through legislation in Portugal and Spain similarly in the year 2007.

Portugal, being smaller in population and in size of economy, may facilitate educational reforms on a national level more rapidly than larger, decentralized countries. The idea of "pathfinder" countries was introduced at the 2012 EHEA Ministerial Conference in Bucharest, to report to the 2015 Ministerial on best practices. Portugal has been among the nine pathfinder countries that have been exemplary in finding ways to implement the automatic academic recognition criteria of the EHEA, as the culmination of achieving policy reforms. While Portugal initially implemented some reforms more quickly and has increased attainment at a faster pace, Spain has had greater total attainment in higher education (Eurydice 2015). This book explains that government structure, as well as political support and institutional leadership, is key to policy reform. Even prior to the Bologna Process, because of transitions to democratic rule under new constitutions in the 1970s, there were ongoing higher education policy reforms in the Iberian countries at a national level that intersected with the European reforms introduced in 1999.

With the method of difference applied to these most similar country cases, there was a distinct outcome on the dependent variable of interest, namely, the expansion of higher education has progressed more rapidly in Portugal than in Spain. The average annual change in higher education attainment rate, over the period 2011–2014, was 5.5 percent for Portugal and less than 0.5 percent for Spain (European Commission 2015). There is an important diverging explanatory or independent variable, which is the structure of government, alongside other similar independent variables (Bennett 2004: 31; George and Bennett 2005: 50). Portugal has a unitary government and a population of approximately 11 million people. Spain has a quasi-federal governmental structure and approximately 44 million people, four times greater than the national population of Portugal. Other independent variables provide explanations concerning the extent of national support for reforms, politically and economically. In addition, it is pertinent to consider the starting points, from the beginning of the Bologna Process, to evaluate higher education policy criteria in each national context.

The recent pressures from the global recession and Eurozone crisis are considered for Portugal and Spain. The pressures of globalization acting on economy, politics, and society are ongoing. The greater than 100 percent debt to GDP for the Iberian countries remains burdensome as they emerge from economic assistance programs. These trends in the economy during the global financial crisis (2007–2009) preceded changes in political party leadership in the countries. In Iberia in 2011, the electorate voted to replace the Socialist leaders in the Prime Minister's office in both countries; in June in Portugal and in November in Spain. Then in late 2015, Portugal returned to Socialist party leadership. Spain remained without a new government for most of 2016. National priorities and EU priorities are occasionally aligned and are often in tension, for interest groups and political parties. Since Portugal's government agreed to accept EU funds in 2011 and Spain agreed to accept funds for the banking sector in 2012, there were opportunities for enhanced cooperation between the national leadership and the EU. The role of stakeholders—from the academic, public, and private sectors—is discussed in the qualitative case studies. More than a decade of reform provides an appropriate time period for application of the Advocacy Coalition Framework (ACF) to assess the roles of stakeholders from the academic, public, and private sectors (Sabatier and Weible 2007). The outcomes in policy reform, to achieve the Bologna Process objectives, are influenced by the international political economy processes of intergovernmentalism and Europeanization (Bickerton 2015; Börzel and Risse 2000, 2012).

COMPLEMENTING THE SINGLE MARKET: THE CASE FOR THE BOLOGNA PROCESS

The Bologna Process and the EHEA have been created to complement the common market and its four freedoms: labor, capital, goods, and services. This common market in Europe is known as the Single Market, formally established in 1992 with the Single European Act, and it is a model for common markets globally (Egan 2015). There remain opportunities and challenges in the political economy to achieve regional integration in higher education. This under-researched area is an emerging field of academic inquiry. The knowledge economy of the twenty-first century is central to the analysis of the Bologna Process objectives in the second decade. In the second decade, many of the 48 participating countries have achieved the policy convergence objectives. However, there is an opportunity to provide institutional support, at the European level working in cooperation with the European Commission, to countries that can continue to advance on the policy reforms (Lagier 2016; Tyson 2016).

Within the context of regional integration, the Bologna Process is the most ambitious undertaking in the world for policy coordination of higher education. Given that the region of Europe is the most economically and politically integrated region, it is appropriate that this continent drives an unprecedented initiative toward convergence of higher education credits, degrees, educational quality, and recognition across sovereign states.

The following chapter considers the policy processes of intergovernmentalism, a state-driven process, present alongside Europeanization, a top-down process influencing the states. A historical institutional approach is taken to understand trends in regional integration and higher education cooperation through these policy processes. This provides historical explanations for the development of the Bologna Process—as international cooperation in higher education that is part of the process of regional integration that began in the post-World War II era.

NOTES

1. The Lisbon Recognition Convention is the Convention on the Recognition of Qualifications concerning Higher Education in the European Region. This was developed by the Council of Europe and the United National Educational, Scientific, and Cultural Organization (UNESCO). It was adopted by national representatives meeting in Lisbon on April 8–11, 1997. As countries join the Bologna Process, they adopt the Lisbon Recognition Convention. See Appendix C.
2. The 2012 Ministerial Conference and Third Bologna Policy Forum documents available at: http://www.bologna-bucharest2012.ehea.info/background-documents.html.
3. The mobility of students was earlier supported by the European Commission with the Erasmus program established in 1986. This is explained in Chap. 4.

4. The Bologna Declaration was signed on June 19, 1999, in Bologna, Italy, by 29 ministers of education. Please see Appendix C for the full text of the Bologna Declaration.
5. See Appendix D for the Treaty of Lisbon, Article 165 in Part 3, Title XII, on the EU role in education.
6. The statistical analysis does not include the countries of Luxembourg or Croatia, for which there is limited data. Therefore, 26 of the 28 current EU member states are included in the data analysis in Chap. 5.
7. The Europe 2020 economic growth strategy was launched in March 2010 by the European Commission. More information is available at: http://ec.europa.eu/europe2020/index_en.htm.
8. A method for determining the research design and selected countries for case-study analysis comes from John Stuart Mill's logic of comparisons in *A System of Logic* (1843).

References

Amaral, A. (2013). Founding Director, Centre for Research on Higher Education Policies (CIPES), Matosinhos (Porto) and President of the Administration Council, A3ES Portuguese National Qualifications Agency; May 28, 2013.

Bennett, A. (2004). Case study methods: Design, use, and comparative advantages. In D. F. Sprinz, & Y. Wolinsky-Nahmias (Eds.), *Models, numbers, and cases: Methods for studying international relations* (pp. 19–55). Ann Arbor: University of Michigan Press.

Berry, F. S., & Berry, W. D. (2014). Innovation and diffusion models in policy research. In P. Sabatier & C. M. Weible (Eds.), *Theories of the policy process* (3rd ed.). Boulder, CO: Westview Press.

Bickerton, C. J., Hodson, D., & Puetter, U. (2015). *The new interngovernmentalism: States and supranational actors in a post-Maastricht era.* Oxford: Oxford University Press.

Bologna Process. (1999). The Bologna Declaration of 19 June 1999: Joint declaration of the European Ministers of Education.

Bologna Process. (2001). The Prague Communiqué of 19 May 2001: Towards the European Higher Education Area. Communiqué of the meeting of European Ministers in charge of Higher Education.

Bologna Process. (2009, April 28–29). Communiqué of the conference of European ministers responsible for higher education, Leuven and Louvain-la-Neuve.

Bologna Process Researchers' Conference. (2014, November 24–26). Report: The future of higher education, 2nd ed. Bucharest, Romania.

Börzel, T. A. (2000, Spring). From competitive regionalism to cooperative federalism: The Europeanization of the Spanish state of the autonomies. *The Journal of Federalism, 30*(2), 17–42.

Börzel, T. A., & Risse, T. (2012). From Europeanisation to diffusion: Introduction. *West European Politics, 35*(1), 1–19.

Börzel, T. A., & Thomas R. (2000). When Europe hits home: Europeanization and domestic change. *European Integration online Papers (EIoP), 4*(15). Retrieved from http://eiop.or.at/eiop/texte/2000-015a.htm.

Cerych, L., & Sabatier, P. (1986). *Great expectations and mixed performance: implementation of higher education reforms in Europe.* Stoke-on-Trent: Trentham Books.

Christiansen, T., Jorgensen, K. E., et al. (2001). *Social construction of Europe.* London: Sage.

Egan, M. (2015). *Single markets: Economic integration in Europe and the United States.* Oxford: Oxford University Press.

EHEA Ministerial Conference. (2012). Bucharest Communiqué: Making the most of our potential: Consolidating the European higher education area. Retrieved from http://www.ehea.info/Uploads/%281%29/Bucharest%20 Communique%202012%281%29.pdf.

EHEA Ministerial Conference. (2015). Yerevan Communiqué. Retrieved from http://bologna-yerevan2015.ehea.info/files/YerevanCommuniqueFinal.pdf.

European Commission. (2015, November 26). European semester thematic fiche: Tertiary education attainment.

European Higher Education Area. (2010, March 12). Budapest-Vienna Declaration on the European Higher Education Area.

Eurydice: Education, Audiovisual and Culture Executive Agency. (2012). The European higher education area in 2012: Bologna process implementation report. Retrieved from http://eacea.ec.europa.eu/education/eurydice/documents/thematic_reports/138EN.pdf.

Eurydice/European Commission/EACEA. (2015). *The European Higher Education Area in 2015: Bologna process implementation report.* Luxembourg: Publications Office of the European Union.

George, A. L., & Bennett, A. (2005). *Case studies and theory development in the social sciences.* Cambridge, MA: MIT Press.

Goertz, G., & Mahoney, J. (2012). *A tale of two cultures: Qualitative and quantitative research in the social sciences.* Princeton: Princeton University Press.

Gornitzka, Å. (2007). The Lisbon process: A supranational policy perspective: Institutionalizing the open method of coordination. In P. Maassen & J. P. Olsen (Eds.), *University dynamics and European integration.* Dordrecht: Springer.

Haas, E. B. (1964). *Beyond the nation state: Functionalism and international organization.* Stanford: Stanford University Press.

Hall, P. A. (2010). Historical institutionalism in rational and sociological perspective. In J. Mahoney & K. Thelen (Eds.), *Explaining institutional change: Ambiguity, agency, and power*. Cambridge: Cambridge University Press.

Hall, P. A., & Taylor R. C. R. (1996). Political science and the three new institutionalisms. *Political Studies, XLIV*, 936–957.

Kania, K. (2012, 2016). European Commission, Policy Officer, Directorate General for Education and Culture (DG EAC). Directorate A—Lifelong learning: horizontal policy issues and 2020 strategy, Unit A1—Education and Training in Europe 2020; country analysis. Correspondence December 2012; September 7, 2016.

Keeling, R. (2006). The Bologna Process and the Lisbon Research Agenda: The European commission's expanding role in higher education discourse. *European Journal of Education, 41*(2), 203–223.

Keohane, R. O., & Hoffmann, S. (Eds.). (1991). *The new European community: Decisionmaking and institutional change*. Boulder: Westview Press.

Keohane, R. O., & Milner, H. M. (Eds.). (1996). *Internationalization and domestic politics*. New York: Cambridge University Press.

Lagier, H. (2013, 2016). Direction des Relations Européennes et Internationales et de la Coopération (DREIC). Ministère de l'Enseignement supérieur et de la Recherche. Program Officer, European and International Cooperation, Ministry of Higher Education and Research, France. Correspondence February 2013; September 1, 2016.

Lavdas, K. A., Papadakis, N. E., & Gidarakou, M. (2006). Policies and networks in the construction of the European higher education area. *Higher Education Management and Policy, 18*(1), 121–131.

Lijphart, A. (1999). *Patterns of democracy: Government forms and performance in 36 countries*. New Haven: Yale University Press.

Llavori de Micheo, R. (2013, 2016). Director of International Relations ANECA (National Agency for Quality Assessment and Accreditation of Spain) and Board Member, ENQA (European Association for Quality Assurance in Higher Education), May 24, 2013; November 16, 2016.

Maassen, P., & Olsen, J. P. (Eds.). (2007). *University dynamics and European integration*. Dordrecht: Springer.

Mill, J. S. (1843). *A system of logic, ratiocinative and inductive: Being a connected view of the principles of evidence and the methods of scientific investigation*.

Milner, H. V. (1992). Theories of international cooperation among nations: Strengths and weaknesses. *World Politics, 44*(3), 466–496.

Milner, H. V. (1997). *Interests, institutions, and information: Domestic politics and international relations*. Princeton: Princeton University Press.

Mitrany, D. (1943). *A working peace system. An argument for the functional development of international organization*. London: Royal Institute of International Affairs.

Moravcsik, A. (1998). *The choice for Europe: Social purpose and state power from Messina to Maastricht*. Ithaca: Cornell University Press.

Moravcsik, A., & Schimmelfennig, F. (2009). Liberal intergovernmentalism. In A. Wiener & T. Diez (Eds.), *European integration theory* (2nd ed.). Oxford: Oxford University Press.

Nokkola, T. (2007). The Bologna process and the role of higher education: Discursive construction of the European higher education area. In J. Enders & B. Jongbloed (Eds.), *Public-private dynamics in higher education: Expectations, developments and outcomes* (pp. 221–245). Piscataway: Transaction.

Nokkola, T. (2012). Institutional autonomy and the attractiveness of the European higher education area—Facts or tokenistic discourse. In A. Curaj, P. Scott, L. Vlasceanu, & L. Wilson (Eds.), *European higher education at the crossroad: Between the Bologna process and national reforms. Parts 1 and 2*. Dordrecht: Springer Science+Business Media.

North, D. C. (1990). *Institutions, institutional change, and economic performance*. Cambridge: Cambridge University Press.

North, D. C. (2005). *Understanding the process of economic change*. Princeton: Princeton University Press.

Olsen, J. P. (2009a). Change and continuity: An institutional approach to institutions of democratic government. *European Political Science Review, 1*(1), 3–32.

Olsen, J. P. (2009b, January). Democratic government, institutional autonomy and the dynamics of change (Working Paper No. 01), ARENA Working Paper. Retrieved from http://www.sv.uio.no/arena/english/research/publications/arena-publications/workingpapers/.

Olsen, J. P. (2010). *Governing through institution building: Institutional theory and recent European experiments in democratic organization*. Oxford: Oxford University Press.

Peters, B. G. (2012). *Institutional theory in political science: The new institutionalism* (3rd ed.). New York: Continuum Books.

Pierson, P. (1996). The path to European integration: A historical institutionalist analysis. *Comparative Political Studies, 29*(2), 123–163.

Pierson, P. (2004). *Politics in time: History, analysis, and social analysis*. Princeton: Princeton University Press.

Putnam, R. D. (1988, Summer). Diplomacy and domestic politics: The logic of two-level games. *International Organization, 42*(3), 427–460.

Rauhvargers, A., Deane, C., & Pauwels, W. (2009). *Bologna process stocktaking (Report 2009): Report from working groups appointed by the Bologna follow-up group to the ministerial conference in Leuven/Louvain-la-Neuve*. Benelux: Bologna Process.

Reinalda, B., & Kulesza, E. (2006). *The Bologna Process—Harmonizing European's higher education* (2nd revised edition). Opladen & Farmington Hills: Barbara Budrich.

Risse, T. (2009). Social constructivism and European integration. In A. Wiener & T. Diez (Eds.), *European integration theory* (2nd ed., pp. 144–169). Oxford: Oxford University Press.

Rodrik, D. (2000). Institutions for high-quality growth: What they are and how to acquire them. *Studies in Comparative International Development, 35*(3), 3–31.

Rodrik, D. (2011). *The globalization paradox: Democracy and the future of the world economy.* New York: W.W. Norton and Company.

Rosamond, B. (2002). Imagining the European economy: 'Competitiveness' and the social construction of 'Europe' as an economic space. *New Political Economy, 7*(2), 157–177.

Sabatier, P. A., & Weible C. M. (2007). The advocacy coalition framework. In P. A. Sabatier (Ed.), *Theories of the policy process* (pp. 189–220). Cambridge: Westview Press.

Schmidt, V. A. (2009). The EU and its member states: From bottom up to top down. In D. Phinnemore & A. Warleigh-Lack (Eds.), *Reflections on European integration: 50 years of the treaty of Rome* (pp. 194–211). London: Palgrave Macmillan.

Spring, J. (2009). *Globalization of education: An introduction.* New York: Routledge.

Tyson, A. (2012, 2016). Acting Director for Strategy and Evaluation, Former Head of UnitC1, Higher Education and Erasmus, Directorate-General Education and Culture, European Commission, April 25, 2012; September 6, 2016.

Veiga, A., & Amaral, A. (2009a). Policy implementation tools and European governance. In A. Amaral, G. Neave, C. Musselin, & P. Maassen (Eds.), *European integration and the governance of higher education research* (pp. 133–157). Dordrecht: Springer.

Veiga, A., & Amaral, A. (2009b). Survey on the implementation of the Bologna process in Portugal. *Higher Education, 57*(1), 57–69.

CHAPTER 3

Historical Institutionalism and Change in Higher Education

Building on the achievements so far in the Bologna Process, we wish to establish a European Higher Education Area based on the principles of quality and transparency. We must cherish our rich heritage and cultural diversity in contributing to a knowledge-based society. We commit ourselves to upholding the principle of public responsibility for higher education in the context of complex modern societies.
Bergen Communiqué (excerpt), May 20, 2005

A driving purpose of the Bologna Process and the European Higher Education Area (EHEA) is to complement the economic competitiveness generated by the European Union (EU) Single Market. The EU Member States and cooperating countries in the region have agreed—over time—to commitments to the Bologna Process at EHEA ministerial conferences. With origins in the Treaty of Paris, which formed the European Coal and Steel Community (ECSC) (1951), and the Treaty of Rome (1957), which established the European Economic Community (EEC), the predecessor of the EU, the Single Market provides mobility of labor, capital, goods, and services. The mobility of higher educational degrees envisaged by the EHEA is an evolution of enhanced economic and political cooperation. The cooperation at the national level, of state and non-state actors, brings about the change in higher education in the Bologna Process.

© The Author(s) 2017
B. Barrett, *Globalization and Change in Higher Education*,
DOI 10.1007/978-3-319-52368-2_3

> This evidence on policy-making in higher education though the Bologna process leads me to conclude that what we are seeing is a new kind of partnership, with state actors and with non-state actors, suggesting a new conception of European policy-making in higher education based on cooperation not legislation...But it is precisely because of the engagement of national actors who are determined to get change within national systems that the process has a legitimacy which keeps it in being. (Corbett 2005:203)

In the context of global governance of knowledge, this book considers how higher education is made accessible over time across the region of Europe (Amaral et al. 2009; Chou and Gornitzka 2014). This chapter provides the historical evolution of higher education policy in Europe since the origins of integration in forming the EU following World War II. This legacy gives a substantive background and perspective to current developments in the EU Member States and across the region of Europe. An assessment of higher education policy in Europe through the years, in a historical institutional perspective, provides a launching point from which to analyze the political and economic dimensions in the global governance of knowledge. Since the EHEA, created by the Bologna Process, is the largest regional integration scheme for higher education in the world, there are lessons to apply to higher education coordination efforts in other regions of the world. Regional integration is the appropriate analytical framework for understanding historical developments and contemporary concerns across the spectrum of policy issues in international cooperation, in particular higher education policy. Scholars have recognized the policy reform and cooperation taking place to varying extents, depending on national socioeconomic and political contexts, to be differentiated integration (Amaral et al. 2015; Furlong 2010; Kölliker 2001; Schimmelfennig 2015).

This chapter examines the chronology of regional integration and enlargement, as it relates to higher education policy, analyzing three periods of historical analysis:

1. 1957 to 1999: from the Treaty of Rome to the launch of the Bologna Process
2. 1999 to 2010: from the launch of the Bologna Process to the creation of the EHEA
3. 2010 to today: from the creation of the EHEA into the second decade of the Bologna Process

The Bologna Process tells the larger story of institutional changes in Europe over the past two decades. It provides the background for understanding the emphasis on the Europe 2020 economic growth strategy indicators for higher education attainment. Additional indicators in the strategy are research innovation, employability, social cohesion, and climate sustainability. The Bologna Process provides a new architecture for governance of higher education, and it challenges traditional notions of the state role in knowledge policies (related to research and development [R&D] and innovation) in the region of Europe and beyond (Sørensen et al. 2015). Since the development of higher education policy in Europe, higher education institutions have been recipients of policy change. The 1972 founding of the European University Institute (EUI) in Fiesole near Florence, Italy, is an example of European policy entrepreneurship in higher education (Corbett 2005). The purpose has been to establish a world-class institution to study the region's history, its integration through the years, and its future in world affairs. Since then, access to higher education has expanded and become a policy objective as part of Europe 2020. Higher education institutions have evolved into a second role, as agents for change in the global economy, which is explained in Chap. 4. There is particular interest in the role that education may play in economic growth, given not only the global recession, between 2007 and 2009, but also the double-dip recession in 2012 in countries in the EU.

Historical institutionalism is the overarching explanatory theory for framing the changes over time, especially as it bridges rational and sociological institutionalisms (Hall 2010; Hall and Taylor 1996). Academic fields draw upon their own literature, using distinct terms to explain similar processes. The field of Political Science explains institutional change (Hall 2010; March and Olsen 1984, 1989; Peters 2012; Pierson 2004). In the fields of Education and Business, scholar James March has bridged the Social Sciences and Business disciplines, as has sociologist scholar W. Richard Scott (Scott 2014). Business literature explains organizational change (Cyert and March 1963; Pettigrew 1990). This Social Sciences paradigm for this research has relevance to the field of Business, given the economic and workforce development implications of higher education policy. A social constructivist analysis contributes to an understanding, through the lens of ideas, the increasing integration of Europe (Risse 2007, 2009, 2010).

Despite various economic, political, and social circumstances, the 28 countries in the EU and the 20 additional countries that have become participating members of the EHEA share educational values inherent in the Bologna Process. The shared values for participatory governance and human rights are upheld in the European Cultural Convention, which was ratified by the Council of Europe in 1954. Each country must adopt the European Cultural Convention to accede to the Bologna Process. The social norm of adopting the European Cultural Convention is evidence that these European values have completed the norm life-cycle through internalization, which is a concept of social constructivism (Finnemore and Sikkink 1998). In sequence, following norm emergence and norm cascade, there is norm internalization by participating members in the EHEA. The internalization of policies has led to new institutional frameworks, at the national and higher education institution levels, that have come to define knowledge policies in the twenty-first century (Chou and Gornitzka 2014).

THREE PERIODS OF HISTORICAL ANALYSIS IN REGIONAL INTEGRATION

As stated earlier in this chapter, there are three important periods on which to focus for a historical analysis of regional integration for higher education in Europe.

1957–1999: From the Treaty of Rome to Launch of Bologna Process

The six original countries of the European Union—Belgium, France, Germany, Italy, Luxembourg, and The Netherlands—that agreed to the Treaty of Rome launched the regional integration that has enlarged over decades. By the end of the century, when the Bologna Process was launched, some of the significant subsequent treaties had been the Single European Act (1986), the Treaty of Maastricht (1992), and the Treaty of Amsterdam (1997). The Treaty of Amsterdam became effective in May 1999, the month before the Bologna Process was launched.

After the original six countries created the EEC and Euratom in 1957 with the Treaty of Rome, nine more Member States joined to make 15 total Member States by the turn to the twenty-first century. At the negotiations in Messina on the island of Sicily during the summer 1955, the policy entrepreneur Walter Hallstein, Foreign Minister of the German

Federal Republic, planted the seeds that in later decades were foundational for higher education policy for the region (Corbett 2005:17, 25). The consideration for the place of education in public policy from the European Community's earliest days demonstrates historic consideration for how best to serve the states and the region of Europe. Some important dates to note are (Corbett 2005:19):

- 1957: Euratom, established by the Treaty of Rome, granted that the European Atomic Energy Community may establish a university institution.
- 1972: The decision to found the European University Institute in Florence, Italy, was actualized by the treaty among the six founding members of the EEC at the "Convention Setting Up a European University Institute" on April 19, 1972.
- 1976: The Action Program in Education was established, following the previous treaty's commitment among the EEC's six ministers of education to pursue education policy for the EEC.
- 1987: Erasmus was created by the Council Decision of June 15, 1987, which was the first decision of the EEC on education that completely utilized Community rules to create the international higher education study-abroad program.

The regional integration of Europe, which advanced for nearly half a century before the Bologna Process, ensured that the economic and political architecture was in place to support the intergovernmental cooperation in higher education that came into fruition at the start of the twenty-first century. From 1968, following social revolutions across Europe such as in France, Germany, and Czechoslovakia, traditions changed in the relationships between the politicians and university administrators (Fridenson 2010; Trow 2005). Stakeholders beyond government and the academic sector, such as students and the broader society, were becoming vocal about education policy. The year 1968 was pivotal for the role of university governance, since this was when students assumed greater engagement in governance. Politics began to influence higher education, and higher education administration wanted to be involved in politics (Temesi 2012). While at the European level, the 1960s and 1970s were marked by a period of "euro-sclerosis," or euro-skepticism, an opening evolved in the early 1970s that created new opportunities for higher education policy (Corbett 2005:60).

Among the European Commission officials, Altiero Spinelli, European Commissioner for Industry and Research in the early 1970s, and Félix-Paul Mercereau, who had been responsible for the education portfolio since the early years of Euratom, influenced the agreement among education ministers at a November 1971 meeting. The new "active cooperation" by the EEC soon led to the European University Institute established by convention in 1972, following political negotiations between France and Italy, and eventually led to the Community Action Programme in Education initiated in 1976 (Corbett 2005:70). Before that time, the EEC had hardly any role in education, which was considered in an intergovernmental manner addressed by the Council of Europe. After that time, the policy tools of intergovernmentalism and community competence, from ministers working within the European Council, ensured this notable success, charting a new direction for higher education in Europe (Corbett 2017). This Community Action Programme in 1976 was significant, giving the EU an active role in higher education policy. The first broadly coordinated policy undertaking in higher education, defined as a nonbinding resolution, the program focused on six priorities for action: "actions educating the children of migrant workers, closer relations between education systems in Europe, the compilation of documentation and statistics, higher education, the teaching of foreign languages, and equal opportunities" (European Commission 2006, 2013). Head of Education and Youth (1973–1976) and Director of Education, Training, and Youth (1985–1987), Hywel Ceri Jones shaped European education policy for two decades, between 1973 and 1993, distinguishing himself with his longevity in service and policy entrepreneurship. As well as advancing the Community Action Programme in Education, he was instrumental in delivering Erasmus, which took effect in 1987 (Corbett 2005:136). By working within the institutions of the European Commission, the European Council, and the European Parliament in order to secure budget appropriations, Jones was effective as a policy entrepreneur. Jones and Spinelli are among the eight higher education policy entrepreneurs presented, between 1955 and 2005, in *Universities and the Europe of Knowledge* (Corbett 2005:211–212).

During 1972 the six Member States of the Treaty of Rome committed to creating the European University Institute at the Convention in Florence, Italy, which took place on April 19, 1972. The next year, in 1973, the European Community experienced its first expansion when it grew from six to nine Member States with the addition of Denmark,

Ireland, and the United Kingdom (UK). The UK has among the most reputable universities in the region and the world, most notably Cambridge and Oxford. The high quality of elite research universities in the UK serves as a benchmark to which higher institutions aspire, particularly given the emphasis on global rankings today.[1] Countries collaborate with the European Quality Assurance Registrar (EQAR) on quality standards, a central component of the Bologna Process.

The Single European Act (SEA) in 1986 came about under the leadership of Jacques Delors, President of the European Commission from 1985 to 1995. The SEA set the European common market in motion, establishing the Single Market in by 1993. Among the four freedoms of the common market, for goods, services, capital, and movement of labor or people, the movement of labor has particular relevance for graduates and for higher education policy in the Single Market and the neighboring countries.[2]

The same year that the SEA was ratified, the Mediterranean countries of Portugal and Spain joined the European Community.Greece had joined five years prior, and there were 12 total European Economic Community countries by 1986. These three Mediterranean countries were emerging from four decades of authoritarian rule. Their educational systems devolved, resulting in greater institutional autonomy as the countries democratized across functions of domestic policy. Portugal's Reform Act of July 25, 1973 ("Act 5/73") established a binary system of higher education, separating the administration for the polytechnic institutions and research universities. Spain's constitution of 1978 established the constitutional monarchy with quasi-federal government that assigned educational authority to the 17 autonomous communities known in Spanish as "*autonomías.*" The government of Spain determined that Germany had provided a good example of federal-type administration following World War II, having devolved governance to the regional provinces in key policy areas (Bonete 2013). Provincial authority in education, media, and police affairs is afforded to the regions through the 1949 Basic Law for the Federal Republic of Germany in order to ensure a robust administrative system that shares power with the regional governments. The preceding decades of cooperation among some of the world's most powerful sovereign states affirmed the observations of functionalist scholar David Mitrany, who said "It would indeed be sounder and wiser to speak not of the surrender but of a sharing of sovereignty" (1943:31).

1999–2010: From Launch of the Bologna Process to Creation of the EHEA

The EU, as a political entity, underwent significant transformations in regional integration, from being an emergent federation of sovereign states to a currency union for some of its members with the Economic and Monetary Union (EMU) in 1999. The twenty-first century started off with the significant undertaking to adopt a common currency to create a monetary union. When the euro currency began to be offered on the financial markets in 1999, there were 11 participating countries in the EMU. (Denmark, Sweden, and United Kingdom did not participate, and Greece joined in 2001.) Between 1999 and 2010, the decade shifted attitudes from optimism for European integration to skepticism for the grand experiment of European integration, owing to the global financial crisis from 2007 to 2009. At the beginning of the new millennium the introduction of the euro by the EMU brought enthusiasm for the expansion of European governance into new policy domains such as currency and related financial functions. The introduction of the Bologna Process in 1999 occurred the same year that the EMU started trading the euro on international currency markets ahead of the circulation of the physical currency in 2002.

In this first decade of the twenty-first century, countries began to take measures to establish the EHEA. At the end of the first decade, the euro began to falter when the debt crisis in Greece came to be realized in the spring of 2010. The onset of the euro zone crisis in May 2010, starting in Greece, followed soon after the global recession of 2008, from which advanced economies continued to be affected by slower economic growth into the second decade of the century. During 2011, Ireland and Portugal received financial assistance from the troika (European Central Bank, European Union, and International Monetary Fund), and during 2012 Spain received financial assistance, supporting its banking financial sector. There remains an element of uncertainty because of the participation of countries with severe fiscal imbalances and because the monetary union exists without a fiscal union. However, the higher education initiative of the Bologna Process continues to progress with relatively less skepticism about the objectives affirmed for achievement by the year 2020 and beyond (EHEA 2012a, b, 2015).

The European enlargement in the first decade of the twenty-first century brought the accession of 12 new Member States. Eight (8) of the

10 that joined in 2004, along with the two that joined in 2007, had communist educational traditions that had been in place during the post-World War II decades through the Cold War. Post-communist countries embraced international economic integration and the opportunity to join capital markets in their unique ways (Kanet and Kirschbaum 2007). These new Member States combated the social costs of mitigating poverty and inequality while embracing a return to European institutional norms (Bohle and Greskovits 2009:54). The addition of post-communist countries raised concerns about a culture of corruption in higher education, since the decentralization of educational administration created openings for corruption in administration of educational degrees. The effect of educational corruption is similar to the effect of lower quality education (Heyneman et al. 2008:21). Although some corruption existed under communism, the extent of educational corruption heightened along with decentralization of educational administration (Heyneman et al. 2008:21). The controls of educational corruption and respect for human rights, including the rights of students, have been a consideration for countries seeking to join the EHEA. The country of Belarus joined in 2015 after postponement of its application in 2012. The Kyrgyz Republic, along with Israel and Kosovo, did not have their membership request to join the Bologna Process accepted in 2007 on the grounds that they had not yet ratified the European Cultural Convention (Mundell 2012).

The post-communist countries that joined the EU in 2004 and 2007 were eager to join the knowledge society (without restrictions on areas of academic inquiry) that was being constructed in the Bologna Process. The political values and practices of Western Europe were attractive to the aspiring member states, and there was no real opposition to the Bologna Process from Central and Eastern Europe. Accession to the EU mattered most; the absolutely decisive factor for countries to participate in the EHEA was to be accepted as a member of the EU (Matei 2012). The European economic space became expanded with the entry of 12 new Member States during the first decade of the twenty-first century in 2004 and 2007 (Rosamond 2002). Beginning in 1989 it was a new era for higher education institutions in Central and Eastern Europe. They had some catching up to do, since the later years under communism had relatively weak institutions (Scott 2002:138). In the decades of the mid-twentieth century, the region had stronger higher education institutions with core competencies in the natural sciences. The natural sciences were strengths for higher education institutions in communist states during the Cold War years (Heyneman 1998:23; Scott 2002:138). There were strong programs and a greater number of students and researchers in the natural sciences because they are not ideologically oriented like the social sciences. The strength of the natural sciences was owing to the resources invested in these fields, which were not ideologically debatable concerning political and social values. The humanities and social sciences in Central and Eastern Europe reflected communist values that were challenged by the U.S., Western Europe, and their allies. Therefore, the communist countries gained an internationally competitive edge in the natural sciences without ideologically confronting nations with democratic and capitalist values. A stronger impetus to offer academic fields of business administration and international management among the new Member States arrived with the expansion of the European economic space within the global economy and that of its neighbors in the early years of globalization in the 1990s and 2000s (Risse 2007; Rosamond 2002).

As political openness and economic development of these countries advanced, the trend for educators and students to move into the Social Sciences field grew. After 1989, while most of the people in Central and Eastern Europe were pleased with new political freedoms, economically there were frustrations, uncertainty, and unemployment (Temesi 2012). Social problems, including poverty and decline in educational quality, abounded in the early years of transition. Teachers had living standard problems, given their decrease in compensation, and they were not as dedicated as they were before 1989. By comparison, in the decades prior, there had been the "illusion of knowledge" that once a student had completed university and had applied that knowledge through employment, their quality of life would improve. The national commitment to public education in these countries initially declined because of economic and social uncertainty (Temesi 2012). A former vice-rector at the Cornivus University of Budapest between 2000 and 2001, JózsefTemesi said that while educational quality became lower, students had other employment interests and life skills that were prioritized as more options became available for participating in the economic market (2012). After 1989, earning money and the employment networks became more important and immediate priorities than completion of higher education, for the traditional-age university student population and their families. The trend in educational quality and participation of students in Central and Eastern European countries in the initial years after 1989 was downward from the European average, while simultaneously the trend for these countries in the post-Cold War years was upward in economic advancement as national GDP grew (Temesi 2012).

The Bologna Process has been blamed, some may argue, for keeping Central and Eastern European countries' educational accomplishments relatively low since 1989 (Temesi 2012). Countries such as Bulgaria, Hungary, and Romania saw the quality of university professors decline and blamed this on the Bologna Process rather than on national factors. Consequentially, in the ensuing decade joining the Bologna Process in 1999 was merely automatic for the 12 candidate countries which joined the EU in 2004 and 2007. Joining the Bologna Process was a political decision: Countries did whatever that had to do to align themselves with European-led policies in their pursuit of EU membership (Matei 2012). According to some Central and Eastern European countries' educational administrators, the acceptance of the Bologna Process prevented educational recovery and simplified education (Temesi 2012). However, rather than the Bologna Process being a cause of educational decline within the countries, it seems to be a coincidence that the countries joined a decade following the political freedoms that were accompanied by institutional changes in education. Education was one of many sectors in the economy, alongside healthcare and utilities services, that decentralized administration following democratization in Central and Eastern Europe.

The Lisbon Strategy and the Open Method of Coordination

The Lisbon Strategyalso known as the Lisbon Agenda, was introduced in 2000, providing an opening for the Europeanization of higher education. The Bologna Process is recognized as a convergence of national efforts driven by the Lisbon Strategy, and the participating countries and higher education institutions are recipients of change (Veiga and Amaral 2009:134). The ideational constructs from the European level of government influence countries and higher education institutions, which are recipients of influence from Europeanization. The process of Europeanization, like the Bologna Process, has two dimensions: sociocultural and economic (Börzel and Risse 2000). "The construction of the EHEA could contribute to a social Europe if it helps to strengthen the social capital, although a content analysis of the core documents of the Bologna Process suggests the domain of the political and economic factors over the cultural dimension" (Veiga and Amaral 2006:284).

In the second decade the Bologna Process has emphasized social concerns and the student dimension, notably in the Yerevan Communiqué (EHEA 2015).

The European Commission has taken an active role in advancing higher education policy and has shaped discourse in the creation of the higher education policy space (Keeling 2006:209). The Open Method of Coordination (OMC) was created in 2000 as part of the Lisbon Strategy to be a soft-power instrument to create a "social Europe" (Barcevičius et al. 2014).[3] The OMC is useful in "soft policy" areas such as education, employment, and the environment, for which decisions on policy competencies remain with the Member States rather than with the EU. These policy areas are delegated to the states under the subsidiarity principle of the EU, which is embedded in the treaties that define political power. By comparison, some competencies for which states pool their sovereignty at the European level are agriculture and trade policies. The discourse scripts that created the EHEA through the Bologna Process are interpreted according to each country's cultural traditions (Capano and Piattoni 2011:585). An understanding emerged with the Lisbon Strategy—that best practices of each country would spillover to model excellence for the region of Europe (European Union 2016). Through the OMC, the European Commission would formally take a lesser role in the intergovernmental policies that were driven by the states. Nevertheless, once the Lisbon Strategy began in 2000, the European Commission heightened its engagement with the Bologna Process as a partner along with the participating countries. The "governance architecture" of the Lisbon Strategy script was applied to advance the higher education agenda (Capano and Piattoni 2011). In the face of challenges for coordination of multi-level governance, the soft power of the Bologna Process continues to exert its influence on participating countries in the absence of European legislation.

At the national level, legislation has been introduced at unique points in time in each country to reform systems of higher education in the three areas of the Bologna Process. These areas are (1) credit and degree structure, (2) quality assurance that concurs with the European Standards and Guidelines (ESG), and (3) recognition of academic degrees across countries. These three areas were measured in 10 dimensions in the Stocktaking Reports prepared for the EHEA Ministerial Conferences in 2005, 2007, and 2009. Between the launch of the Bologna Process in 1999 and the creation of the EHEA in 2010 at the Budapest-Vienna ministerial meeting, the education ministers met five times to advance the vision of the EHEA and its policy implementation in participating countries. These ministerial meetings took place in Prague 2001, Berlin 2003, Bergen 2005, London 2007, and Leuven/Louvain-la-Neuve 2009.

2010–2015: Creation of EHEA to the Ninth Ministerial Conference (Yerevan, Armenia, May 2015)

When the ministers of education met in Budapest and Vienna in 2010, they established the European Higher Education Area. On March 12, 2010, the Budapest-Vienna Declaration on the EHEA announced the ongoing commitment to the intergovernmental initiative. Even though the vision that the Bologna Process set into motion a decade previously was officially attained by establishing the EHEA, many Member States still had implementation objectives yet to be met. As is characteristic of OMC coordination, there are concerns about accountability of national governments to implement the EHEA objectives without a strong governing mechanism of formal law (Jayasuriya 2010). Complexity exists among levels of governance in the implementation of the Bologna Process, and the OMC does not take into account the influence of the numerous agents at the institutional level of higher education (Veiga and Amaral 2006:292).

The year 2010 began with the EU's new governing Treaty of Lisbon in place, which had become effective on December 1, 2009. In March 2010, the announcement of the European Commission's economic growth strategy, Europe 2020, provided substantive guidance on objectives for Member States. Europe 2020 was presented by the European Commission president, José Manuel Barroso, to offer a vision for the decade. Politically there has been resistance to European initiatives because of national economic growth concerns. In the face of European-defined objectives across policy areas, select countries have faced the concurrent challenges of responding to the euro area crisis and confronting growing euro-skepticism in domestic politics. Far-right nationalistic parties have become more active in some countries, including Germany (Alternative for Germany/*Deutschland* [AfD]), The Netherlands (Party for Freedom), and Finland (where the True Finns earned significant representation and became the Finns Party). An increasing number of representatives from non-traditional parties earned seats in the 2014 elections for the European Parliament, which has had elections every five years since 1979.

This increasing pluralism demonstrates a greater range of political voices, which have challenged the influence of EU policies that rely on cooperation through supranationalism and intergovernmentalism. Historically, periods of economic downtown have caused social and political actors in countries to advance national priorities at the expense of international cooperation (Lefkofridi and Schmitter 2015).

The Lisbon Strategy, aspects of which evolved into the Europe 2020 economic growth strategy with its emphasis on competitiveness in the knowledge economy, was complementary to the Bologna Process (Jayasuria 2010; Robertson 2010). Education, along with employment, innovation, social inclusion, and climate-energy sustainability, is one of the five key areas of Europe 2020. The significance of education in its relationship to each of the other four key areas in the strategy, is the enhancement of the competitiveness and innovativeness of the European region. The five key areas are interdependent and are supported by the central goal of achievement in education. Europe 2020 is an example of how strategy in education is assumed to be connected to economic outcomes, and it articulates the aspirations of the EU to compete successfully in the rapidly changing global economy. These policies have a built-in assumption that higher education institutions are agents for positive outcomes in the economy. The EU objective for an average of 40% of 30–34 year olds to attain higher education is a benchmark in this strategy, which is assessed in Chap. 4. The EHEA Yerevan Ministerial Conference in May 2015 was more about attention to the social dimension of student concerns, with relatively less emphasis on economic concerns of employability (Tyson 2016). Major challenges for the EU are managing crises and efficient decision making. The EU and the world today, which are increasingly technologically driven, are vastly different than when the Bologna Process was launched (Prats-Monné 2016). The advancement of international mobility complements the Europe 2020 objective of higher education attainment, alongside the structural change criteria for harmonization of credits and degrees, quality assurance, and automatic recognition in the Bologna Process.

Summary

As countries joined the EU their traditions shaped the contours of higher education governance in Europe. Neighboring countries have engaged in political cooperation over time, and preceding years of interactions have fostered openness among countries willing to cooperate in the area of higher education policy. The Bologna Process is large enough, in the ideological sense, to accommodate various higher educational traditions from across countries. The criteria put forward by the Bologna Process—on credits and degrees, quality assurance, and recognition across countries—while demanding, are not as stringent as to restrict higher education institutions from continuing to develop in line with national traditions. In some cases, such as countries that had emerged from authoritarian rule in previous decades, the Bologna Process has coincided with the opportunity to embrace new democratic values and global business and international economics academic studies.

Since the beginning of European regional integration post-World War II, the Member States' intergovernmental policy cooperation occasionally provided support for higher education and research in Europe (Corbett 2005). The year 1999 was important because of the launch of the Bologna Process, signifying that over time higher education institutions can become agents of regional and global change. When higher education institutions are agents of change, the intended policy outcomes are greater social cohesion and economic growth nationally, as well as greater opportunities for academic and professional mobility internationally. An aspect of Europeanization that comes into effect is the financial leverage of the European Commission to induce higher education institutions to be agents of change (Keeling 2006). This has continued with the Erasmus international exchange program, which remains an important aspect of higher education supported by the Lisbon Strategy and Bologna Process agendas (Batory and Lindstrom 2011).

> The Commission shapes higher education reform and does this not simply by facilitating learning and emulation through fostering transnational linkages, as OMC accounts suggest, or by persuading national governments to adapt, but rather by directly intervening in the higher education sector itself. (Batory and Lindstrom 2011:324)

While the EU has enlarged over the decades and is engaged extensively in its eastern and southern neighborhood of countries, the efforts to regionally integrate higher education are an unprecedented initiative on a global scale. Governments in Europe began to take an active role in the education of their citizens to advance literacy in the eighteenth century agricultural economy, such as under the rule of Maria Theresa, Holy Roman Empress of the Hapsburg dynasty . In the mid-twentieth century, the demand for universal higher education supported the industrial economy growth after World War II (Burrage 2010; Trow 2005). The appropriate role of government in education has remained a central issue in public policy, as it is today in the twenty-first century knowledge economy that emphasizes technology and services (Heyneman 1998). Across the EHEA countries, higher education is delivered through a variety of institutions, public and private, and some institutions have closer alignments with the state than others (Enders and Jongbloed 2007). The Bologna Process has impacts on both Europe and other world regions that can learn from its example of international cooperation and institutional change.The coordination between countries in Latin America and the Iberian countries Portugal and Spain demonstrates an interest to learn from countries to which there are historical and cultural ties.[4]

The following chapter explains how national commitments to institutional change in the Bologna Process have conferred dual roles on higher education institutions, as both recipients of policy change and agents of policy change in the knowledge economy. The influences of intergovernmental cooperation and the Europeanization of national interests have acted upon higher education institutions to become recipients of institutional change before they become agents of change. Higher education institutions are recipients of changes that are driven by intergovernmentalism at the national level and Europeanization at the supranational. Higher education institutions become agents of change, as envisaged by Europe 2020, as they cultivate graduates and researchers with knowledge of a socially defined Europe and skills to succeed through employability in the global economy.

NOTES

1. Global rankings that are widely referenced are Academic Ranking of World Universities (ARWU) from Shanghai Jiao Tong University and the British-published *Times Higher Education* World University Rankings.
2. The European Neighbourhood Policy (ENP) is maintained by the European External Action Service (EEAS). The ENP engages with neighboring countries to support civic and economic development.
3. The Lisbon Strategy was the European Commission and European Union strategy that preceded the ratification of the Lisbon Treaty. The

Lisbon Treaty governing the EU went into effect of December 1, 2009. This EU initiative is distinct from the 1997 Lisbon Convention on the "Recognition of Qualifications concerning Higher Education in the European Region."

4. *El Centro Interuniversitario de Desarollo* (CINDA), the Inter-University Center for Development, presents periodic reports on higher education trends in Ibero-America.

REFERENCES

Amaral, A., Neave, G., Musselin, C., & Maassen, P. (Eds.). (2009). *European integration and the Governance of Higher Education and Research*. Dordrecht: Springer.

Amaral, A., Magalhães, A., & Veiga, A. (2015). Differentiated integration and the Bologna Process. *Journal of Contemporary European Research, 11*(1), 84–102.

Barcevičius, E, Weishaupt, J., & Zeitlin, J. (2014). *Assessing the Open Method Coordination: Institutional Design and National Influence on EU Social Policy Coordination*. London: Palgrave Macmillan.

Batory, A., & Nicole L. (2011). The power of the purse: Supranational entrepreneurship, financial incentives, and European Higher Education Policy. *Governance: An International Journal of Policy, Administration, and Institutions, 24*(2), 311–329.

Bohle, D., & Greskovits, B. (2009). East-Central Europe's Quandary. *Journal of Democracy, 20*(4), 50–63.

Bonete Perales, R. (2012, June 28, 2013, May 30). Associate Professor of Applied Economics, and Assessor for the Vice-Chancellor of Internationalization, University of Salamanca. Counselor for Education to the Permanent Delegations of Spain to OECD, UNESCO and the Council of Europe (July 2010–July 2012). Member of the Bologna Follow Up Group for Spain (2008–2012).

Börzel, T. A., & Risse, T. (2000). When Europe hits home: Europeanization and domestic change. *European Integration online Papers (EIoP), 4*, 15. Retrieved from http://eiop.or.at/eiop/texte/2000-015a.htm.

Burrage, J. (Ed.). (2010). *Martin Trow: Twentieth-century higher education: Elite to mass to universal*. Baltimore: Johns Hopkins University Press.

Cappano, G., & Piattoni, S. (2011). From Bologna to Lisbon: The political uses of the Lisbon 'script' in European Higher Education Policy. *Journal of European Public Policy, 18*(4), 584–606.

Chou, M. H., & Gornitzka, Å. (2014). *Building the knowledge economy in Europe: New constellations in European Research and Higher Education Governance*. Cheltenham: Edward Elgar.

Corbett, A. (2005). *Universities and the Europe of knowledge: Ideas, institutions and policy entrepreneurship in European Union Higher Education 1955–2005.* New York: Palgrave Macmillan.

Corbett, A. (2017, February 27). Senior Associate, LSE Enterprise. London School of Economics and Political Science. Correspondence.

Cyert, R., & March, J. (1963). *A Behavioral Theory of the Firm.* Englewood Cliffs, NJ: Prentice Hall.

EHEA Ministerial Conference. (2012a). Bucharest Communiqué: Making the most of our potential: Consolidating the European Higher Education Area. Retrieved from http://www.ehea.info/Uploads/%281%29/Bucharest%20Communique%202012%281%29.pdf.

EHEA Ministerial Conference. (2012b). Mobility for better learning: Mobility strategy 2020 for the European Higher Education Area (EHEA). Retrieved from http://www.ehea.info/Uploads/(1)/2012%20EHEA%20Mobility%20Strategy.pdf.

EHEA Ministerial Conference. (2015). Yerevan Communiqué. Retrieved from http://bologna-yerevan2015.ehea.info/files/YerevanCommuniqueFinal.pdf.

EHEA Pathfinder Group on Automatic Recognition. (2015, January). Report by the EHEA Pathfinder Group on Automatic Recognition. To Present to the Ministers of the Bologna Ministerial in Yerevan, Armenia.

Enders, J., & Jongbloed, B. (Eds.). (2007). *Public-private dynamics in Higher Education: Expectations, developments and outcomes.* Piscataway: Transaction.

European Commission. (2006). The history of European cooperation in education and training: Europe in the Making—An Example. Report.

European Commission. (2013). "History of European co-operation in education" Education and training. Updated 7 February 2013. Retrieved from http://ec.europa.eu/education/more-information/former-programmes_en.htm.

European Union. (1957). Treaty Establishing the European Economic Community (EEC), Treaty of Rome.

European Union. (1986). Treaties Establishing the European Communities: Treaties Amending these Treaties. *Single European Act.*

European Union. (1997). Treaty of Amsterdam Amending the Treaty on European Union: The Treaties Establishing the European Communities and Certain Related Acts.

European Union. (1992). Treaty on European Union (TEU), Treaty of Maastricht.

European Union. (2016). The Lisbon strategy in short. Retrieved from https://portal.cor.europa.eu/europe2020/Profiles/Pages/TheLisbonStrategyinshort.aspx.

Finnemore, M., & Sikkink, K. (1998). International norm dynamics and political change. *International Organization, 52*(4), 887–917.

Fridenson, P. (2010). La Politique Universitaire depuis 1968. *Le Mouvement Social* 2010/4: 233, 47–67.

Furlong, P. (2010). "Bologna's deepening empire: Higher education policy in Europe." In Kenneth Dyson & Angelos Sepos (Eds.). *Which Europe?: The politics of differentiated integration.* Houndmills, UK: Palgrave Macmillan.

Hall, P. A. (2010). Historical institutionalism in rational and sociological perspective. In James Mahoney & Kathleen Thelen (Eds.), *Explaining institutional change: Ambiguity, agency, and power.* Cambridge: Cambridge University Press.

Hall, P. A., & Taylor, R. C. R. (1996). *Political science and the three new institutionalisms. Political Studies, XLIV,* 936–957.

Heyneman, S. P. (1998). The transition from party/state to open democracy: The role of education. *International Journal of Educational Development, 18*(1), 21–40.

Heyneman, S. P., Anderson, K. H., & Nuraliyeva, N. (2008). The cost of corruption in Higher Education. *Comparative Education Review, 52*(1), 1–25.

Jayasuriya, K. (2010). Learning by the market: Regulatory regionalism, Bologna, and accountability communities. *Globalisation Societies and Education, 8*(1), 7–22.

Kanet, R. E., & Kirschbaum, S. (Eds.). (2007). *The meaning of Europe: Central Europe and the EU.* Houndmills: Palgrave Macmillan.

Keeling, R. (2006). The Bologna Process and the Lisbon Research Agenda: The European Commission's expanding role in Higher Education discourse. *European Journal of Education, 41*(2), 203–223.

Kölliker, A. (2001). Bringing together or Driving apart the Union? Towards a theory of differentiated integration. Preprints aus der Max-Planck-Projektgruppe Recht der Gemeinschaftsgüter. Bonn: Gemeinschaftsgüter: Recht, Politik und Ökonomie, 2001/5.

Lefkofridi, Z., & Schmitter, P. C. (2015). Transcending or descending? European integration in times of crisis. *European Political Science Review, 7,* 3–22.

March, J. G., & Olsen, J. P. (1989). *Rediscovering institutions: The organizational basis of politics.* New York: Free Press.

March, J. G., & Johan P. O. (1984). The new institutionalism: Organizational factors in political life. *American Political Science Review, 78*(3), 734–749.

Matei, L. (2012, July 18). Chief operating officer and Professor of Public Policy, Central European University, Budapest, Hungary.

Mitrany, D. (1943). A working peace system. *An argument for the functional development of international organization.* London: Royal Institute of International Affairs.

Mundell, I. (2012). No Bologna for Belarus. *European Voice*. Retrieved April 4, 2012, from http://www.europeanvoice.com/article/imported/no-bologna-for-belarus/74079.aspx.

Peters, B. G. (2012). *Institutional theory in political science: The new institutionalism* (3rd ed.). New York: Continuum Books.

Pettigrew, A. (1990). Longitudonal field research on change: Theory and practice. *Organization Science, 1*(3), 267–292.

Pierson, P. (2004). *Politics in time: History, analysis, and social analysis*. Princeton: Princeton University Press.

Prats-Monné, X. (2012, April, 2016, September 6). Director-general for heath and food safety; Former Director General for Education and Culture, European Commission; Correspondence.

Risse, T. (2007). Social constructivism meets globalization. In A. Held and D. McGrew (Eds.), *Globalization theory: Approaches and controversies* (pp. 126–147). Cambridge: Polity Press.

Risse, T. (2009). Social constructivism and European integration. In A. Wiener & Thomas Diez (Eds.), *European Integration theory* (2nd ed., pp. 144–169). Oxford: Oxford University Press.

Risse, T. (2010). *A community of Europeans? Transnational identities and public spheres*. Ithaca: Cornell University Press.

Robertson, S. L. (2010). The EU, 'Regulatory State Regionalism' and new modes of Higher Education Governance. *Globalisation Societies and Education, 8*(1), 23–37.

Rosamond, B. (2002). Imagining the European economy: 'Competitiveness' and the social construction of 'Europe' as an economic space. *New Political Economy, 7*(2), 157–177.

Schimmelfennig, F. (2015). Differentiated integration before and after the crisis. In O. Cramme & S. B. Hobolt (Eds.). 2015. *Democratic Politics in an EU under stress* (pp. 120–134). Oxford: Oxford University Press.

Scott, P. (2002). Reflections on the reform of Higher Education in Central and Eastern Europe. *Higher Education in Europe, 27*(1–2), 137–152.

Scott, W. R. (2014). *Institutions and organizations: Ideas, interests, and identities* (4th ed.). Los Angeles: SAGE.

Sørensen, M. P., Bloch, C., & Young, M. (2015). Excellence in the knowledge-based economy: From scientific to research excellence. *European Journal of Higher Education*, 1–20.

Temesi, J. (2012, July 12). Director, Center for International Higher Education Studies and Vice Rector 1995–2004, Corvinus University of Budapest, Hungary.

Trow, M. (2005). Reflections on the transition from elite to mass to universal access: Forms and phases of Higher Education in modern societies since

WWII. Working Papers, Institute of governmental studies, University of California-Berkeley.

Tyson, A. (2012, April 25, 2016, September 6). Acting Director for strategy and evaluation, Former Head of UnitC1, Higher Education and Erasmus, Directorate-General Education and Culture, European Commission.

Veiga, A., & Amaral, A. (2006). The open method of coordination and the implementation of the Bologna Process. *Tertiary Education and Management, 12,* 283–295.

Veiga, A., & Amaral, A. (2009). Policy implementation tools and European Governance. In A. Amaral, G. Neave, C. Musselin, & P. Maassen (Eds.), *European Integration and the Governance of Higher Education Research* (pp. 133–157). Dordrecht: Springer.

.

CHAPTER 4

The Dual Roles of Higher Education Institutions in the Knowledge Economy

The Europe we are building up is not only the one of the euro, of the banks and of the economy; it must be a Europe of knowledge as well. We must strengthen and build upon the intellectual, cultural, social and technical dimensions of our continent. These have to a large extent been shaped by its universities, which continue to play a pivotal role for their development.
The Sorbonne Declaration (excerpt), May 25, 1998

In a historical institutional perspective, this chapter presents the policy processes of Europeanization (top-down and state-responsive) and inter-governmentalism (bottom-up and state-driven) and their application to higher education policy. Since the Bologna Process began in 1999, the European Commission is a partner alongside the 48 countries in the European Higher Education Area (EHEA). There are dual roles of higher education institutions, supporting objectives for increased mobility in the social dimension of higher education and objectives for competitiveness in the knowledge economy. This EHEA commitment to student mobility objectives through the year 2020 is described within the Bucharest Communiqué (EHEA 2012a). Institutional changes of recent years place higher education policy in the context of the European Commission's economic growth strategy, Europe 2020, which outlines the motivations and benchmarks for a region that is "smart, sustainable, and inclusive" (European Commission 2016a).

© The Author(s) 2017
B. Barrett, *Globalization and Change in Higher Education*,
DOI 10.1007/978-3-319-52368-2_4

The place of higher education institutions in the economy and society has dual roles, contributing to their significance as agents of change. Higher education institutions are both recipients and agents of change in the political economy context. Initially, the Bologna Process and Europe 2020 objectives highlight that higher education institutions are intended to be recipients of change in the policy process.[1] Ultimately, higher education institutions are intended by stakeholders (academic, public, private) to bring about a change through increased knowledge of graduates, leading to enhanced competitiveness in the global economy. Sociological and historical institutional perspectives frame the analysis of Europeanization (Schmidt 2005, 2009) and intergovernmentalism (Pierson 1996; Moravcsik 1998).

The EHEA is placing more emphasis on making higher education institutions agents of change. This is aligned with the intentions of the Europe 2020 economic growth strategy of the European Commission, which was launched in 2010. The communiqués of the EHEA ministers at the Bologna Process conferences state that the following are the intended policy outcomes of higher education institutions as agents of change (Bologna Process Secretariat 2016):

- Increased social cohesion nationally and regionally together with economic growth
- Increased social mobility and opportunities for employability within the country
- Increased opportunities for academic and professional mobility internationally

A primary challenge in Social Sciences research is attributing these economic and social outcomes to higher education policy reform. The outcomes may come from fiscal policies or monetary policies that incentivize economic growth, or other variables that are not identified in research. A second challenge is the relatively long time—years, decades, or generations—that it takes to see effects of higher education policy reform. Because states and markets fall short in providing productive-use systems over the long term, communities depend on institutions (Ostrom 1990:1). The policies of higher education are a hybrid of state and market interests, reflecting neither the state nor the market alone in their governance (Dobbins and Knill 2009, 2014).

A New Kind of Regional Integration Through Higher Education

The coordination of higher education policy in the EHEA aligns with the economic growth strategy of Europe 2020 for the 28 EU Member States. The headline target of the strategy for higher education is attainment by 40 percent of graduates, 30–34 years old. In turn, they will be equipped to contribute knowledge in the socioeconomic dimension within the region and globally. The Strategic Framework for Education and Training outlines the priorities of the European Commission (European Commission 2016b). These strategies provide an informative context for the 20 additional countries in the Bologna Process that are not in the EU. The emphasis on higher education attainment serves as a proxy for a wider range of measures (Tyson 2016).

This wider range of measures includes:

- Secondary education preparation
- Higher education access requirements
- Nontraditional routes to higher education for first-generation students
- The appeal of the curricula and degree requirements for higher education

The Bologna Process is a response of internationalization to the pressures of globalization, and with it comes changing conceptions of the modern university (European Commission 2011; Eurydice 2012). The idea behind the Bologna Process drives a new kind of regional integration, supported by a discourse and a vision that is socially constructed as it unfolds (Christiansen 2001; Nokkola 2007). The motto of the European Union, "unity in diversity", is especially true for the regional integration of higher education policy. Over history, regional integration in higher education was pursued by policy entrepreneurs shaping the historical institutions of the EU. The entrepreneurs included their policy priorities along with broader initiatives in regional integration (Corbett 2005; Dinan 2014).

An important, increasingly supported initiative for European education has been the Erasmus international student exchange, established in 1987 by the European Commission. The success of Erasmus gave momentum to the 1998 Sorbonne Declaration—formulated by the education ministers of Italy, France, Germany, and the United Kingdom—which paved the way for the Bologna Process that created the EHEA (Neave 2003a:33, 2003b). Erasmus was initially proposed in 1986 and ultimately adopted in 1987 by the European Commission as the European Community Action Scheme for the Mobility of University Students (Erasmus). Over three decades, the initiative has evolved into Erasmus Mundus and, later, Erasmus+ to include students and exchanges beyond Europe. The mobility of students in Erasmus, for semester or year-abroad study, paved the way for convergence of higher education degrees across countries.

> Erasmus demonstrated the need for a single system of transferable credits (ECTS), for rules on the recognition of qualifications (Lisbon Convention), and for quality assurance to be underpinned by common principles (the European Standards and Guidelines) as a basis of trust between higher education systems. (Tyson 2012)

Beyond the Bologna Process and Erasmus, there are regional programs for higher education, lifelong learning, vocational training, and ongoing student exchanges in Europe. Additional educational programs of the EU include those for Vocational and Education Training (VET) such as Grundtvig and Leonardo, those for languages such as Lingua and Socrates, and those for young students such as IRIS and Petra.[2] The education policy initiatives of the European Communities include the COMmunity programme for Education and Training in Technology (COMETT) and Erasmus.

Globalization and internationalization have been shaping Europe, and the commitment to higher education reform is an outcome resulting from these pressures in recent years. As countries have joined the EU and the EHEA, they have brought distinct traditions and values that affect their views of higher education. The EU is "becoming" rather than "being" (Moravcsik 2005:350), and this applies to the region beyond the 28 Member States. The agenda and space of the EHEA have been socially constructed through discourse (Nokkola 2007:221), and they are complementary to the construction of the European economic agenda and space (Rosamond 2002). Sociological institutionalism explains that regional scripts of appropriate behavior are acted out as norms that become established in these public spaces (Risse 2007).

This emphasis on the European social model reflects a policy concern with developing human capital (or 'intangible assets') as the basis of European competitiveness. It also reflects a recent tendency within EU policy circles to make claims about those elements of a European model that should remain robust in the face of globalisation. (Rosamond 2002:171)

Tracing the development of educational policy through historical analysis of regional integration explains how the region arrived at international cooperation in the higher education dimension, which has synergistically advanced regional integration in Europe. Regional integration since the start of the European project considers the three central dynamics that are explanatory factors throughout this book: competitive economic pressures through globalization, domestic politics through intergovernmentalism, and sociological and ideational processes stemming from the EU and European institutions through Europeanization. Considering globalization, advancements in communications and technology bring speed to most elements of daily life and bring additional pressure to governmental priorities. Because of intergovernmentalism, countries coordinate domestic policies through intergovernmental bargaining. Because of Europeanization, European-level leadership influences the national level of policy implementation through legislative procedures (Schmidt 2002, 2009). National cooperation generated by intergovernmentalism and social norm diffusion resulting from Europeanization are dynamics that have driven the policy process in higher education reform. The complementary influences of intergovernmentalism and Europeanization have impacted policy reform to varying extents within each country.

The traditions in the relationship of the state to the governance of higher education vary across the region of Europe (Dobbins and Knill 2009, 2014; Heyneman 2009, 2010). The Bologna Process countries inside and outside the EU are influenced by the higher education governance of states in their geographic proximity (Scott 2002). There are traditions in higher education corresponding to various social models particular to regions, such as Anglo-Saxon, Continental, Mediterranean, Central and Eastern European, and Scandinavian. The institutional nature of the EU itself is challenged by the results of enlargement, immigration, nationalism, and security among other concerns that have arisen since the process of integration began after World War II. Through each stage of EU enlargement, Member States that joined the European Community brought along higher education traditions. The policy entrepreneurs influenced the higher education traditions and created the social constructs upon which institutions that implement policies were built (Hall and Taylor 1996:951). Broader economic and governance policies unfolded in the region through treaties that impacted countries and their higher education institutions.

EUROPEANIZATION AND INTERGOVERNMENTALISM IN HIGHER EDUCATION POLICY

Historical institutionalism frames the policy relationships across levels of governance that make evident both intergovernmentalism and Europeanization in the Bologna Process. Although they are unique phenomena moving in different directions, they both influence the progress toward reforms at the institutional and national levels. To distinguish between intergovernmentalism and Europeanization: Europeanization is the overall regional influence of Europe acting on national and institutional levels (Schmidt 2009); intergovernmentalism is led by the states to make policy at the European level (Moravcsik 1998, 2005). The internationalization of higher education through Europeanization is part of the process to build the EHEA (Bache 2006; Batory and Lindstrom 2011). Europeanization is described by scholars as a top-down effect from the EU on the Member States that affects national institutional structures and national policy-making processes (Schmidt 2009:204–206). Although Europeanization is distinct from European integration, they influence each other in a dynamic relationship (Schmidt 2009:211; 2005). European integration in the context of intergovernmentalism is Member State—driven. Europeanization operates at the supranational level that influences the national level.

Depending on national circumstances, intergovernmentalism or Europeanization may be a stronger policy process. The higher education institution stakeholders or constituencies are important influences. The academic institutions, the state in the public sector, and the market in the private sector are the key stakeholders in modern European university (Regini 2011). The theory of liberal intergovernmentalism put forward by Moravcsik claims that the states have led the initiative for international cooperation (1998). An analysis of policy implementation across levels of governance emphasizes the importance of the national level due to the "domestic nature of Bologna reforms" (Veiga

2012:389). Within social and economic policy spaces, Europeanization has been taking place at the national level, which in turn influences the institutional level. "The point is that the examination of Europeanization effects (positive integration, negative integration and 'framing' integration) linked to the implementation of a single policy framework (Bologna Process and Lisbon Strategy) deals with a policy area where European policies require incremental changes in national frameworks" (Veiga and Amaral 2006:293).

The Europeanization top-down influence of the Bologna Process, in which the direction of agency proceeds from the greater region to the state, is explained in this book for Portugal and Spain. These countries incorporated European standards alongside their domestic reforms that had taken place before the start of the Bologna Process. In Portugal, the policy processes incorporated the principles from the domestic University Autonomy Act (1988) with subsequent domestic laws on higher education policy. In Spain, European principles were incorporated into the domestic legislations *LOU: Ley de Ordinación Universitaria* (2001) Act on Universities and the amended *LOMLOU* Act Modifying the Act on Universities (2007).

The dynamics of intergovernmentalism work in a contrary direction, in which agency proceeds from the state to the greater regional initiative. Both directions of influence, Europeanization and intergovernmentalism, are complementary dynamics in regional integration and coexist, albeit with some imbalance, in each national circumstance.

Europeanization does not take place consistently across countries in Europe (Bulmer and Radaelli 2004). The Bologna Process is a soft power policy, and there are not political ramifications for noncompliance other than reputational effects. The Open Method of Coordination (OMC) that emerged from the Lisbon Strategy in 2000 is a mechanism to deliver this policy cooperation in higher education. Challenges exist in implementation because an enforcement mechanism is lacking. Soft policies such as the EHEA, ERA, Lisbon Strategy, and Europe 2020 have weaknesses in policy coordination, since there is no governance enforcement (Amaral 2011). Alberto Amaral, founding director of the Portuguese national accreditation agency, concludes that:

> Building a strong Europe will probably need stronger mechanisms for coordinating policy implementation and an agreement of member states on clear objectives for those policies. Eventually, policy implementation

will become more coordinated, not only at the level of national interpretation but also at the pace of implementation. Whatever the future, the present turmoil resulting from the economic crisis will result in significant changes in European policy implementation. (Amaral 2011:47)

Intergovernmentalism explains the expansion of national cooperation in the regional policy domain of higher education in Europe (Neave and Maassen 2007). The origins of explanations for this international cooperation relates to neofunctionalist principles, which explained the first efforts toward regional integration in the mid-twentieth century. When the Treaty of Rome came into effect in 1958, Ernst Hass completed the neofunctionalist treatise *The Uniting of Europe*. The two principles that Haas contributed to neofunctionalism remain relevant to why countries pursue intergovernmental policy in recent years:

1. Integration progresses when organized economic interests pressure governments to manage economic interdependence to their advantage by centralizing policies and institutions.

2. Initial decisions to integrate economically create economic and political spillovers—unintended or unwanted consequences of earlier decisions—which are the major force propelling regional integration further forward (Moravcsik 2005:351–352).

The spillovers that resulted from integration in functional areas continued to expand through the decades until reaching the policy domain of higher education. The active role of the state in intergovernmental policy cooperation shows:

Major steps toward regional integration results, as does global economic integration, from a three-step process: (a) national preferences develop in response to exogenous changes in the nature of issue-specific functional interdependence; (b) interstate negotiation proceeds on the basis of relative bargaining power; and (c) delegation to supranational institutions is designed to facilitate credible commitments. (Moravcsik 2005:358)

These three steps explain the response of European national governments and higher education institutions to the exogenous influence of globalization, and the continued negotiations to define the steps forward.

After having agreed to a "grand bargain" at the international negotiating table, policies are changed at the national level when it comes to
implementation. To understand the political and economic influences on
policy implementation and international coordination, it is necessary to
consider the explanatory power of political institutions and the potential for compromise. Political institutions may shape outcomes by providing or withholding resources and by representing political parties that
convey values and a policy agenda (March and Olsen 1989). Institutions
are here defined on multiple levels of governance: the supranational level
of the EU, the national level of the state, and the sub-national level of
the higher education institution. Through an institutional approach,
one identifies the underlying processes and mechanisms that contribute to institutional change. However, scholars attest that there remain
many unexplained factors to investigate in explaining institutional change
(Olsen 2009:27).

> Institutional arrangements are usually a product of situation-specific com-
> promises. They fit more or less into a coherent order and they function
> through a mix of co-existing organizational and normative principles,
> behavioral logics, and legitimate resources. (Olsen 2009:18)

Given the Member States' proactive position in intergovernmental theory, the states influence in an upward governance direction toward the
supranational level of European initiatives. The European political entities, such as the Council of Europe and the European Commission,
influence the higher education institutions (Bache 2006:236; Keeling
2006). Europeanization, and participating countries at the national level
in the Bologna Process, influence, in turn, the higher education institutions' governance. Institutions experience dual pressures from both
supranational and national levels. Figure 4.1 shows the path of agency
from the Member States to the European institutions and the higher
education institutions. Figure 4.2 shows the role of higher education
institutions as agents of change in the region as they build European
economic competitiveness.

International Mobility in Higher Education

Around the world, the internationalization of higher education has
become a twenty-first century objective for increasing numbers of higher

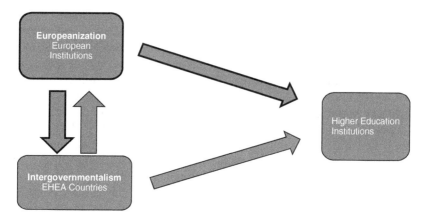

Fig. 4.1 Higher Education Institutions (HEIs) as recipients of change. Reciprocity between the influences of Europeanization and the influences of intergovernmentalism. Europeanization from institutions influences EHEA participating countries and higher education institutions. Intergovernmental from EHEA countries influences the European level policy and higher education institutions

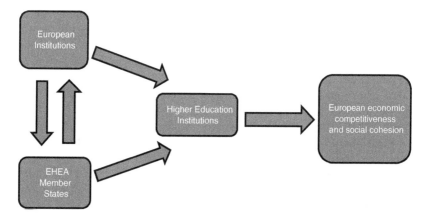

Fig. 4.2 Higher Education Institutions (HEIs) as agents of change. Following the influence of European institutions and EHEA participating countries on higher education institutions, the institutions influence European economic competitiveness and social cohesion. HEIs are recipients and agents of institutional change

education institutions (Martens et al. 2014; Spring 2009). There is growing interest in the internationalization of curriculum and the mobility of students, which provides a complement for mobility of labor in the EU common market.[3]

> In fact, every substantial policy document of the Bologna Process explicitly emphasizes student mobility as both a means to establish the EHEA as well as an indicator to measure its success in terms of competitiveness and compatibility. As a central policy outcome, the trajectory of student mobility can thus be viewed as a benchmark against which to measure the success of Bologna reforms. (Fulge and Vögtle 2014:68)

Student mobility as a goal in the Bologna Process was emphasized at the EHEA Bucharest Ministerial Conference in April 2012 (EHEA 2012b). The mobility strategy was presented that set the objective for 20 percent of students to spend a period of study abroad by the year 2020.[4]Higher education institutions are agents of mobility by providing opportunities for students and researchers to study and to work beyond their home country. There are administrative barriers such as quotas limiting enrollment and higher tuition costs for foreign students; however, the mobility of students and the international recognition of academic credits and degrees are expected to enhance educational quality, student learning outcomes, and economic development (EHEA 2012a, b). The discourse in the Bologna Process and the EHEA proclamations reveals that mobility is a value. The importance of mobility is specified in the Bologna Declaration (1999) and the Prague Communiqué (2001):

> Promotion of *mobility* by overcoming obstacles to the effective exercise of free movement with particular attention to:
>
> - for students, access to study and training opportunities and to related services
> - for teachers, researchers and administrative staff, recognition and valorisation of periods spent in a European context researching, teaching and training, without prejudicing their statutory rights. (Bologna Declaration 1999)

> Ministers reaffirmed that efforts to promote *mobility* must be continued to enable students, teachers, researchers and administrative staff to benefit from the richness of the European Higher Education Area, including its

democratic values, diversity of cultures and languages and the diversity of higher educational systems. (Prague Communiqué 2001)

Diversity of educational experiences through an international study period is highly desirable in today's global society in order to develop adaptability to, and understanding of, foreign cultures (Spring 2009). The inherent influence of globalization is pressure for internationalization of higher education that encourages students to spend at least some of their educational experience beyond their home country in order to cultivate an international perspective through living abroad. This diverse academic experience is expected to provide greater preparedness for graduates when looking for employment in the global knowledge economy. Personal knowledge of various countries and their cultures and traditions is an important strength for students seeking employment in the knowledge economy (Martens et al. 2014).

The Erasmus exchange program has provided students with a period of study abroad since 1987. The Marie Curie Action programs, which began in 1996, support mobility of researchers. These programs make Europe an attractive place to study and to research. There is competition within Europe and internationally for locations to study and to research. Beyond the region of Europe, China and India have been increasing their students' enrollments in the higher education systems of the U.S. and the EU. The growing student and researcher diaspora of Chinese and Indians provides new networks of information sharing and transmits knowledge through informal channels of policy diffusion. A joint report of the Migration Policy Institute and the European University Institute compared mobility challenges and opportunities for the EU and the U.S. (Fargues et al. 2011). These two regions, among the most economically advanced in the world, together receive the majority of the world's migrants who seek relocation for education and employment opportunities.

The limited availability of funding at the individual, national, and regional levels is a barrier to educational mobility. The European Commission is committed to mobility of education and to providing funds through the flagship higher education program Erasmus. The European Commission—funded study abroad scheme has been among the most lauded policy programs, providing for limited periods of study abroad, for a semester or an academic year. There was a debate during the second half of 2012 over the appropriate level of Erasmus funding for the EU Multiannual Financial Framework (MFF) 2014–2020

(European Commission 2012). In the EU's MFF 2014–2020, the early announcement of the initiative Erasmus+ was one of the only programs to have received an expansion and a budget increase. At the end of 2013, the then director general for Education and Culture, Androulla Vassiliou, announced Erasmus+, a program to include countries beyond the EU in the educational exchange beginning in 2014.[5] The number of Erasmus students per year has increased from 3264 in the initial academic year 1987–1988 to more than 250,000 in the academic year 2011–2012. There was steady progress toward the 3-million-student mobility target, which was reached in July 2013 (European Commission 2013b). Higher education mobility programs from the EHEA and Erasmus have been simulated by other regions of the world, and outcomes thus far provide lessons for understanding successes and challenges.

The dual role of higher education institutions as recipients and as agents of change makes them important subjects in analyzing the political economy and policy reform. Europe's recent history of regional integration and international collaboration in higher education has contributed to the role that the region plays in the world and to the conception of a global governance of knowledge. The emphasis on higher education attainment reflects a recognition of twenty-first-century society and economy as forces in increasing the importance of knowledge and human mobility. This may be attributed to the growing reliance on technology and the prominence of the services sectors, which often require advanced skills through education. Recognizing the distinctions between attainment and quality, an assessment of the political economy factors that influence higher education attainment is presented in the following chapter.

Notes

1. Since the institutions are not engaged in the European-level policy process, they are recipients of policy decided at the European level and national level. While the institutions may influence the national level, often they have received policy directives—especially in the cases of Portugal and Spain—where faculty described those countries as policy takers.
2. Comett and Grundtvig are vocational adult education programs. Leonardo da Vinci is a European Community vocational training and lifelong-learning program. Lingua and Socrates are language training programs. IRIS is Improvement through Research in the Inclusive School. Petra is European Community vocational training of young people in preparation for adult and working life.

3. Beginning in 2017 the United Kingdom will negotiate its ability to access the European Single Market as part of the process of the British exit from the EU (Brexit).
4. European Higher Education Area Ministerial Conference. 2012. "Mobility for Better Learning: Mobility Strategy 2020 for the European Higher Education Area (EHEA)".
5. European Commission. (2013a). "Erasmus+ is the new EU programme for education, training, youth and sport for 2014–2020, starting in January 2014". Available from: http://ec.europa.eu/education/erasmus-plus/index_en.htm.

REFERENCES

Amaral, A. (2011). ERA and the Bologna Process: Implementation problems and the human resource factor. In S. Avveduto (Ed.), *Convergence or differentiation. Human resources for research in a changing European scenario* (pp. 13–54). Naples: ScriptaWeb.
Bache, I. (2006). The Europeanization of higher education: Markets, politics or learning? *Journal of Common Market Studies, 44*(2), 231–248.
Batory, A., & Lindstrom, N. (2011, April). The power of the purse: Supranational entrepreneurship, financial incentives, and European higher education policy. *Governance: An International Journal of Policy, Administration, and Institutions, 24*(2), 311–329.
Bologna Process. (1999). The Bologna Declaration of 19 June 1999: Joint declaration of the European Ministers of Education.
Bologna Process. (2001). The Prague Communiqué of 19 May 2001: Towards the European Higher Education Area. Communiqué of the meeting of European Ministers in charge of Higher Education.
Bologna Process Secretariat. (2016). European higher education area. http://www.ehea.info/#.
Bulmer, S. J., & Radaelli, C. M. (2004). The Europeanisation of National Policy? Queen's University Belfast Papers on Europeanisation. No. 1/2004. http://www.qub.ac.uk/schools/SchoolofPoliticsInternationalStudiesandPhilosophy/FileStore/EuropeanisationFiles/Filetoupload,38405,en.pdf.
Christiansen, T. J., et al. (2001). *Social construction of Europe*. London: SAGE.
Corbett, A. (2005). *Universities and the Europe of knowledge: Ideas, institutions and policy entrepreneurship in European Union higher education 1955–2005*. New York: Palgrave Macmillan.
Dinan, D. (2014). *Origins and evolution of the European Union* (2nd ed.). The New European Union Series. Oxford: Oxford University Press.
Dobbins, M., & Knill, C. (2009). Higher education policies in central and Eastern Europe: Convergence toward a common model? *Governance: An International Journal of Policy Administration, and Institutions, 22*(3), 397–430.

Dobbins, M., & Knill, C. (2014). *Higher education governance and policy change in Western Europe*. London: Palgrave Macmillan.

EHEA Ministerial Conference. (2012a). Bucharest Communiqué: Making the most of our potential: Consolidating the European Higher Education Area. http://www.ehea.info/Uploads/%281%29/Bucharest%20Communique%20 2012%281%29.pdf.

EHEA Ministerial Conference. (2012b). Mobility for better learning: Mobility strategy 2020 for the European Higher Education Area (EHEA). http:// www.ehea.info/Uploads/(1)/2012%20EHEA%20Mobility%20Strategy.pdf.

European Commission. (2011, September 20). Supporting growth and jobs— an agenda for the modernisation of Europe's higher education systems. Communication from the Commission to the European Parliament, the Council, the European Economic and Social Committee and the Committee of the Regions. COM 2011 (567) Final.

European Commission. (2012). The EU averts funding crisis for Erasmus. Press Release. December 12, 2012. http://ec.europa.eu/education/ news/20121212_en.htm.

European Commission. (2013a). Erasmus+ is the new EU programme for education, training, youth and sport for 2014–2020, starting in January 2014. http://ec.europa.eu/education/erasmus-plus/index_en.htm.

European Commission. (2013b). Memo: Erasmus Programme in 2011–2012: The Figures Explained. July 8, 2013.

European Commission. (2016a). European Commission: Europe 2020. http:// ec.europa.eu/europe2020/index_en.htm.

European Commission. (2016b). Strategic Framework—Education & Training. http://ec.europa.eu/education/policy/strategic-framework_en.

Eurydice: Education, Audiovisual and Culture Executive Agency. (2012). The European Higher Education Area in 2012: Bologna Process Implementation Report. http://eacea.ec.europa.eu/education/eurydice/documents/thematic_reports/138EN.pdf.

Fargues, P., Papademetriou, D. G., Salinari, G., & Sumption, M. (2011). Shared challenges and opportunities for EU and US immigration policymakers. European University Institute and Migration Policy Institute Report.

Fulge, T., & Vögtle, E. M. (2014). Sweeping change—but does it matter? The Bologna Process and determinants of student mobility. In K. Martens, P. Knodel, & M. Windzio (Eds.), *Internationalization of education policy: A new constellation of statehood in education?*. London: Palgrave Macmillan.

Hall, P. A., & Taylor, R. C. R. (1996). Political science and the three new institutionalisms. *Political Studies, XLIV,* 936–957.

Heyneman, S. P. (2009). What is appropriate role for government in education? *Journal of Higher Education Policy, 3,* 135–157.

Heyneman, S. P. (2010). A comment on the changes in higher education in the post-soviet union. *European Education, 42*(1), 76–87.

Keeling, R. (2006). The Bologna Process and the Lisbon research agenda: The European commission's expanding role in higher education discourse. *European Journal of Education, 41*(2), 203–223.

March, J. G., & Olsen, J. P. (1989). *Rediscovering institutions: The organizational basis of politics.* New York: Free Press.

Martens, K., Knodel, P., & Windzio, M. (2014). *Internationalization of education policy: A new constellation of statehood in education?*. London: Palgrave Macmillan.

Moravcsik, A. (1998). *The choice for Europe: Social purpose and state power from Messina to Maastricht.* Ithaca: Cornell University Press.

Moravcsik, A. (2005). The European constitutional compromise and the neo-functionalist legacy. *Journal of European Public Policy, 12,* 349–389.

Neave, G. (2003a). On the return from Babylon: A long voyage around history, ideology and systems change. In J. File & L. Geodegebuure (Eds.), *Reflections on higher education in the Czech Republic, Hungary, Poland and Slovenia.* Twente: CHEPS (Center for Higher Education Policy Studies).

Neave, G. (2003b). The Bologna Declaration: Some of the historic dilemmas posed by the reconstruction of the community in Europe's systems of higher education. *Educational Policy, 17,* 141–164.

Neave, G., & Maassen, P. (2007). The Bologna Process: An intergovernmental policy perspective. In P. Maassen & J. P. Olsen (Eds.), *University dynamics and European integration.* Dordrecht: Springer.

Nokkola, T. (2007). The Bologna Process and the role of higher education: Discursive construction of the European higher education area. In J. Enders & B. Jongbloed (Eds.), *Public-Private dynamics in higher education: Expectations, developments and outcomes* (pp. 221–245). Piscataway: Transaction.

Olsen, J. P. (2009). Change and continuity: An institutional approach to institutions of democratic government. *European Political Science Review, 1*(1), 3–32.

Ostrom, E. (1990). Governing the Commons: The Evolution of Institutions for Collective Action. New York: Cambridge University Press.

Pierson, P. (1996). The path to European integration: A historical institutionalist analysis. *Comparative Political Studies, 29*(2), 123–163.

Regini, M. (2011). *European universities and the challenge of the market: A comparative analysis.* Cheltenham: Edward Elgar.

Risse, T. (2007). Social constructivism meets globalization. In A. Held & D. McGrew (Eds.), *Globalization theory: Approaches and controversies* (pp. 126–147). Cambridge: Polity Press.

Rosamond, B. (2002). Imagining the European economy: 'Competitiveness' and the social construction of 'Europe' as an economic space. *New Political Economy, 7*(2), 157–177.

Schmidt, V. A. (2002). Europeanization and the mechanics of economic policy adjustment. *Journal of European Public Policy, 9*(6), 894–912.

Schmidt, V. A. (2005, December). Democracy in Europe: The impact of European integration. Perspectives on Politics, 3(4), 761–779.

Schmidt, V. A. (2009). The EU and its member states: From bottom up to top down. In D. Phinnemore & A. Warleigh-Lack (Eds.), *Reflections on European integration: 50 years of the treaty of Rome* (pp. 194–211). London: Palgrave Macmillan.

Scott, P. (2002). Reflections on the reform of higher education in central and Eastern Europe. *Higher Education in Europe, 27*(1/2), 137–152.

Spring, J. (2009). *Globalization of education: An introduction.* New York: Routledge.

Tyson, A. (2012, 2016). Acting Director for Strategy and Evaluation, Former Head of UnitC1, Higher Education and Erasmus, Directorate-General Education and Culture, European Commission; April 25, 2012; September 6, 2016.

Veiga, A. (2010). The moment of truth? *European Journal of Education, 47*(3), 378–391.

Veiga, A., & Amaral, A. (2006). The open method of coordination and the implementation of the Bologna Process. *Tertiary Education and Management, 12,* 283–295.

CHAPTER 5

The Context for Higher Education Attainment: A Quantitative Assessment

Higher education is an important part of the solution to our current difficulties. Strong and accountable higher education systems provide the foundations for thriving knowledge societies. Higher education should be at the heart of our efforts to overcome the crisis—now more than ever.
Bucharest Communiqué (excerpt), April 27, 2012, EHEA Ministerial Conference

The Bologna Process builds upon more than half a century of history of regional integration. The previous chapter provided a look backward, through the stages of regional integration since World War II, and described the historical circumstances that have given rise to the Bologna Process. It is useful to understand this twenty-first century regional initiative against the backdrop of European Commission-led initiatives for higher education. The European Commission is a partner in the European Higher Education Area (EHEA); it develops national policy recommendations for the European Union (EU) Member States. The objectives of the Lisbon Strategy (2000–2010) and Europe 2020 (2010–2020) are specifically for the EU countries. Nevertheless, the additional countries involved in the Bologna Process find the EU strategic benchmarks to be informative as objectives in higher education for the broader region. The progress toward the benchmarks is important to consider for all 48 countries in the EHEA, beyond the 28 EU Member States (Tyson 2016). This chapter considers how the EU countries are converging upon the Europe 2020 benchmark target

© The Author(s) 2017
B. Barrett, *Globalization and Change in Higher Education*,
DOI 10.1007/978-3-319-52368-2_5

of an average of 40 percent higher education attainment by 30–34-year-olds, which is greater than the national targets for more than a half of the EU countries (European Commission 2015b). This quantitative analysis of attainment is separate from an analysis of quality. Educational quality is a generally accepted indicator to demonstrate the effectiveness of education (European Commission 2009; European Union 2013; Rosa et al. 2016).

This chapter places the EU countries in a group to relate the national-level independent variables in the political economy to the dependent variable of higher education attainment. The findings reveal that the most statistically significant relationship is that between gross GDP per capita and higher education attainment. While considering countries in aggregate in order to understand EU trends, it is noted that it not possible to fully capture socioeconomic variations among regions within Europe that are significant, such as the variations in culture and in economy between the southern Mediterranean and northern Nordic countries. Analyzing the region of Europe as an entity is useful as a comparison to the distinguishing characteristics in the case countries of Portugal and Spain.

Reconciling the objectives for higher education attainment within a European social dimension, as with opportunities for participation in the global economy, remains challenging. Assessing the trends in higher education initiated by the Bologna Process considers the progress toward the Europe 2020 objective. Building upon themes from the Lisbon Strategy in the first decade of the twenty-first century, the economic growth strategy of Europe 2020 addresses the global context of slowed growth in developed countries that was the reality following the 2007–2009 global financial crisis. In the euro area, the double-dip recession, in the years 2009 and 2012, created stress on the fiscal budgets of southern European countries such as Portugal and Spain. However, the governments remained committed to higher education and its internationalization.

The Bologna Process recognized higher education attainment as important in the Bucharest Communiqué (2012a). At the following meeting of the EHEA Ministers several years later, the Yerevan Conference (2015) recognized this significance:

> The effective outcomes of higher education, that is, higher education attainment and completion on the one hand, and the employability of graduates on the other have been an important focus of the Bologna Process from the very beginning. The 2012 Bucharest Communiqué

further strengthens this output-oriented focus by reaffirming that both raising completion rates and enhancing employability are among the main goals of the "consolidation" process within the European Higher Education Area (EHEA).

Bologna Process Implementation Report (Eurydice 2015: 167).

This chapter discusses the theoretical background of the factors that have influenced the Bologna Process, namely the political economy and policy diffusion across countries. It discusses opportunities and challenges in the Bologna Process and the objectives for higher education attainment, as defined by Europe 2020. The opportunities with the Bologna Process are higher education attainment, internationalization, and innovation. The challenges are funding and leadership at national and institutional levels. The quantitative analysis uses panel data for 26 countries in the EU from 2000 to 2014.[1] There is specific analysis for the two Iberian countries, Portugal and Spain, which precedes the qualitative analysis in the four chapters following. Although the encompassing Bologna Process reforms include credit and degree structure, quality assurance, and recognition of academic degrees across countries, they are not part of this analysis. In conclusion, GDP per capita is the most significant variable in relation to higher education attainment.[2] This chapter examines how the momentum for reforms through the Bologna Process aligns with the Europe 2020 objective for higher education attainment in the EU countries.

THEORETICAL BACKGROUND FOR POLICY DIFFUSION

The convergence objectives in higher education policy are part of reforms that build upon the regional integration put in motion after World War II. Although higher education became more inclusive in Europe and the U.S. in the mid-twentieth century, this objective was not implemented by the Iberian countries until their transition to democracy in the late 1970s. Embracing the constructivist value placed on ideas, higher education is cultural and important, given its rituals and respect for authority that shape people's perceptions and values (McNamara 2015: 25). The national cultures and European cultures intersect in the policy space of the EHEA. Since the global financial crises in 2008, followed by Europe's sovereign debt crisis taking hold in select countries in 2010, economic uncertainty has added to the skepticism within European culture (Cramme and Hobolt 2015).

The preferences of the state, and influences of European institutions such as the EU and the EHEA, interact in the policy space between supranational and national power. In intergovernmentalist theory, the states are seen as the primary actors and drivers of policy; this perspective has been widely applied to the implementation of the Bologna Process (Moravcsik 1998; Neave and Maassen 2007). Three explanatory factors in the political economy—economic, political, and social—continue to influence the outcomes of the Bologna Process. These factors which are operational in the processes—globalization, intergovernmentalism, and Europeanization—work through institutions and ideas to shape and reform policy. Institutional perspectives in previous research on intergovernmentalism and the diffusion of ideas in Europeanization inform this analysis (Moravcsik 1998; Schmidt 2009; Börzel and Risse 2012). Diffusion is seen as "inherently intergovernmental"—that national governments implement policies to mimic adoptions by other national governments (Berry and Berry 2014: 308). Regional diffusion models, such as in the EHEA, assume channels of influence across governments in the region, even though that influence is not equal among governments (Berry and Berry 2014: 308).

The regional diffusion of policy in the Bologna Process began with the Sorbonne Declaration on May 25, 1998, when four countries recommended convergence of higher education in Europe. At this historic university in Paris, the ministers of France, Germany, Italy, and the United Kingdom (UK) made a commitment to coordinate voluntarily. As the initiative gained momentum, the following year 28 countries signed the Bologna Declaration on June 19, 1999 to create the EHEA. Governments are influenced primarily by other governments in proximity, according to the regional diffusion model (Berry and Berry 2014: 317). Once the four leading and largest countries in the EU had made the commitment to higher education reform, the other EU countries also committed. The 12 candidate countries accepted into the EU for its enlargements in 2004 and 2007 were eager to cooperate with the initiative to demonstrate their commitment to western Europe (Matei 2012).

This chapter explains the factors relating to the political economy, embedded in institutions and ideas that influence the national-level objectives for the Bologna Process. The power of institutions (Keohane and Nye 2012; Moravcsik 1998; Simmons et al. 2006) and the diffusion of ideas (Börzel and Risse 2012; Katzenstein 2005; Risse 2007) explain the regional trend in higher education reform, unparalleled in the number of participating countries. Neoliberal institutions, within the context of international cooperation, and ideas of social cohesion, within a highly integrated regional political economy, provide a backdrop for public policy (Schmidt and Thatcher 2013). The regionally integrated institutions of Europe and the EU's Single Market have expanded voluntarily to include minimum standards for higher education. This complements the freedom of movement for labor in the Single Market, which takes place together with the freedom of movement for goods, services, and capital. The idea, namely the Europe of Knowledge, brings a European dimension to higher education and is a foundational driver of the Bologna Process (European Commission 1997).

A historical institutional perspective is useful to identify the opportunities and challenges for policy reform and implementation in the Bologna Process.

> Though social policy is widely seen as an area of firm member state control with a minimal European Community role, a historical institutionalist perspective highlights the growing significance of European policy, the influence of actors other than member states, and the mounting constraints on Member State initiatives (Pierson 1996: 156).

Policies at the national and supranational levels reflect national and Europe 2020 objectives, which ideally are complementary. Higher education attainment has become an accepted national and supranational objective, which underscores its central place in the twenty-first century knowledge economy. This objective is simultaneously sociocultural to strengthen an understanding of European citizenship within a global perspective and economic to support national growth and the regional economy (European Commission 2016).

As the number of higher education graduates increases, a greater proportion of the population demonstrates readiness for employment and productivity, contributing to economic growth. Reconciling the objective for higher education attainment with opportunities for participation in the economy during periods of relatively high unemployment remains among the greatest challenges in the knowledge economy. Within European higher education institutions, the objective of achieving a global perspective through internationalization is increasingly dominant. "There is no doubt that the trend for internationalisation is growing, and that this offers great potential for higher education institutions in the EHEA. However, limits on funding as well as inflexible national legal frameworks may hinder development in some countries" (European Commission 2015a, b: 22).

OPPORTUNITIES

Opportunities for the Bologna Process policy reform are higher education attainment, internationalization, and economic growth through innovation. Higher education attainment and innovation have received extensive attention from the European Commission throughout the Bologna Process period since 2000. These two objectives have target benchmarks, set by the European Commission's Europe 2020 economic growth strategy. Economic growth through innovation is measured against the average national target for R&D/GDP, wherein 3 percent has been the target since the Lisbon Strategy and has continued with Europe 2020. Introduced in 2000, the European Research Area (ERA) has reinforced the objective of reaching the 3 percent goal, with 2 percent of GDP to originate from the private sector and 1 percent of GDP to originate from the public sector (European Commission 2000). Since then, budget austerity, after the financial and sovereign debt crises of the last decade, has strained public sector finances. Many private sector research institutions that were dependent upon public sector funds have received less funding for research and development (R&D) since the financial crisis.

Although innovation is attractive, it is not enough without a robust employment context. What matters is how effectively it is channeled through the labor force (Rodrik 2016). Higher education institutions have an opportunity to foster innovation at a time when the private and public sectors have experienced economic constraints. The partnerships between the academic and private sectors in the U.S. can serve as a model for the EU (Mazza et al. 2008). Horizon 2020 is the EU's flagship R&D and innovation initiative for the years 2014–2020. A multimethod study by United Nations University (UNU) and Maastricht University shows that university education and research positively impact innovation (Hoareau 2012: 14). The UNU policy report found that funding, together with policy and managerial autonomy, contributes to innovation in education research (Hoareau 2012: 17). The report's recommendation is that "more governments could adopt integrated or coordinated governance structures to promote a coherent strategy between higher education and innovation, if they want higher education to work for innovation" (Hoareau 2012: 36). In view of innovation and higher education attainment opportunities, "with funds and good policies it is possible to induce change" (Matei 2012a).

Higher Education Attainment and Internationalization

The widening of access to higher education that brings opportunities for knowledge, skills, and training to more people is supported by national investments in education spending. Most countries increased their higher education spending, even in the years of the financial crisis (Eurostat 2012). The demand for more educated people to meet the industrial society's demands and the desire for social mobility are complementary explanations for the broadening of higher education in the post-World War II decades (Regini 2011: 202). "Massification" of higher education has been on an upward trajectory since the mid-twentieth century as greater numbers of students have become enrolled in higher education.[3] University attendance became more accessible to society and widespread beyond the traditional elites in the post-World War II years. Advanced economies in Europe and the U.S. concentrated their production in the services sector beyond the preceding agricultural and industrial modes of production. The importance of access to higher education is evident in the Bologna Process and the Europe 2020 target of 40 percent higher education attainment, for 30–34-year-olds in the population, by 2020. In the 1970s, Martin Trow initially described higher education systems as follows (Trow 1974):

- Elite systems: University students are less than 15 percent of their age cohort
- Mass systems: University students are 15–35 percent of their age cohort
- Universal or generalized-access systems: University students are 35 percent or greater in their age cohort

Although "generalized access" is a driver of change in the Bologna Process, it has an economic cost for the state, and funding remains a challenge in fiscal policy. Rationales of the shorter degree cycle were to support inclusivity, to spend less on the cost of higher education per individual, and to move graduates more quickly into the workforce to contribute to the economy (Tyson 2012). The massification of higher education has shaped the purposes of higher education in recent decades.

Rather than being a traditional regimen for the elites as in previous years, higher education has become preparatory training for professional development to match the skills and knowledge demands of the evolving economy (Cantwell and Kauppinnen 2014). Simultaneous with the recent decades of massification in higher education, the economic demands for human capital labor have changed as technology has become more ubiquitous and has made it necessary to reinvent traditional employment functions that have become obsolete. This major transformation in the purposes of higher education in the post-World War II decades has been described in this way:

> The major impact of the transition to mass university was probably the destabilization of the traditional function of socializing the political, administrative, and economic elites via cultural codes that were not demanded by student-users but defined by the academic oligarchy. As access to higher education expanded, it became clear that curricula should be more concerned with the employability of their graduates and with problems of mismatch between demand and supply. Everywhere, a growing emphasis was put on such services as counseling, internships, job placements, monitoring the transition to work and graduates' careers (Regini 2011: 203).

The emphasis on student services in higher education to provide training and preparation for work that is knowledge based continues to accelerate. Aligned with a liberal intergovernmental process, the states, in pursuit of their interests, are the driving force in educational policy coordination and in the subsequent step of policy implementation (Moravcsik and Schimmelfennig 2009). In international policy cooperation, national governments pursue their own interests, which become shared across borders with regional diffusion (Berry and Berry 2014). Since the Bologna Process is a voluntary, soft policy, there is no enforcement mechanism, other than the limitation of not earning recognition of academic degrees abroad if an institution or country does not meet the minimum qualifications standards.

CHALLENGES

The most relevant challenges for higher education reform are economic scarcity that limits funds at national and institutional levels and, to a lesser extent, uncertainty about EU political leadership and organization. Regarding economic support for higher education, there are areas of uncertainty at multiple levels of governance. There is uncertainty about various policy aspects of the EU: the political union, the monetary union, and the feasibility of a fiscal union. The European Commission higher education flagship initiative, Erasmus, which provides students with mobility for academic study abroad, faced an uncertain fate in the last months of 2012 (European Commission 2013c). Erasmus funding is part of negotiations for the Multiannual Financial Framework (MFF), which budgets for seven-year cycles. In recent years, the EU spent approximately €1 trillion over seven years, or approximately €135 billion each year, in the MFF budget cycle.

In late 2012, there were petitions and testimonials to support this program, which has been in effect since 1987. Erasmus funding in the MFF 2014–2020, through the Directorate General for Education and Culture in the European Commission, is important to the Bologna Process objectives because the program provides for a period of student mobility in studying abroad. The European Parliament and the European Council agreed to a 40 percent increase in spending on the new Erasmus+ program for 2014–2020 (European Commission 2013b). The continuation and expansion of Erasmus supports the EHEA mobility goal of 20 percent student mobility by the year 2020 (EHEA 2012b). Erasmus funds for 2013 are approximately €500 million per year, and account for approximately 0.4 percent of the EU budget (European Commission 2013a).

By comparison to Erasmus, the Bologna Process primarily is funded by the states, as part of national spending on higher education, rather than by the EU. Therefore, the future of the Bologna Process has not hinged much on the MFF negotiations:

> Member States are increasingly striving to maximise the value of resources invested, including through targeted performance agreements with institutions, competitive funding arrangements, and channeling finance directly to individuals. They are looking to diversify funding sources, using public investment to lever funds from elsewhere and drawing to a larger extent on private funding; tuition fees are becoming more widespread particularly at the master level and above (European Commission 2011: 9).

The tuition fees that are often higher at the master-degree level necessitate self-financing, which has become a byproduct of the Bologna Process reforms that have established new degree cycles. Although the basis for higher education is public investment, the large scale of funding necessary may draw on additional sources of funds from the private sector (European Commission 2011: 8). As a spur to change, given the necessity that arises to coordinate when less resources are available, "budgetary starvation or reduced slack is likely to generate demands for joint decisions and coordination, and such demands tend to make conflict and change more likely" (Olsen 2009a: 16).[4]

A source of funds from the supranational level of the EU, namely Cohesion Funds and Structural Funds, can make economic development more balanced across the broader region. These funds are provided directly to develop specific sub-regional areas within Member States. They are an important part of the MFF, accounting for approximately 35 percent of the overall budget (€376 billion over seven years) and are the second highest in overall budget allotment, after the common agricultural policy and rural development allotment (European Union 2013). "Structural and cohesion funds to upgrade universities could improve the performance of higher education in less economically developed regions", concluded The State of University Policy for Progress in Europe policy report (Hoareau 2012: 38).

The Provost and Professor of Public Policy at Central European University, Liviu Matei, sees the Bologna Process as an overall success (Matei 2012: 679). There have been specific policy achievements in functional areas like degree structure, quality standards, and mobility. "The Bologna Process has evolved as a specific European answer to the challenges of globalisation, displaying a remarkable European capacity to innovate in higher education" (Matei 2012: 679). Amid the relative success of the Bologna Process, the willingness of states to fund higher education is an element of uncertainty at the national level. Among the many criteria for the Bologna Process, the absence of specific policy on funding leaves the responsibility to the participating states. The concept of a "funding gap" has become the common vernacular among practitioners and policymakers in the EHEA. The most ambitious higher education funding initiative of the EU is the Erasmus student exchange programs, specifically the Erasmus bilateral program among EU countries and the Erasmus Mundus program among EU and non-EU universities. In 2013, Erasmus+ consolidated these and other educational programs, as well as provided additional funding for student exchanges in the neighborhood of Europe.

Beyond the funding gap there is a "funding policy gap" in the area of financing the Bologna Process (Matei 2012: 685). For the first time, at the Leuven/Louvain-la-Neuve ministerial conference in 2009, funding was recognized as a priority for the Bologna Process. As a guideline to address the funding policy gap, the way forward is twofold according to Matei, the rapporteur for the International Conference on Funding of Higher Education in September 2011 in Yerevan, Armenia (the location of the 2015 EHEA Ministerial Conference). First, the public responsibility for funding higher education needs to be reaffirmed as a priority. This integral public sector role is possible through an established framework that advances priorities for funding, including that which comes from beyond the public sector. Second, "a European space for dialogue in higher education" about funding is essential to consider the opportunities for financing the Bologna Process" (Matei 2012: 687). Despite the diversity of national policy approaches across Europe, it is a policy option to establish similar public policy objectives for higher education funding that include a plan for long-term growth, accountability, and openness.

General uncertainty about the future of the EU leadership and organization has had a relatively weak impact on EHEA implementation. Because 20 of the 48 members of the Bologna Process are not in the EU, many of the countries in the EHEA are not affected directly by EU political uncertainty. In most cases, the domestic political concerns of EU Member States have not extended to create uncertain circumstances in the EHEA. For example, concerns about Britain's future membership in the EU, given the Prime Minister's February 2013 announcement of a future referendum, have not extended to uncertainty about its or other countries' commitments to the EHEA criteria.[5] Even though Britain voted on June 23, 2016, to leave the EU, it remains part of the EHEA. The soft politics area of higher education seems to be protected from binding political issues of EU membership and the monetary union. The uncertainty about the monetary union, in the absence of a fiscal union, has not been an insurmountable challenge to implementing the objectives for the EHEA.

Instead, challenges to implementation have been those of changing the institutional design in university governance, leadership at the national level, and limited funding. These challenges include limitations on domestic economic resources available to support higher education reform and countries' institutional capacities. The importance of economic resources is affirmed by the data analysis demonstrating a statistically significant relationship between GDP per capita and higher education attainment.

RESEARCH METHODOLOGY

There is a mixed methodological approach for the research in this book. In this chapter, the quantitative analysis assesses data and reports by Eurostat on higher education attainment, which is the dependent variable of interest. Indicating a rising value trend for this indicator among the youngest generation, "the Bologna median value is now 37.3 percent for the 25–34 age group, 29.4 percent for the 35–44 age group, and 22.9 percent for the 45–64 age group" (European Commission 2015: 168). Broader qualitative analysis of case-study countries—Portugal, in Chaps. 6 and 7, and Spain—in Chaps. 8 and 9, considers higher education governance at national and supranational levels and the role of stakeholders (academic, public, and private sectors) in policy reform.

To address the hypothesis that the political economy context influences the Bologna Process implementation, there are three explanatory factors traced throughout this book: competitive economic pressures through globalization, domestic politics through intergovernmentalism, and sociological and ideational processes in Europeanization. These three factors have temporal influences on the Bologna Process implementation (over time). Giving importance to the temporal dimension of social science asserts that "history matters" (Pierson 2004: 2, 6).

Participating countries prefer to be part of the policy network, rather than outside. The opportunity to be part of the network comes with the costs of implementing policies at the national level to attain the degree structure, quality assurance, and recognition objectives of the EHEA. Reputational benefits from participating in the policy network may present opportunities, since countries seek the benefits of the "network good" (Kölliker 2001). There are sociological reputational benefits to attaining the objectives of the Bologna Process and EHEA. The idea of "pathfinder" countries was introduced at the 2012 EHEA Ministerial Conference in Bucharest. The pathfinder countries were designated to demonstrate ways to implement the automatic recognition criteria of the EHEA, and they reflect a variety of higher education systems. These pathfinder countries collaborated with the European Commission soon after the Bucharest Ministerial, and in 2015 they reported to the EHEA Yerevan Ministerial Conference with recommendations. The pathfinder countries have been Belgium (Flemish Region and Walloon French Region), Croatia, Denmark, Estonia, Germany, Luxembourg, The Netherlands, Portugal, and Slovenia. The case studies in this research are

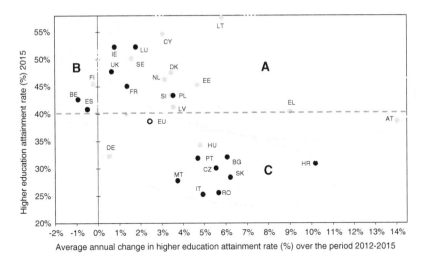

Fig. 5.1 "Higher Education Attainment (2014): Current performance (Y) and recent change (X)." European Commission (2015). European Semester Thematic Fiche: Higher Education Attainment. November 26, 2015. Page 3

the Iberian countries, Portugal and Spain. Portugal has demonstrated notable progress in higher education attainment increase across its population in the recent decades (see Fig. 5.1).

The book's hypothesis is tested with statistical analysis to explain the significance of the relationship between explanatory variables in the political economy and the dependent variable of higher education attainment. Although higher education attainment does not explain the process of implementation, it is important to measure because of the objective for 40 percent of the population, ages 30–34, to have higher education qualifications by the year 2020.

Hypothesis: Influences of Macroeconomic Performance on Higher Education Attainment

Hypothesis for Research Question (*Political Economy Explanations for Policy Reform*):

Hypothesis: A higher level of economic development, measured by GDP per capita, has a relationship with progress on higher education reform—especially higher education attainment. Countries with weaker levels of economic development may have higher opportunity costs and lesser capacities for policy reform.

The hypothesis provides that when countries have greater GDP per capita, there will be more progress on higher education attainment (indicated by a statistically significant relationship). The focus is on the dependent variable of higher education attainment. The influences of the independent and control variables, GDP per capita, R&D/GDP, employment, trade/GDP, and population, are in relationship to higher education attainment.

This rests on premises of positive feedback within path dependency, which are central to a historical institutional perspective (Pierson 2004: 22). Countries may continue on a positive performance trajectory unless a significant outside shock exerts influence. The positive feedback in path dependency supports the hypothesis that countries will stay on a trajectory of high performance as it relates to positive economic and educational indicators (Pierson 2004: 17). Pierson's contributions to describing long-term processes as causal chains and to framing institutional design are meaningful to this research and to the complementary qualitative analysis. Causal chains, cumulative causes, and threshold effects are three types of slow-moving causal processes (Pierson 2004: 82). The Bologna Process implementation is similar to a causal chain from which impetus proceeds at multiple levels of governance: supranational, national, and institutional. A policy change may lead to several intervening factors for stakeholders before outcomes are known. These causal chains become illuminated with process-tracing in qualitative research. "Causal chain arguments are typically utilized when key institutional, policy, or organizational outcomes lie some distance in time from initial points of crucial political choice" (Pierson 2004: 88).

Considering how the macroeconomic context influences higher education reforms, there are panel data linear regression models that address the hypothesis quantitatively, using higher education attainment as the dependent variable. Model 1 is a regression analysis of aggregate data over 15 years (2000–2014) in 26 countries in the EU. Model 2 introduces the variable of time (t) to emphasize the impact of the independent variables. The theoretical framework of historical institutionalism emphasizes path dependence, for which increasing returns to the dependent variable are explained by rationales from the field of economics (Pierson 2000: 253).

Quantitative Data Analysis

This research recognizes that national cultures and traditions, as they act on legislative processes and institutional change, provide a relatively more complete explanation for policy reform, when taken together with quantitative factors. Qualitative analysis is necessary to reveal the influences of history, culture, and tradition that cannot be captured by statistical analysis. The relationship indicated by the value of the coefficients informs the strength and the direction of the relationship between the variables. The regression function provides coefficient values for the variables, and p-values provide determination of whether the variables are statistically significant by being at an appropriate level to accept or to reject the null hypothesis. The following analysis uses regression and correlation to consider the relationships among variables for EU countries in aggregate. There are 26 country cases over 15 years (2000–2014) in this longitudinal or cross-sectional panel data analysis.

The dependent variable of higher education attainment is regressed on the observations from the independent and control variables:

1. GDP per capita.
2. Investment in R&D as percentage of GDP.
3. Trade/GDP as a measure of economic integration.
4. Employment as percentage of population.
5. Population.

The linear regression model is:

Higher education attainment = a + $b1$(GDP per capita) + $b2$(Investment in R&D) + $b3$(Trade/GDP) + $b4$(Employment) + $b5$(Population)

The two models used are:

Model 1: panel data aggregate of variables over fifteen years (2000–2014).

Model 2: introduction of model with time (t).

Pearson Correlation describes the direction and the strength of a linear bivariate relationship between two variables. There are strong correlations between some variables, notably correlations of approximately |0.5| (absolute value of 0.5 ($\pm$)) or greater, which raise concerns about the presence of autocorrelation among variables. The number 1 describes perfect correlation between the same variables.

Future research may utilize an interaction variable in the model, with the variables RD/GDP and GDP per capita interacting together, given that these variables are highly correlated. The presence of auto-correlation gives reason to test different models to attempt to limit this influence on the regression model specification. Model 2 introduces time (t) as a control variable to measure the relationship of independent variables to the dependent variable of higher education attainment.

REGRESSION ANALYSIS OF DATA AND OUTCOMES

Model 1

For Model 1, the Hausman test was run to determine which model, fixed-effects or random-effects, is to be used to measure this relationship among variables. The fixed-effects model assumes that the effects of time-invariant characteristics are removed from the predictor variables in order to measure the predictors' net effect. Additionally, the fixed-effects model accounts for omitted variables, such as cultural differences, that differ between cases but are constant over time. By comparison, the random-effects regression model accounts for omitted variables that may be fixed between cases yet vary throughout time.

The results of the Hausman test indicate that it is appropriate to use the fixed-effects, rather than random-effects, regression model. By determining if the more efficient model of fixed effects would provide as consistent results as those given by random-effects model, which is less efficient, the fixed-effects model is desirable for the most efficient results with this regression relationship. The fixed-effects model controls for all time-invariant differences between the countries. Therefore, the estimated coefficients of the fixed-effects models cannot be biased because of omitted time-invariant characteristic. Fixed-effects models are intended to analyze causes of change within entities. One limitation of the features of fixed-effects models is that they cannot be used to investigate time-invariant causes of the dependent variables. Time-invariant causes may be cultural variations, which are not captured by the fixed-effects model. The time-invariant causes are constant for each entity or country. When the time variable (t) is introduced in Model 2, GDP per capita is the only variable that is statistically significant.

The Wooldridge test demonstrates significant first-order auto-correlation. For example, GDP per capita and R&D/GDP are highly correlated at 0.71, and it is assumed that there is significant first-order auto-correlation between the variables over time. The presence of autocorrelation reveals the imperfections with this data set. The analysis of the fixed-effects regression model reveals that several of the independent and control variables are statistically significant with the panel data in Model 1 and only GDP per capita in Model 2 with time (t) as a variable.

Statistical Analysis of Coefficients

The dependent variable, higher education attainment, is chosen to represent higher education reform. There are limitations in its relevance, given that it shows outcomes rather than processes. Nevertheless, it is an important variable due to the emphasis placed on it by the European Commission and by select Bologna Process countries. The EU Member States have adopted the average 40 percent target for higher education attainment, for 30–34-year-olds, by the year 2020. Qualitative analysis is used to explain the cultural, historical, and political aspects of the policy process that cannot be captured by this quantitative variable.

The European Commission target, defined in the Europe 2020 economic growth strategy, is a benchmark that gives meaning to the dependent variable of higher education attainment, on which the following variables are regressed. In relation to higher education attainment, four of the five independent variables are significant at the most significant ($***p < 0.01$) level, and one variable (Population) is significant at the $**p < 0.05$ level. The analysis of the coefficients for the independent variables in relation to higher education attainment for Model 1 is as follows and the readers are referred to Table 5.1 in the Appendix.

1. *GDP Per Capita*
   This variable is significant at the highest level in both Models 1 and 2. As noted for Variable 2, Investment in R&D as a percentage of GDP, GDP per capita and R&D/GDP are strongly correlated. The statistical significance of GDP per capita (coefficient $b = 0.0015$ and $p < 0.001$)*** has the same level of statistical significance with R&D/GDP. This may be because auto-correlations limit the unique interpretation of each variable. When variables are correlated, it weakens the understanding of the true coefficient value. GDP growth has a positive relationship with educational quality (Hanushek and Woessmann 2009).

Table 5.1   Pearson Correlation Table: Variables for 26 Countries (Years 2000–2014)

	Higher Ed*	GDP PC*	RD/GDP*	Trade/GDP*	Emp.*	Pop.
Higher Ed	1.000	0.526	0.473	0.098	0.276	−0.002
GDP PC	0.526	1.000	0.710	−0.028	0.307	0.236
RD/GDP	0.453	0.710	1.000	−0.144	0.332	0.175
Trade/DGP	0.098	−0.028	−0.144	1.000	0.036	−0.585
Employment	0.276	0.307	0.332	0.036	1.000	−0.205
Population	−0.002	0.232	0.175	−0.585	−0.205	1.000

2. *Investment in R&D as percentage of GDP*
   Considering the European Commission target for 3 percent (public and private combined) R&D spending over GDP, the EC has promoted both this target and the 40 percent target for higher education attainment as part of Europe 2020. The data indicate that the relationship between variables is statistically significant at the highest level, since $p < 0.001***$ is less than the critical value $p < 0.10$ under which the null hypothesis would be rejected. Since R&D/GDP and GDP are strongly correlated, at 0.7, the statistical significance of GDP may contribute to the statistical significance of R&D/GDP.

3. *Trade/GDP as a measure of economic integration*
   The coefficient for trade/GDP as a measure of economic integration ($b = 0.044$, $p = 0.021$)** has a positive relationship with higher education attainment. The data indicate that the relationship between variables is statistically significant, given that the p-value is less than the critical value of $p < 0.05$ under which the null hypothesis would be rejected. There is a positive relationship between trade/GDP and higher education attainment in the regression, strengthening the premise that trade as a percentage of GDP has a positive relationship with higher education attainment. However, if trade volume rather than a percentage of trade/GDP had been measured, there may be different statistical results. A country that has a relatively low percentage of trade/GDP, such as Germany, would have a higher volume of trade in comparison to some countries that have a higher percentage of trade/GDP.

4. *Employment as percentage of population*

The noteworthy aspect of this relationship between employment and higher education attainment is the negative direction of the relationship. Employment as a percentage of population is statistically significant (coefficient $b = -0.868$ and $p < 0.001)***$. As employment increases by one unit, higher education attainment decreases by -0.868 units. When individuals are employed, there is less incentive to pursue higher education. An explanation is that as the workforce diminishes, the number of students completing higher education increases. As the opportunities for employment decrease, individuals may pursue higher education as an alternative.

5. *Population*

There is a significant relationship between population and higher education attainment. A unit change in higher education attainment has the relationship, $b = 1.90$ e6 $(p < 0.001)***$. At the $***p < 0.001$ level, this relationship is as statistically significant as are the relationships of the dependent variable higher education attainment with RD/GDP, employment, and GDP per capita. Only trade/GDP has a weaker level of statistical significance at the $**p < 0.05$ level.

The R^2 indicates the explanatory power of the regression model to describe variance in the model. The Overall $R^2 = 0.03$ is relatively weak, and may reflect the significant first-order autocorrelation between variables. The independent variables explain, or account for, approximately 3 percent of the variance in the dependent variable higher education attainment. Overall R^2 is low enough not to be concerned with multicollinearity given that the Overall $R^2 < 0.8$. The Within $R^2 = 0.68$ shows the variance explained within countries to be 68 percent, which is a meaningful explanation.

Model 2

In Model 2, the time variable (t) is used to provide greater specificity about the impact of the independent variables, in which the GDP per capita is the only statistically significant variable. The analysis of the coefficients for the independent variables in relation to higher education attainment for Model 2 is as follows and the readers are referred to Table 5.2. The time variable is statistically significant with coefficient $b = 1.082 \ (p < 0.001)***$ (Table 5.3).

Table 5.2   Model 1: Effect of Macroeconomic Indicators on Higher Education Attainment Panel Regression with Fixed-effects & Autocorrelation

Variables Attainment	Fixed-effects model regressed on tertiary ed. Unstandardized coefficients and standard error
GDP per capita	0.002***
	(<0.001)
R&D/GDP	6.394***
	(0.956)
Trade/GDP	0.044**
	(0.019)
Employment	−0.868***
	(0.108)
Population	1.90 e6***
	(2.42 e7)

***$p < 0.01$, **$p < 0.05$, *$p < 0.10$
Overall $R^2 = 0.0334$
Within $R^2 = 0.6830$
Between $R^2 = 0.0278$

In Model 2, the Overall $R^2 = 0.30$ is relatively high indicating that the independent variables provide 30 percent of the variance explained in the dependent variable higher education attainment. This is higher than the R^2 in the first model, compared to merely 0.03 overall in Model 1. An analysis of the independent variables in Model 2 provides that among the five independent variables the statistical significance is present only with GDP per capita at the *$p < 0.1$ level with *$p = 0.051$.

Models 1 and 2 affirm the hypothesis that stronger performing economies may have an advantage to attain greater higher education attainment, toward the 40 percent target. The statistically significant relationship of GDP per capita with higher education attainment is of greatest interest to explain the hypothesis. GDP per capita within a country indicates availability of economic resources, and therefore greater economic support available for higher education attainment. This may take place through more economic resources available at higher education institutions from public funding, at a higher level when the country performs stronger in GDP. Support for higher education may come from private funding, scholarships, or the ability of individuals to finance higher education when there is greater GDP per capita within a country. Although GDP per capita is not a specific measure of economic

Table 5.3 Model 2: Effect of Macroeconomic Indicators on Higher Education Attainment Regression with Time Variable (t)

Variables	Model regressed on higher education attainment Unstandardized coefficients and standard error
GDP per capita	0.0002*
	(<0.001)
R&D/GDP	0.222
	(1.896)
Trade/GDP	0.019
	(0.016)
Employment	0.0008
	(0.108)
Population	1.14 e7
	(2.36 e7)
Time	1.082***
	(0.078)

$***p < 0.01$, $**p < 0.05$, $*p < 0.10$
Overall $R^2 = 0.3220$
Within $R^2 = 0.7923$
Between $R^2 = 0.1286$

integration, it is supported by the international economy, given the economic interconnectedness—through trade, finance, and multi-nationalization of production—of countries in Europe and globally.

REGRESSION ANALYSIS FOR PORTUGAL AND SPAIN

There are many intangible and unquantifiable factors, stemming from culture and history that explain higher education completion and Bologna Process reforms. To explain statistical relationships with the dependent variable, higher education attainment, a regression analysis follows for the years 2000–2011, which include the variable of education spending, and for the years 2000–2014. These five independent variables are used in both data sets, which are GDP per capita, R&D/GDP, trade/GDP, employment, and population. In Portugal and Spain between 2000 and 2011, the negative relationship between education spending and higher education attainment is consistent with expectations for the Bologna Process. The intention has been that fewer state funds and private funds are spent per student as the shorter first-cycle degree became implemented (EHEA 2012). The first-cycle degree may be a minimum of three years as compared to the traditional five to six-year *Licenciatura* degree. In Portugal, employment is statistically significant at the $p < 0.01$ level. Given each unit of increase in higher education attainment, there has been a 0.349 unit decrease in employment between 2000 and 2011. The independent control variable of population has a statistically significant positive relationship in both countries. As the population increases in both countries, higher education attainment increases as well. The standardized coefficient $B = 2.026$ in Spain is greater than the $B = 0.349$ in Portugal. Notably, the R^2 indicating variance explained by the model is exceptionally high for both Portugal and Spain (Table 5.4).

Between the years 2000 and 2014 in Portugal, the only statistically significant relationship ($p < 0.01***$) is between employment (which has a negative relationship $B = -0.989$) and higher education attainment. This is a negative direction relationship for a nearly one-unit change in employment resulting in a one-unit change in higher education attainment. In Spain both R&D/GDP (at the level of $p < 0.05**$) and Population (at $p < 0.01***$) have a statistically significant relationship with higher education attainment. That the results are different between the two countries demonstrates the unique political economy context within each country, impacting higher education attainment. Portugal and Spain suffered during the global financial crisis, and soon afterward as Portugal had a debt crisis, Spain had a banking crisis. They have completed the financial assistance programs with the European Union, and

Table 5.4 Portugal and Spain: Standardized Coefficients of Regression on Higher Education Attainment (Years 2000–2011)

Independent variables	OLS model regressed on higher education attainment	
	Standardized coefficients	
	Portugal	Spain
EdSpending/GDP (%)	−0.192**	−0.750**
GDP per capita	0.307	−0.616
R&D/GDP (%)	0.174	0.160
Trade/GDP (%)	−0.026	−0.018
Employment	−0.349***	−0.172
Population	0.349***	2.026**

***$p < 0.01$, **$p < 0.05$, *$p < 0.10$
Portugal $R^2 = 0.998$, Spain $R^2 = 0.991$

they remain committed to continuing with the Bologna Process reforms. Although these countries joined the EU at the same time, in 1986, they have had different approaches to policy reform for the Bologna Process given that Spain has a quasi-federal government structure with 17 autonomous regions and Portugal has a unitary government structure. The unitary government structure providing more direct institutional authority, and the consistent support for Bologna Process reforms across the changing political leadership, may have contributed to Portugal serving as a "pathfinder" country between the 2012 and 2015 EHEA Ministerial conferences (Table 5.5).

SUMMARY: THE CONTEXT FOR HIGHER EDUCATION ATTAINMENT

The perseverance of ideas and the change in institutions have constructed the EHEA through the Bologna Process. The origins trace to previous decades where higher education policy entrepreneurs influenced the initial treaties, which are the historical roots of the EU (Corbett 2005). The ideas and institutions have been strengthened over time by open economic and policy cooperation across countries. This neoliberal institutional design in Europe has maintained its appeal throughout history. The generality and diversity of neoliberal ideas, together with their institutionalization, have contributed to their enduring appeal (Schmidt and Thatcher 2013: xix). Globalization, intergovernmentalism, and Europeanization are the processes evident in the Bologna Process' internationalization of higher education. Given Europeanization, policies in higher education progress in influence from the European level to the national level of education, where the Open Method of Coordination has been a mechanism to share best practices (Dale and Robertson 2009a).

The path dependency in historical institutionalism supports the hypothesis, proposing a trajectory of economic growth and higher education expansion (Pierson 1996, 2004). There is a relationship between strength in economies, measured by GDP per capita, and higher education attainment. Although countries with weaker economies may have incentives to catch up, they may have challenges such as weaker institutional capacity, financial resources, and organizational leadership. The directionally positive and statistically significant relationship between economic performance measured by GDP per capita and higher education attainment has been demonstrated in the data between the years 2010 and 2014 for the

Table 5.5 Portugal and Spain: Standardized Coefficients of Regression on Higher Education Attainment (Years 2000–2014)

Independent variables	OLS model regressed on higher education attainment	
	Standardized coefficients	
	Portugal	Spain
GDP per capita	0.300	0.137
R&D/GDP	0.005	−1.196**
Trade/GDP (%)	0.070	−0.122
Employment	−0.989***	0.127
Population	0.042	2.090***

***$p < 0.01$, **$p < 0.05$, *$p < 0.10$
Portugal $R^2 = 0.979$, Spain $R^2 = 0.976$

countries in the EU. The independent variables of GDP per capita (which is strongly correlated with R&D/GDP), trade/GDP, employment, and population each have statistically significant relationships with higher education attainment. Beyond factors in the political economy, the cultural and political influences that are unobserved in quantitative analysis are traced through qualitative analysis. The political economy context since the Bologna Process initiated in 1999 has had a positive impact on higher education attainment in the countries in the EU, which has been demonstrated by the collective increasing trend over time.

This chapter has discussed the opportunities and challenges for higher education policy reform. The opportunities are expanded higher education attainment and internationalization, together with innovation to support economic growth. The key challenges to policy reform are national limits on funding and a funding policy gap at multiple levels of governance. Although the uncertainty about the economic and political future of the EU affects domestic politics and global financial markets, this uncertainty is less of an obstacle to Bologna Process reforms than is organizational capacity for institutional change. Institutional change requires leadership that provides realistic vision, personnel resources, financial resources, and stakeholders invested in the process of change (Olsen 2009a, b). Innovation and R&D competitiveness are promising for economic growth, and incorporated into Europe 2020 strategy and the Horizon 2020 framework of the European Commission (Sørensen et al. 2016).

They are opportunities, to pursue alongside higher education attainment, given the attractiveness for countries to have these economic attributes.

Notwithstanding the opportunities, the economic conditions at national and supranational levels of governance may be obstacles for the Bologna Process implementation (Matei 2012; Veiga and Amaral 2006). As the decades of regional integration have progressed, from the European Economic Community founded with the Treaty of Rome (1957), the policy focus has progressed from regional security to economic concerns such as trade and agriculture to soft policy areas including education. The bureaucratic expansion has grown into additional policy areas including political cooperation in immigration, energy, and transport (Lefkofridi and Schmitter 2015: 6). These policy areas increasingly have been brought under the authority of EU competencies in the successive treaties and legislation. Higher education policy remains distinctive, as a soft policy initiative, given that it remains a national competency. The regional organization of the EU is unique in being able to cope with successive crises, and explanations stem from three extraordinary qualities:

- The high level of supranationality, stemming from the design of the European Coal and Steel Community (ESCS) with the Treaty of Paris (1951);
- The diffusion of non-state organizations and interest groups at the regional level that advocate for EU policies transnationally;
- The EU Member States are liberal democracies supportive of supranational policies and transnational organizations (Lefkofridi and Schmitter 2015: 7).

These historical characteristics ensure that, even in times of economic and political crises, the EU will continue to be robust as a policy actor in serving the Member States and the region of Europe while setting norms for global affairs. As regional integration has expanded beyond the EU's Single Market, it has encompassed areas of higher education, research, and knowledge policies that historically are the competencies of EU Member States. The interests of the states in intergovernmentalism and the ideas of the supranational European level of leadership in Europeanization, that began with the Sorbonne Declaration nearly 20 years ago, continue to develop in the EHEA. The trends for higher education attainment among the EU countries in the Bologna Process have been upward, since its origination at the beginning of the millennium. This upward trend supports the objectives for higher education attainment and broader policy reforms that have been diffused regionally throughout Europe. The sustained momentum for policy reform has captured interest globally given the connection to the twenty-first century context of the knowledge economy. Beyond these variables in the political economy, the social and cultural influences that are absent in quantitative analysis are traced through the following qualitative analysis that compares Portugal and Spain.

NOTES

1. The EU member states Luxembourg and Croatia are not included because of unavailability of data.
2. The term "higher education" is synonymous with "higher education".
3. The term "massification" is used in the literature to describe widening access to higher education since the mid-twentieth century. John Burrage (Ed.). 2010. *Martin Trow: Twentieth-Century Higher Education: Elite to Mass to Universal.* Baltimore: Johns Hopkins University Press.
4. Richard Cyert and James March's *A Behavioral Theory of the Firm* (1963) remains a foundational contribution to institutional change analysis and discusses budgetary starvation.
5. Though part of the United Kingdom, Scotland has its own representation in the Bologna Process and the EHEA. The most recent referendum, in September 2014, for Scotland to separate from the UK did not receive a majority of votes to succeed. In Belgium, Flanders and Wallonia also have their own representation in the Bologna Process.

DATA SOURCES

Tertiary Education Attainment

Eurostat. 2016. Tertiary educational attainment by sex, age group 30–34; Tertiary educational attainment—total. Available from: http://epp.eurostat.ec.europa.eu/tgm/table.do?tab=table&init=1&plugin=0&language=en&pcode=t2020_41 Short Description: "The share of the population aged 30–34 years who have successfully completed university or university-like (tertiary-level) education with an education level

ISCED 1997 (International Standard Classification of Education) of 5–6. This indicator measures the Europe 2020 strategy's headline target to increase the share of the 30–34-year-olds having completed tertiary or equivalent education to at least 40% in 2020".

For Austria years 2000–2003, OECD. Education: Key tables from OECD—ISSN 2075-5120—© OECD. 2010. Tertiary education graduation rates; Percentage of graduates to the population at the typical age of graduation.

Educational Spending as percentage of GDP

Eurostat. 2012. Expenditure on education as % of GDP or public expenditure [educ_figdp]. INDIC_ED. Total public expenditure on education as % of GDP, for all levels of education combined. Available from: http://epp.eurostat.ec.europa.eu/statistics_explained/index.php/Educational_expenditure_statistics.

Missing data note: All countries for 2010 and 2011 take the previous value for 2009 and 2010. Belgium and Slovenia 2000 take next value for 2001. Malta 2000 and 2001 take the next value for 2002. Romania 2006 takes the value for 2005, and 2008 takes the value for 2007.

R&D as percentage of GDP

Eurostat. 2016. The indicator provided is GERD (Gross domestic expenditure on R&D) as a percentage of GDP. "Research and experimental development (R&D) comprise creative work undertaken on a systematic basis in order to increase the stock of knowledge, including knowledge of man, culture and society and the use of this stock of knowledge to devise new applications" (Frascati Manual, 2002 edition, § 63). Available from: http://epp.eurostat.ec.europa.eu/tgm/table.do?tab=table&init=1&plugin=0&language=en&pcode=t2020_20.

Missing data note: Greece 2000 takes the value for 2001; Greece 2002 takes the average value for 2001 and 2003. Sweden 2000 takes the value for 2001; Sweden 2002 takes the average value for 2001 and 2003.

Trade as percentage of GDP

World Bank. 2016. Trade is the sum of exports and imports of goods and services measured as a share of gross domestic product. Code:

NE.TRD.GNFS.ZS. Source: World Bank national accounts data, and OECD National Accounts data files. Available from: http://data.world-bank.org/indicator/NE.EXP.GNFS.ZS.

Missing data note: For Malta missing the years 2012, 2013, and 2014 take 2011 value.

Employment as percentage of population

World Bank. 2016. Employment to population ratio, 15+, total (%) (modeled ILO estimate). International Labour Organization, Key Indicators of the Labour Market database. Available from: http://data.worldbank.org/indicator/SL.EMP.TOTL.SP.ZS.

GDP per capita

World Bank. 2016. GDP per capita, PPP (constant 2011 international $).

GDP per capita based on purchasing power parity (PPP). PPP GDP is gross domestic product converted to international dollars using purchasing power parity rates. An international dollar has the same purchasing power over GDP as the U.S. dollar has in the United States. GDP at purchaser's prices is the sum of gross value added by all resident producers in the economy plus any product taxes and minus any subsidies not included in the value of the products. It is calculated without making deductions for depreciation of fabricated assets or for depletion and degradation of natural resources. Code: NY.GDP.PCAP.PP.KD.

Missing data note: Malta has the same values for 2013, 2014, and 2015 (2013 value for missing 2014 and 2015).

Source: World Bank, International Comparison Program database.

Available from: http://data.worldbank.org/indicator/NY.GDP.PCAP.PP.KD. **GDPpercapita** based on purchasing power parity (PPP). PPP **GDP** is gross domestic product converted to international dollars using purchasing power parity rates. An international dollar has the same purchasing power over **GDP** as the U.S. dollar has in the United States. **GDP** at purchaser's prices is the sum of gross.

Population

World Bank. 2016. Population, total refers to the total population. (1) United Nations Population Division. World Population Prospects, (2) United Nations Statistical Division. Population and Vital Statistics Report (various years), (3) Census reports and other statistical publications from national statistical offices, (4) Eurostat: Demographic Statistics, (5) Secretariat of the Pacific Community: Statistics and Demography Programme, and (6) U.S. Census Bureau: International Database. Catalog Sources World Development Indicators. Available from: http://data.worldbank.org/indicator/SP.POP.TOTL. See Table 5.1.

REFERENCES

Berry, F. S., & Berry, W. D. (2014). Innovation and diffusion models in policy research. In P. Sabatier & C. M. Weible (Eds.), *Theories of the policy process* (3rd ed.). Boulder, CO: Westview Press.

Börzel, T. A., & Risse, T. (2012). From Europeanisation to diffusion: Introduction. *West European Politics, 35*(1), 1–19.

Cantwell, B., & Kauppinen, I. (Eds.). (2014). *Academic capitalism in the age of globalization.* Baltimore: Johns Hopkins University Press.

Corbett, A. (2005). *Universities and the Europe of knowledge: Ideas, institutions and policy entrepreneurship in European Union Higher Education 1955–2005.* New York: Palgrave Macmillan.

Cramme, O., & Hobolt, S. B. (Eds.). (2015). *Democratic politics in an EU under stress.* Oxford: Oxford University Press.

Dale, R. and Robertson, S. (2009a). *Globalisation and Europeanisation in Education.* Cambridge: Symposium Press.

EHEA Ministerial Conference. (2012a). Bucharest Communiqué: Making the most of our potential: Consolidating the European Higher Education Area. Retrieved from http://www.ehea.info/Uploads/%281%29/Bucharest%20Communique%202012%281%29.pdf.

EHEA Ministerial Conference. (2015). Yerevan Communiqué. Retrieved from http://bologna-yerevan2015.ehea.info/files/YerevanCommuniqueFinal.pdf.

EHEA Ministerial Conference. (2012b). Mobility for better learning: Mobility strategy 2020 for the European Higher Education Area (EHEA). Retrieved from http://www.ehea.info/Uploads/(1)/2012%20EHEA%20Mobility%20Strategy.pdf.

European Commission. (1997). Towards a Europe of Knowledge. COM(97) 563 final. Communication from the Commission tothe Council, the

European Parliament, the Economic and Social Committee and the Committee of the Regions. November 12,1997.

European Commission. (2000, January 18). Towards a European research area. COM (2000) 6 final. Communication from the Commission to the Council, the European Parliament, the Economic and Social Committee and the Committee of the Regions.

European Commission. (2009, September 21). *Report on progress in quality assurance in higher education*. Brussels, COM (2009) 487 final.

European Commission. (2011). 'Supporting growth and jobs – an agenda for the modernisation of Europe's higher education systems.' Communication from the Commission to the European Parliament, the Council, the European Economic and Social Committee and the Committee of the Regions. COM 2011 (567) Final. September 20, 2011.

European Commission. (2013a, July 11). *European Higher Education in the World*. Communication from the Commission to the European Parliament, the European Council, the European Economic and Social Committee and the Committee of the Regions. COM (2013) 499 final.

European Commission. (2013b). History of European co-operation in education and training, Retrieved February 7, 2013, from http://ec.europa.eu/education/more-information/former-programmes_en.htm.

European Commission. (2013c, July 8). Memo: Erasmus programme in 2011–2012: The figures explained.

European Commission. (2015, November 26). European semester thematic fiche: Tertiary education attainment.

European Commission. (2015a). The Bologna Process—towards the European higher education area. Updated July 23,2015. Retrieved from http://europa.eu/legislation_summaries/education_training_youth/lifelong_learning/c11088_en.htm.

European Commission. (2015b). European Semester Thematic Fiche: Tertiary Education Attainment. November 26, 2015.

European Commission. (2016). European Commission: Europe 2020. Available from: http://ec.europa.eu/europe2020/index_en.htm.

European Union. (1951). Treaty establishing the European Coal and Steel Community (ECSC), Treaty of Paris.

European Union: High Level Group on the Modernisation of Higher Education. (2013). *Report to the European Commission: Improving the quality of teaching and learning in Europe's higher education institutions.* Luxembourg: Publications Office of the European Union.

European Union. (1957). Treaty establishing the European Economic Community (EEC), Treaty of Rome.

Eurostat. (2012). European Commission statistics historical database.

Eurostat. (2016). European Commission statistics historical database

Eurydice & Eurostat. (2012). *Key data on education in Europe*. Brussels: Education, Audiovisual and Culture Executive Agency (EACA 9) and European Commission.

Eurydice/European Commission/EACEA. (2015). *The European Higher Education Area in 2015: Bologna Process Implementation Report*. Luxembourg: Publications Office of the European Union.

Hanushek, E. A., & Woessmann L. (2009, November). *Do better schools lead to more growth? Cognitive skills, economic outcomes, and causation* (IZA Discussion Papers, No. 4575).

Hoareau, C. (2012). Deliberative governance in the European Higher Education Area: The Bologna Process as a case of alternative governance architecture in Europe. *Journal of European Public Policy, 19*(4), 530–548.

Katzenstein, P. J. (2005). *World of regions*. Ithaca: Cornell University Press.

Keohane, R. O., & J. Nye. (2012). *Power and interdependence* (4th ed.). Longman Classics in Political Science.

Kölliker, A. (2001). Bringing together or driving apart the union?: Towards a theory of differentiated integration. Preprints aus der Max-Planck-Projektgruppe Recht der Gemeinschaftsgüter. Bonn: Gemeinschaftsgüter: Recht, Politik und Ökonomie, 2001/5.

Lefkofridi, Z., & Schmitter, P. C. (2015). Transcending or descending? European integration in times of crisis. *European Political Science Review, 7*, 3–22.

Matei, L. (2012, July 18). Chief Operating Officer and Professor of Public Policy, Central European University, Budapest, Hungary.

Matei, L. (2012a). Chief Operating Officer and Professor of Public Policy, Central European University, Budapest, Hungary. July 18, 2012.

Matei, L. (2012b). A policy gap financing in the European higher education area. In Curaj, A., Scott, P., Vlasceanu, L., & Wilson, L. (Eds.), European higher education at the crossroad: Between the bologna process and national reforms. Parts 1 and 2. Dordrecht: Springer Science+Business Media.

Mazza, C., Paolo, Q., & Angelo, R. (Eds.). (2008). *European universities in transition: Issues, models, and cases*. Northampton: Edward Elgar.

McNamara, K. (2015). *The politics of everyday Europe*. Oxford: Oxford University Press.

Moravcsik, A. (1998). *The choice for Europe: Social purpose and state power from Messina to Maastricht*. Ithaca: Cornell University Press.

Moravcsik, A., & Schimmelfennig, F. (2009). Liberal intergovernmentalism. In A. Wiener & T. Diez (Eds.), *European integration theory* (2nd ed.). Oxford: Oxford University Press.

Neave, G., & Maassen, P. (2007). The Bologna Process: An intergovernmental policy perspective. In P. Maassen & J. P. Olsen (Eds.), *University dynamics and European integration*. Dordrecht: Springer.

Olsen, J. (2009a). Change and continuity: An institutional approach to institutions of democratic government. *European Political Science Review, 1*(1), 3–32.

Olsen, Johan. P. 2009b. Democratic Government, Institutional Autonomy and the Dynamics of Change, Working Paper No. 01, January 2009 ARENA Working Paper. Available from: http://www.sv.uio.no/arena/english/research/publications/arena-publications/workingpapers/.

Pierson, P. (2004). *Politics in time: History, analysis, and social analysis.* Princeton: Princeton University Press.

Pierson, P. (1996). The path to European integration: A historical institutionalist analysis. *Comparative Political Studies, 29*(2), 123–163.

Pierson, P. (2000). Increasing returns, path dependence and the study of politics. *American Political Science Review, 94, 2.*

Regini, M. (2011). *European universities and the challenge of the market: A comparative analysis.* Cheltenham: Edward Elgar.

Risse, T. (2007). Social constructivism meets globalization. In H. Anthony & M. David (Eds.). *Globalization theory: Approaches and controversies* (pp. 126–147). Cambridge: Polity Press.

Rodrik, D. (2016, June 9). Innovation is not enough. *Project Syndicate.*

Rosa, M. J., Sarrico, C. S., Tavares, O., & Amaral, A. (2016). *Cross-border higher education and quality assurance: Commerce, the service directive and governing higher education.* London: Palgrave Macmillan.

Schmidt, V. A. (2009). The EU and its member states: From bottom up to top down. In D. Phinnemore & A. Warleigh-Lack (Eds.), *Reflections on European integration: 50 years of the Treaty of Rome* (pp. 194–211). London: Palgrave Macmillan.

Schmidt, V. A., & Thatcher, M. (Eds.). (2013). *Resilient liberalism in Europe's political economy.* Cambridge: Cambridge University Press.

Simmons, B. A., Dobbin, F., & Garrett, G. (2006). The institutional diffusion of liberalism. *International Organization, 60*(4), 781–810.

Sørensen, M. P., Carter B., & Mitchell Y. (2016). Excellence in the knowledge-based economy: From scientific to research excellence. *European Journal of Higher Education,* 6:3, 217–236.

Trow, M. (1974). Policies for higher education general report; 26–29 June 1973. Conference on Future Structures of Post-Secondary Education. Paris: Organisation for Economic Co-operation and Development (OECD).

Tyson, A. (2012, 2016). Acting Director for Strategy and Evaluation, Former Head of UnitC1, Higher Education and Erasmus, Directorate-General Education and Culture, European Commission; April 25, 2012; September 6, 2016.

Veiga, A., & Amaral, A. (2006). The open method of coordination and the implementation of the Bologna Process. *Tertiary Education and Management, 12,* 283–295.

World Bank Group. (2016). The Worldwide Governance Indicators (WGI) project. Retrieved from http://info.worldbank.org/governance/wgi/index.aspx.

CHAPTER 6

Portugal: Political Economy Explanations for Centralized Reforms

The state shall promote the democratisation of education and the other conditions needed for an education conducted at school and via other means of training to contribute to equal opportunities, the overcoming of economic, social and cultural inequalities, the development of the personality and the spirit of tolerance, mutual understanding, solidarity and responsibility, to social progress and to democratic participation in public life.
Constitution of the Portuguese Republic, Part 1, Article 73.2 (April 1976)

A historical institutional analysis of the Iberian countries provides the context to explain the processes of higher education policy reform in Portugal and Spain. After peace was established with the Treaty of Zamora in 1143, the earlier kingdoms for the most part turned their backs on each other until the Iberian dynastic union (1580–1640). After Portuguese independence in 1640, they proceeded through the following centuries with fierce independence from each other. Both countries experienced authoritarian rule between the 1930s and 1970s. As part of the third wave of democratization, Portugal and Spain developed closer ties in the last decades of the twentieth century (Huntington 1991). They founded new democracies in the Portuguese Constitution of 1976 and the Spanish Constitution of 1978. Portugal and Spain reformed their economic and political systems to join the European Economic Community (EEC), the predecessor to the European Union, in 1986. When the Iberian countries acceded to the EEC, they became the

© The Author(s) 2017
B. Barrett, *Globalization and Change in Higher Education*,
DOI 10.1007/978-3-319-52368-2_6

eleventh and twelfth Member States. The social sciences method of difference used in this research design demonstrates that, despite similar factors in the political economy of each country, there have been distinct outcomes in higher education attainment at the national level.[1]

In comparing Portugal and Spain, there are strong distinctions in national identity despite some historical parallels. An important similarity between Portugal and Spain is that they are both "policy takers" rather than "policy makers" in Bologna Process reforms (Bonete 2013). The impetus for Bologna came from France, Germany, Italy, and the United Kingdom with the Sorbonne Declaration in 1998. One aspect of being a policy taker is evidenced by relatively delayed implementation (until 2007) in initial reforms to establish the National Qualifications Framework (NQF) after this objective was introduced a year earlier. The method of difference used in this qualitative research design demonstrates that, with similar factors in the political economy of each country and the key variable of difference being government structure, Portugal has made greater increases in higher education attainment than Spain (Fig. 8.1), but there is a similar outcome in policy change at the national level for the degree structure and NQF criteria in the European Higher Education Area (EHEA). The similar outcome is explained by the policy processes of intergovernmentalism and Europeanization. Although there are many political and cultural explanations unique to each country in the Bologna Process, the substantive reforms were delayed by nearly a decade in the Iberian countries. In these two countries, the national level of governance has been a "taker" rather than an active "maker" of higher education policy constructed at the European level. However, the commitment to the higher education reform has been strong in Portugal. This stems from Portugal's 1986 Education System Act, in the years before the Bologna Process, which was subsequently amended in 2005 to converge with the criteria for the EHEA.

In a political economy perspective, the structure of government defines the bureaucratic process of policy reform. The unitary government structure of Portugal provides (in theory) a more direct manner of governance toward regional and local entities (Lijphart 1999). The quasi-federal government structure of Spain provides an additional level of government in between, with its 17 autonomous communities. This additional level of governance brings complexity and potential delays in policy reform at the sub-regional and university institutional levels. The unitary system of Portugal's government is centralized in national policy making. This coherence of government, together with its status as a relatively small country (population size of approximately 11 million), may lead to greater linearity in the policy implementation process than in a federal system (Lijphart 1999). Given the multi-level governance elements prevalent in higher education, the institutional level of governance has variation in timing and methods of policy reform. Despite the frequent linear theoretical assumption of policy making and implementation, the process is not always linear in practice (Veiga and Amaral 2006, 2009a). Notably, in Portugal there has been national diffusion of interest to reform, once leading universities begin to make changes. There has been a pragmatic approach to policy reform in Portugal, explains Inês Vasques, Portuguese member of the Bologna Follow Up Group.

> The first impressions are that people do not like change. They are not believers from the beginning in the reforms. Only when they see the others, they imitate. The initial reaction is fear of change. Then afterward once they see some results, they do not want to be left out when they observe other institutions reforming (Vasques 2016).

Portugal é um bomaluno da Europa (Portugal is a good student of Europe) was said by the former President of the European Commission, Jacques Delors (1985–1995). The phrase emerged in the 1980s, meaning that Portugal tries hard to comply with European policies even if those policies occasionally challenge the national interest. Portugal is willing to undertake demanding socioeconomic circumstances to be part of the European political community. An example is the general social cohesion despite the austerity reforms negotiated with the troika—the European Union (EU), the European Central Bank (ECB), and the International Monetary Fund (IMF)—in May 2011. Over a history of challenges in recent decades, the education system has reformed in ways described as "exceptional" (Neave and Amaral 2012:20).

QUALITATIVE ANALYSIS: FIVE POINTS OF COMPARISON

This and the following three chapters provide a comparison of the two Iberian countries as they make the Bologna Process policy reforms at the national level. These are the five comparison points: national governance background; political economy context; higher education governance; policy reform; and modernization of the higher education institutions. With the political economy context and policy reform sections, the challenges and opportunities are assessed. In line with the quantitative assessment in the previous chapter, the opportunities are higher education attainment and innovation, as well as the pursuit of internationalization, in Portugal and Spain. The challenges for higher education reform have been limitations on funding, despite some increases in government spending on education, and to a lesser extent uncertainty about the future of the EU. Important challenges are the development of the appropriate institutional capacity and leadership for policy reform. These qualitative case-study chapters identify the key national legislative documents on higher education. The following chapter discusses the role of stakeholders in Portugal's policy reform and the initiatives toward modernization in higher education and research innovation.

Portugal and Spain, after a decade of steady growth from the midnineties, are among the weaker economies in Europe, given their sovereign debt crises in 2011 and 2012, respectively. They have implemented reforms nearly a decade after the Bologna Process began in 1999. Considering GDP per capita (GDP PC) for the years 2000–2014, Portugal is slightly below and Spain is slightly above the EU average (See Table 6.1). Over these 12 years, the average GDP PC for Portugal is approximately $27,000 and for Spain is approximately $33,000. The EU average is in the middle at approximately $31,000 GDP PC for this 15-year period (World Bank 2016). Although there is the variation in GDP PC, the timing of policy reform at the national level in 2007 is similar for establishing for the NQF legal framework. With lower GDP PC, Portugal has made greater advances in higher education attainment than Spain. This may be because it is above a minimum level of GDP that would be a threshold supporting policy reform. Another explanation may be because Spain entered the Bologna Process in 2000 with a relatively high level of attainment, at 29.2 percent, compared to Portugal's 11.3 percent, for 30–34-year-olds (Eurostat 2016).

In Portugal, the *Decree-Law 42/2005* created the instruments to establish the EHEA framework and to introduce the ECTS. The *Law 49/2005* amended the Basic Law for the Education System from 1986. The national legislation for the NQF was adopted by both Portugal and Spain in 2007. They approved these policies at the national level within the same year of the EHEA Ministerial Conference in London (May 2007) that defined the qualifications framework at the European level. There are national and European qualifications frameworks for

Table 6.1   Gross Domestic Product Per Capita (Constant 2011 International $)

Portugal GDP PC 26,693 average (2000–2014)		Spain GDP PC 32,617 average (2000–2014)	
Year	GDP Per Capita	Year	GDP Per Capita
2000	26,147	2000	30,630
2001	26,468	2001	31,470
2002	26,526	2002	31,848
2003	26,180	2003	32,275
2004	26,590	2004	32,727
2005	26,744	2005	33,377
2006	27,111	2006	34,187
2007	27,732	2007	34,825
2008	27,747	2008	34,657
2009	26,895	2009	33,123
2010	27,393	2010	32,976
2011	26,932	2011	32,530
2012	25,953	2012	31,657
2013	25,800	2013	31,230
2014	26,175	2014	31,750
		EU Average 30,529	
		(for 26 countries in quantitative analysis)	

Source World Bank. 2016. GDP per capita, PPP (constant 2011 international $)
Code: NY.GDP.PCAP.PP.KD. *Source* World Bank, International Comparison Program database

each country in the EHEA. Portugal started to create its NQF with the *Decree-Law 276-C/2007 of July 31, 2007* and *Decree-Law 396/2007 of December 31, 2007*. Finally, *Ordinance 782/2009 of July 23, 2009* defined the structure of the Portuguese NQF. By comparison, Spain's law that established the Spanish Framework of Higher Education Qualifications (*El Marco Español de Cualificaciones*) is *Real Decreto 900/2007*. The academic degree structure, taken from the Framework for Higher Education Qualifications (FHEQ-Portugal) in 2010, is given in the Table 6.2. All EU countries in the EHEA are obliged to have a National Qualifications Framework (FHEQ-Portugal), which should be aligned with the European Qualifications Framework (FHEQ-EHEA).

The first-cycle degree with the Bologna Process offers a three-year bachelor's degree, and it has kept the traditional designation of *Licenciatura*. Prior to Bologna, the traditional *Licenciatura* degree was four–six years in duration. Pre-Bologna, a Master degree of usually

Table 6.2 Framework for Higher Education Qualifications in Portugal (FHEQ-Portugal)

FHEQ-Portugal Higher Education Qualifications	Corresponding FQ-EHEA Cycle	Corresponding EQF Levels
Doctoral degrees	Third-cycle qualifications	8
Doctoral course diplomas	/	/
Masters degrees	Second-cycle qualifications	7
Integrated Masters degrees		
Masters course diplomas	/	/
Licenciatura degrees	First-cycle qualifications	6
Technological Specialisation courses	Short-cycle qualifications linked to the first cycle	5

Source The Framework for Higher Education Qualifications in Portugal (FHEQ-Portugal), Page 13. Ministry of Science, Technology, and Education. November 2010

two-years was offered after the *Licenciatura* degree, and it is still offered. The polytechnic degree, *Bacharelato*, was three years in duration prior to the Bologna Process. It is still three-years, although in special cases can be a four-year degree. The Doctorate has been the third-cycle degree before and after the Bologna Process. Given the shorter time period for the first-cycle degree as compared to the historical *Licenciatura*, higher education attainment is presumed to have a lower financial cost after the Bologna Process. Although this coincides with the limited fiscal budgets since the financial crisis and the EU reform package in 2011, Portugal has increased its budget for education overall. Economic strictures have some limitations for government-supported programs such as education, particularly concerning the objective of student mobility. In 2011, Portugal spent more than 5.8 percent of GDP on education overall (Freysson and Wahrig 2013:1). Portugal was above the EU average of 5.3 percent of GDP expenditure on education overall (Eurostat 2012). In subsequent years—2012, 2013, and 2014—budgets have been reduced from this level, reflecting some lessening in overall education expenditures (PORDATA 2016).

There is greater emphasis on polytechnic education since the *Decree-Law 369/2014 of March 18, 2014*, which created and regulates the shorter cycle higher education technical courses called the *Cursos Técnicos Superiores Profissionais* (TeSP) (Vasques 2016). The technical professional higher education courses began to be offered in 2015, with great interest from all stakeholders—public, private, and academic. The government has objectives to modernize the polytechnic institutions, for which there are a greater number than university institutions in Portugal (Table 6.3). This aligns with the national and EHEA objectives for higher education attainment and employability after graduation, and thereby demonstrates the practical approach to policy reform in Portugal.

The five areas of qualitative case-study analysis have been chosen for their inclusion in academic literature on international political economy and higher education policy. The national governance background is similar in that both countries transitioned from authoritarian rule in the 1970s (O'Donnell and Schmitter 1986). Unique aspects of transition in each country have impacted policy reforms. Given lower levels of education following the *Estado Novo*, Portugal has had further to progress in expanding education. This, together with meaningful reforms to expand educational access and quality in the generation since then, has made its progress in higher education reform "exceptional" (Neave and Amaral 2012). The Bologna Process reforms add specification, in quality assurance for example, to reforms that were already underway to increase access to higher education. As the first point of comparison, the unitary structure of Portugal's government makes the policy process more coherent nationally, as compared to Spain's federal government structure. Governance historical background, as the first area of assessment, is broadly understood in this context at a national level, as it influences policy making and bureaucratic administration of higher education.

Table 6.3 Higher Education Institution Types in Portugal and Spain

		Public Sector	*Private Sector*
Portugal	Universities	18	52
Portugal	Polytechnics	30	69
Spain	Universities	50	35

Sources
Portugal A3ES, Links: University Institutions and Polytechnical Institutions, November 2016
Available from: http://www.a3es.pt/en/links
Spain Registro de Universidades, Centros, y Títulos (RUCT), Ministry of Education, November 2016.
Available from: https://www.educacion.gob.es/ruct/listauniversidades?tipo_univ=&d-8320336-p=1& cccaa=&actual=universidades&consulta=1&codigoUniversidad=

Second, the international political economy context is the independent variable, whereas higher education attainment or reform is the dependent variable, in this research. The context is represented in the three explanatory dynamics of global economic forces (globalization), domestic politics (intergovernmentalism), and norm-setting leadership from the EU (Europeanization). These are at play in Portugal, influencing higher education reform. The economic divergence between Portugal and Spain in the first decade of the twenty-first century is explained by the following factors: domestic fiscal policies, EMU accession experience, labor market policies, policy stability, and differences in educational attainment (Royo 2012:196–205). Portugal's employment levels have been higher than Spain's, reflecting fewer labor market rigidities in recent decades. The secondary school completion rates had been among the lowest in the EU, with an early-leavers rate of 40 percent compared to the EU average early-leavers rate of 16 percent (Royo 2012:203). This has influence on limiting the higher education attainment levels. To address these policies, there are incentive programs such as the "Over-23" program to provide a path to higher education for those individuals over 23 who have not completed secondary education (Couto 2012). A weak education sector can have broader effects in the political economy:

> Poor schooling results have a ripple effect on productivity, research, and innovation, which helps account for Portugal's weak competitiveness and slow growth. It is therefore critical for Portugal to narrow this 'human capital gap' in order to improve productivity and resume 'catching up'. (Royo 2012:204)

The Iberian countries' catching up in economic growth and productivity is in relationship to the EU average, to which, in comparison, the countries have lagged. To enter the EEC in 1986, the countries undertook numerous economic reforms that resulted in economic growth in the 1990s. There have been economic strains since then, but also investment in education at multiple levels (secondary and tertiary/higher education in particular) to increase economic competition and to contribute to human capital development. There is not necessarily a lack of funding, but perhaps a need for more efficiency in the education system (Royo 2012:204).

Third, higher education governance is defined by the leadership of the institutions (universities and polytechnic) and the degree of proximity to the state in administration. The analysis considers national legislative documents that are pertinent to Bologna Process reforms in a historical institutional perspective. The binary higher education system in Portugal includes polytechnic institutes similar to the traditional British polytechnics. The polytechnic institutes are vocationally oriented and cannot offer doctorate degrees. The year prior to the democratic Carnation Revolution,[2] the Parliament (called the National Assembly) passed the Reform Act of July 25, 1973 to create a binary system of higher education. The creation of a binary system of higher education provides multiple avenues for entering higher education. This was important given that less than 7 percent of the population of the relevant age cohort attained higher education in the last year of the *Estado Novo* (Amaral and Magalhães 2005:117). Since the Reform Act of 1973, the binary system of higher education, with polytechnic and university institutions, has been maintained with the Bologna Process. The fourth and fifth aspects of qualitative analysis are assessed in Chaps. 7 and 9.

Fourth, considering the role of stakeholders, since the Bologna Process initiative started in 1999, there has been development of coalitions in the organization of stakeholders across sectors. Recognizing the research limitations to gathering specific details on stakeholder organization across the public, academic, and private sectors, a general analysis of stakeholder involvement applies the Advocacy Coalition Framework (ACF) (Sabatier 1991, 1998, 2007). The ACF is especially useful, since it considers a normative reasoning that is social constructivist and rationalist in nature (Sabatier and Weible 2007:194), which is applicable to the social constructivist and rationalist explanations for the Bologna Process. An analysis of policy reform indicates that the public sector is in the dominant stakeholder advocacy coalition role. The government has been the primary driver of national legislation related to the Bologna Process. By comparison, in some countries, such as the United States, the academic sector is a stronger coalition member in higher education. There the academic sector, rather than independent agencies established by national governments, provides quality assurance and accreditation through peer-reviewed university associations. Prior to the Bologna Process, some quality assurance agencies were run by associations of higher education institutions, as in the region of Flanders in Belgium, The Netherlands, and Portugal. The European Standards and Guidelines for quality assurance in Europe require that agencies be independent from higher education institutions and governments. As a private foundation, *Agência de Avaliação e Acreditação do Ensino Superior* (National Agency of Assessment and Accredition of Higher Education), known as A3ES, the quality assurance agency in Portugal has legal independence from both the higher education institutions and the government.

The fifth point of qualitative analysis—the modernization of the higher education institutions—considers research, innovation, and the European Research Area (ERA) as Portugal aims to increase the institutional capacity of universities beyond traditional teaching and learning. The place of research and innovation are central in the knowledge economy. The Europe 2020 and Horizon 2020 research and development initiatives of the European Commission serve as reference points for ongoing initiatives in research in Portugal and in Spain. In the initial decade of the EHEA, from 2000 to 2009, research and development (R&D) in Portugal more than doubled from 0.72 to 1.58 as a percentage of GDP (Eurostat 2016). The ERA was created in 2000, and it is a separate and complementary development to the EHEA with its own unique challenges for implementation (Amaral 2011). The purpose of R&D is to innovate and thereby lead to economic development. This innovation is quantifiable by new patents generated and research partnerships with stakeholders across the public, academic, and private sectors. The following presents reviews of the five points of qualitative analysis for Portugal, three in this chapter and two in Chap. 7.

NATIONAL GOVERNANCE HISTORICAL BACKGROUND

The relationship with Europe is important for Portugal. The historic relationship with the United Kingdom, the Luso-Britannic alliance, has roots in the fourteenth-century Portuguese wine and British cloth trade (Birmingham 2003:4). The Portuguese were part of the Iberian dynastic union (1580–1640) when the Spanish Armada was defeated by the United Kingdom in 1588. Nearly four centuries later, in 1986, Portugal became a member of what is today the European Union. Concerning Portugal's commitment to economic reforms, negotiated by Europe as part of receiving financial assistance between May 2011 and May 2014, Portuguese Foreign Minister Paulo Portas said "Portugal will do whatever it takes to implement reform" (Portas 2012). The disposition of the Portuguese people is that they are more accepting rather than contesting, particularly as compared to their neighbors to the east. Spain and Greece, in the several years since 2010, have protested regularly against austerity measures brought about as part of economic reforms. Although tensions increase, particularly in periods of austerity, historically Portugal has demonstrated fewer protests toward the government and more social cohesion than Spain. Within any limited time period, the greater number of protests in Spain demonstrates that country's stronger tendency toward contestation.[3] Portugal's neighbor to the east, Spain is a quasi-federation of 17 autonomous communities, where citizens that strongly identify with these regions have a greater tendency to voice concerns publicly (Fishman 2004:13).

Today the Bologna Process brings opportunity to study abroad and the opportunity for internationalization of higher education, which are attractive to the Portuguese. Simultaneously, they seek to make their universities an attractive place for non-Portuguese students to study (Correia 2013). Understanding the history preceding higher education policy reform is important, given that this political environment under authoritarian rule in the mid-twentieth century was one where there were limitations to progress through levels of education. In Europe the literacy and education levels were the lowest in Portugal, in the period of the *Estado Novo* (Heitor and Horta 2012:184). In the pursuit of power to control the population by means of limiting knowledge, education as an investment of the state was not a priority. Under authoritarian rule, through the 1970s, approximately 1 percent of the population completed higher education (Pereira and Lains 2012:129). The limited opportunities in education fostered more reliance on the government rather than on individual empowerment which may have ultimately challenged the government.

The period of dictatorial rule under António Salazar became known as "*O Estado Novo*" ("The New State"), Portugal under authoritarianism (Birmingham 2003:162). The era of dictatorship spanned four decades, from the 1930s to the 1970s, and resulted in the distancing of the people from political participation and a collective political silence. "Politics were increasingly dominated by a single dictator who satisfied the aspirations of the old-style army officers while distancing them from the practice of politics" (Birmingham 2003:161). A condition for becoming Minister of Finance in 1928 was that Salazar would take charge of the accounting for all ministries (Birmingham 2003:163). This paved the way for his eventual political rise to become Prime Minister from 1932 to 1968. After illness caused Salazar to resign, in 1968 Marcelo Caetano continued the *Estado Novo* until the peaceful revolution in 1974.

Salazar was a Catholic law professor at the University of Coimbra who eschewed implementation of contemporary economic development theories. Portugal remained the poorest country in western Europe during his rule. A historian describes Salazar's political control of Portugal for more than three decades to be attributed to his advocacy for "patriotism, paternalism, and prudence" in particular:

> [Salazar had] very skilled jugging of the interests of the army, the urban middle class, the monarchists, and the church. The great ideas that were hammered home by the government's propaganda were patriotism, paternalism, and prudence. Patriotism was epitomized by a rejection of the republic and all its values and by a new enthusiasm for Portugal's role as one of the 'great powers' in the African colonies. Paternalism involved an absolute and unquestioning respect for authority and all its agents, including the restored Catholic church. Prudence was enshrined in the virtues of thrift and fortitude for workers and peasants but did not apply to the leisured class who dined well and slept late. Such an agenda satisfied a majority of the army officers who had brought Salazar to power, though not their masonic brethren whose anti-Catholic caste was repressed (Birmingham 2003:165).

When Salazar became ill in 1968, the Prime Minister's authority was granted to Marcelo Caetano who eventually introduced some economic and political reforms. In these years, Portugal remained engaged in combat with the indigenous population of the overseas colonies in Angola, Mozambique, and Portuguese Guinea during their struggles for independence. The years of political silence drew to a close in the late 1960s, as society became more assertive regarding the direction in which the government should go. Accompanying a respect for this new societal openness, traditional weapons of war were not used during the revolution of 1974 that ushered in democracy. In this peaceful revolution there was some resistance by the political police, whereas the army and the government surrendered to the revolutionaries (Birmingham 2003:185). The 1974 Carnation Revolution was a pivotal time.

Afterward, alongside democracy, there was a greater demand for higher education (Neave and Amaral 2012). In the first democratic election after the new 1976 Constitution, Mário Soares was elected Prime Minister. Over the next decade, Soares held office intermittently until winning the Presidency in 1986, becoming the first civilian head of state in 60 years. The Soares years were marked with economic growth during this period of neoliberal market reforms that complied with conditions for joining the EEC. From 1985 to 1995 Prime Minister Aníbal Cavaco Silva took advantage of EU funds to develop the market economy and to liberalize labor regulations. At this time, tuition fees became higher, sparking protests from students. By the mid-1990s, the gross participation rate in higher education had climbed from 7 percent to more than 50 percent (Amaral 2013). In the last years of the *Estado Novo,* the binary system of higher education (polytechnic and university institutions) was established with the Reform Act 5/73 of July 25, 1973 passed by Portugal's Parliament, the National Assembly.

POLITICAL ECONOMY CONTEXT: OPPORTUNITIES AND CHALLENGES

The Bologna Process is a neoliberal approach to higher education (Neave and Amaral 2012:26). To be neoliberal it is necessary to have a market. In the higher education market, the objectives for the EHEA are convergence, openness, and exchange of knowledge, students, and academic degrees. Some objectives of the Bologna Process remained at the discursive level of reform, for a period of time, before advancing on steps in implementation. This book discusses those aspects that have been reformed in Portugal and Spain, given the economic and political context in these Iberian countries.

Alberto Amaral, the Founding Director of the A3ES (National Agency of Assessment and Accreditation of Higher Education) and former Rector of the University of Porto describes a theory on and problems of neoliberalism:

> To implement neoliberal policies in higher education, institutions must have autonomy; otherwise they cannot work in a market. Universities in a market may choose to follow strategies that have nothing to do with government policies and public goods. This forces states to intervene, making sure the institutions do what the states want them to do. Then, it is not fully neoliberalism. It is a paradox. The dilemma is that the Bologna Process is giving some autonomy in the neoliberal market for higher education only to have it sharply monitored. (Amaral 2013)

One of the rules of European Standards and Guidelines for university institutions is that the quality assurance agencies must be fully independent from institutions. This European arrangement is different from the U.S. tradition in which accrediting institutions are run by private regional agencies that are associations of higher education institutions. Considering the relationship between the state and higher education institutions, there is a state-institutional tension (Amaral 2013). This varies across countries as universities have varying extents of autonomy over time (Dobbins and Knill 2009). An example is that although German institutions did not have much autonomy for many years, they have transformed some universities into private foundations. Instead of following public sector rules, they follow private sector rules, and they have more flexibility.

Portugal's economic growth has been unsteady since joining the Bologna Process. Previously, in the second half of the 1990s, GDP annual growth averaged more than 4 percent (World Bank 2016). The economic reforms of Prime Minister Aníbal Cavaco Silva and President Mário Soares, between 1986 and 1996, delivered economic growth that coincided with joining the EEC. The decade earlier, privatization and trade reforms were underway as Portugal and Spain negotiated membership to join the EEC (Royo 2012). The economic restructuring took place in these years of reform prior to accession. The Iberian countries were among those in the Economic and Monetary Union (EMU) that began circulation of the euro currency in 2002. The competition of the Portuguese escudo and the Spanish peseta with stronger currencies in the EMU led to an erosion of export competitiveness during the first decade of the twenty-first century (Dadush 2012). By the second decade, a sovereign debt crisis had taken hold, and GDP measured negative 4.05 percent in 2012 (World Bank 2016). First Portugal, in 2011, and then Spain, in 2012, negotiated economic reform packages with the group known as the troika: the EU, the ECB, and IMF.

In May 2011, Portugal became the third country in the EU, following Greece and Ireland, to receive a bailout from the European Financial Stability Facility (EFSF). The EFSF was created in May 2010 to provide support to the 15 countries in the euro zone area at the time, and it is incorporated in Luxembourg.[4] The Economic Adjustment Programme for Portugal was sponsored by the European Commission's Directorate General of Economic and Financial Affairs. During the sovereign debt crisis, the general election was moved up the calendar after the government lost an important vote in the National

Assembly and resigned. The month following the economic agreement with the troika (EU, IMF, and ECB), in June 2011, Portugal elected a new government. Pedro Passos Coelho became the Prime Minister (Social Democrats, PSD political party), forming a coalition government with the Popular Party. The PSD–PP governing political party led by Prime Minister Coelho replaced the previous government led by José Socrates (Socialist, PS political party) since 2005. Nevertheless, the economic reform agreement received support across party lines (Wise 2012). The PSD–PP government included ministers that were politically independent and were technical experts. The austerity measures as part of the reform program caused uncertainty among the population, which was unsure of the effectiveness of reform measures in the long run (Freire 2013).

Although Portugal experienced slower GDP growth than Spain before the financial recession in 2009, it reached a higher level of growth in 2010 before declining again. The GDPs of both countries declined during the 2008–2009 financial recession in the U.S. and Europe, which was followed by sovereign debt crises in select countries. During 2012, these euro zone area countries experienced a subsequent double-dip recession. This was met with economic assistance from the troika (EU, IMF, and ECB) for Portugal and with economic assistance from the EU for Spain's banking and financial sectors (Fig. 6.1 and Table 6.4).

In the macroeconomic context, having a skilled workforce contributes to productivity for economic growth, which is necessary for a country to pay its debts. Although the support from the public sector for the Bologna Process had moderated in the face of austerity, education remains important as a national value and higher education attainment continues to rise. The link between productivity and human capital is made complete by education. In the face of the economic crisis, the budgets for education have been reduced. This impacts the educational institutions that operate within limited budgets and need to raise tuition costs for second-cycle degrees and above. After peaking in 2010 at 8.5 billion euro, total education spending declined in 2011 and further in 2012 to below 7 billion euro (PORDATA 2013). Between June 2011 and July 2013, Álvaro Santos Pereira served as Minister of the Economy and Business, and, as a professor at a Canadian university, was independent, with no affiliation with a political party. Minister Pereira acknowledged the potential for investment in a knowledge-based economy to improve growth.

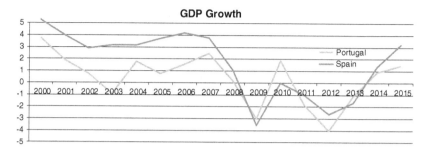

Fig. 6.1 GDP growth annual percentage, Portugal and Spain *Source* World Bank, NY.GDP.MKTP.KD.ZG, 2016

Table 6.4 GDP growth annual percentage, Portugal and Spain

	2000	2001	2002	2003	2004	2005	2006	2007
Portugal	3.79	1.94	0.77	−0.93	1.81	0.77	1.55	2.49
Spain	5.29	4.00	2.88	3.19	3.17	3.72	4.17	3.77
	2008	2009	2010	2011	2012	2013	2014	2015
Portugal	0.20	−2.98	1.90	−1.83	−4.03	−1.13	0.91	1.45
Spain	1.12	−3.57	0.01	−1.00	−2.62	−1.67	1.36	3.21

The disappointing performance of Portugal's economy over the past decade suggests that a return to productivity growth is a necessary prior condition for achieving higher rates of economic growth and thus a rise in the standard of living. Since a strong link exists between productivity and both quality and quantity of human capital, investing in a knowledge-based economy might be an appropriate strategy to bring Portugal's stagnation to an end and improve the country's rate of economic growth (Pereira and Lains 2012: 125).

Other Key Opportunities and Challenges

Higher education access and internationalization are the primary opportunities for higher education reform in Portugal. Chapter 5 assessed these opportunities for higher education attainment, in relation to variables including economic growth and investment in innovation.

Challenges for higher education reform are funding and political uncertainty about the EU. Institutional capacity and leadership, when strong, support opportunities and, when weak, serve as challenges. Institutionally, there are additional places for students in Portuguese higher education institutions, particularly in rural areas (Vasques 2016). This additional capacity presents an opportunity for more students to become enrolled nationally and internationally. Portugal continues to aim to increase educational attainments nationally and to attract students internationally.

After the mid-1990s when the gross participation rate in higher education climbed from 7 percent to more than 50 percent, there was no longer a primary concern about student quantity; instead the government became concerned with quality of higher education (Amaral 2013). The ministry began to issue more competitive rules to influence the quality of higher education opportunities. In Portugal and in Spain, the Ministry of Education places students in universities based on their performance on national entrance exams. The competition for students initially drove implementation of the reforms (Amaral 2013). Previously, in the 1980s, students who received lower scores on placement exams would still have the opportunity to attend university. The more competitive threshold of the late 1990s became institutionalized at the same time as a decline occurred in national birth rates.

This led to competition among universities to attract students. The first-cycle degree had been shortened and would attract more students able to receive their degree in three years. Pre-Bologna, polytechnic institutions offered degrees in three years, whereas university institutions offered *Licenciatura* degrees in four to six years, depending on the field. Once the national laws were passed, mostly in the years 2006–2008, more students applied for higher education. Universities wanted to enroll more students, and they were concerned that students would prefer universities that reformed earlier. The universities did not want to be left out of the reform process and wanted to be attractive to students. Therefore, most universities rushed to implement degree structure reforms in the autumn of 2008 (Correia 2012, 2013).

To increase access, various programs were instituted, including the Over-23 policy, the short polytechnic first-cycle degree, and the quotas for lusophone foreign students. Given the extra capacity for students at some public universities, the government has introduced several opportunities to increase access to higher education. The Over-23 policy provides that potential students over 23 years of age who have not completed secondary education can enter into a higher education institution if they pass an exam. This program to recruit students beyond immediate secondary school graduates and foreign students is an effort to widen access to higher education in Portugal. There is also an initiative to increase access for students from other Portuguese-speaking countries. This provides quotas for students from African Countries with Official Portuguese Language (*Países Africanos de Língua Oficial Portuguesa* [PALOP]). Similarly, many students from lusophone Brazil, a former Portuguese colony, are considered for university enrollment in Portugal.

Internationalization has been an important opportunity. The Bologna Process is a response to the pressures of economic globalization by providing internationalization in higher education. Absent the convergence of policy with the Bologna Process, some countries may have responded with their own reforms. The Bologna Process has been a coordinating mechanism for the internationalization of higher education, every academic program is to comply with the principles of the Bologna Declaration for quality assurance. There are particular EHEA rules in fields such as Architecture, Medicine, and Pharmacy that establish a minimum number of years of study for a degree (World Federation 2005). As a worldwide norm, national professional licensing follows pertinent academic degrees, which have been harmonized internationally across fields in the EHEA. Along with the previously discussed opportunities that accompany higher education reform, and its benefits in relation to economic growth and innovation, other key challenges for higher education reform are funding and, to a lesser extent, political uncertainty about the EU.

HIGHER EDUCATION GOVERNANCE

The delay in changing the Education System Act (1986) explains why Portugal's national legislation did not reform the credit and degree structure until the years between 2005 and 2008. The absence of a Parliamentary majority for several years was the reason the Education Act System Act of 1986 remained in place during the initial years of the 1999 Bologna Process initiative. "To the discontent of ministers and the desperation of higher education institutions, the process dragged on while some heated debates took place" (Veiga and Amaral 2009b:57). The Directorate General for Higher Education (*DGES, Direção-Geral do Ensino Superior*) is the executive administrative agency that faciliates the Bologna Process implementation. The DGES bureau is within the Ministry of Education and Science (*Ministério da Educação e Ciência*). Under previous governments, the DGES was located in the former Ministry of Science, Technology, and Higher Education. "The Bologna Process was a main reason for reform, and it brought aspects of higher education that needed to be changed" (Couto 2012). One aspect was to grant more autonomy to public, private, and polytechnic institutions. With the reforms, they have the ability to design curriculum and to have it approved by the national accrediation agency, which is A3ES in Portugal.

The governance of higher education in Portugal is represented by three groups, which meet approximately on a monthly basis:

- The Council of Rectors of Public Universities (CRUP)
- The Council of Presidents of Public Polytechnics (CCISP)
- The Association of Private Institutions: Universities, Polytechnics, and Specialized Institutions (APESP)

The CRUP is composed of the executive leaders of all public universities and a private one (the Portuguese Catholic University). The CCISP is composed of Presidents of all public Polytechnics. The APESP is composed of representatives of the private institutions that are members of the organization. Occasionally, there is the participation of labor unions when labor relations issues are on the agenda. The National Council of Education and the National Council on Higher Education are diverse groups that advise the government on proposed laws and conduct scholarly research. Among a large number of other members, it has representatives from the three groups.

The DGES role is held by an administrator without a political role in higher education policy. In the decade between the mid-1990s and the mid-2000s, there were four Prime Ministers of Portugal. With less government turnover, in the same decade in Spain, there were two Prime Ministers (José María Aznar of the Popular Party, 1996–2004, and José Luís Rodríguez Zapatero of the Social Democratic Party, 2004–2011). In 2011, both countries changed government leadership from the Socialist parties and established a more conservative leadership in the Social Democrat and Popular Party, respectively. Between June 2011 and October 2015 in Portugal, in the Social Democrat government of Prime Minister Pedro Passos Coelho, the leadership in higher education with Education Minister Nuno Crato had been fairly consistent. Comparatively, in Spain there has been more variation in higher education leadership in these same years under Prime Minister Mariano Rajoy.

The Bologna Process was a good reason to move forward with many reforms that were in Portugal's interest (Couto 2012). By 2006–2007, the academic course credit structure had been changed with the implementation of the ECTS. In the 2008–2009 academic year, the majority of institutions made the degree-cycle changes. Universities compete for students, and they did not want to be overlooked. Particularly, since there are additional places for students at Portuguese universities, they wish to stay attractive to students by complying with the Bologna Process efforts at internationalization. In a survey of the Bologna Process implementation, it was reported, "Leadership was very optimistic about the upcoming challenges, which was not surprising as it is recurrent to see the leadership of higher education institutions being favorable to the Bologna reforms" (Veiga and Amaral 2009b:59).

The Bologna Process reforms became implemented in the second part of the first decade. This took place after the Education System Act of 1986, that needed to be changed, was reformed with the Decree-Law 49/2005 of August 30, 2005. Higher education institutions are obliged to recognize ECTS from other accredited higher education institutions within the country. Ultimately, with the Bologna Process, all countries in the EHEA are obliged to recognize credits in ECTS and academic degrees. The consistency and similar measurement of credits across Portugal is an asset that ensures transferability within the country. The polytechnic institutions offer shorter degree cycles than universities and degrees equivalent in length to the three-year first-cycle Bachelor. The education is particularly technical in focus; it develops individuals for careers in the industrial arts and sciences. The degrees offered by polytechnic institutions may be comparable to those from community colleges in the U.S. that offer technical degrees. There are a greater number of polytechnic institutions than university institutions, and both have experienced reforms in the Bologna Process.

Prior to the Bologna Process launch in 1999, the University Autonomy Act of 1988 gave full pedagogical autonomy to public universities. In the binary system, the universities and polytechnic institutions were ready to reform and did so once the national legislation was approved in the years between 2005 and 2008. Given internationalization, they were knowledgeable of the Bologna Process and eager to participate (Amaral 2013; Freire 2013). As part of the Bologna Process reforms for the new degree cycles and the ECTS, higher education institutions received the directive to implement the first-cycle degree to have relevance for the labor market. This encourages students completing a higher education degree and provides opportunities to participate in the workplace earlier than under the previous *Licenciatura* system. The following is an account of the higher education institutions in the Iberian countries. By comparison with Portugal, within Spain's unified higher education system, the four main polytechnic universities (in Cartagena, Catalunya, Madrid, and Valencia) are included among the public sector universities (Table 6.3).

The account of the higher education institutions in Iberia indicates that overall there are more higher education institutions in Portugal than in Spain. Although the population of Spain is four times larger than that of Portugal, the number of Portuguese higher education institutions is greater. In Portugal, there are more private university-level institutions than public universities. The private university sector includes six universities plus a number of independent, specialized smaller schools offering university degrees. There are more polytechnic institutions than university institutions in Portugal, and the majority of the polytechnic institutions are private. This corresponds with Portugal's priority to offer the degree *Cursos Técnicos Superiores Profissionais* (TeSP) following the Decree-Law 369/2014. All higher education institutions in Spain, including polytechnic universities, are within the university system, making it a unified rather than binary higher education system. Seven of the private universities in Spain are identified as religious universities.

In Portugal and Spain, there are Laws and Decree-Laws. A Law *(Lei, Portuguese; Ley, Spanish)* is passed by the national Parliament. Decree-Laws, *Decreto-Lei* in Portugal and *Real Decreto* in Spain, are enacted by the government and signed by the President of the Republic in Portugal or the King in Spain. This act is called "promulgation," for which the head of state has the responsibility to ensure that legislation complies with the Constitution. The Decree-Law mechanism is allowed by the Constitution to provide the government with the mechanism to legislate in particular areas, including education. There is the option for the legislation to receive judicial review by the Constitutional Court before promulgation.

In Portugal and in Spain, a Decree-Law or Law is necessary to change higher education governance. In Portugal, the Law No. 62/2007 from September 10, 2007 (*Lei No. 62/2007 de 10 de Setembro 2007*) has defined the juridical regime of the higher education institutions (universities and polytechnics, public and private). Decree-Law 276-C/2007 of July 31, 2007 and Decree-Law 396/2007 of December 31, 2007 put into motion the development of the National Qualifications Framework (NQF). The Ordinance 782/2009 of July 23, 2009, defined the structure of the Portuguese NQF, presenting the descriptors for each qualification cycle in terms of knowledge, skills, and competences. The 2010 Framework for Higher Education Qualifications in Portugal (FHEQ-Portugal) demonstrates its alignment with the Framework of Qualifications for the EHEA. Portugal's A3ES and each EHEA country's national agency for quality assurance is registered with the European Quality Assurance Register (EQAR), which assures compliance with the European Standards and Guidelines. Once the agency is registered with EQAR it may operate at the European level, meaning that students and graduates from other countries may use it for academic accreditation.

SUMMARY

When Portugal joined the Bologna Process, the higher education initiative grew from participation of four countries with the Sorbonne Declaration in 1998 to 29 countries in 1999. Portugal and Spain were original signatories to the Bologna Declaration among the 15 EU countries and 14 non-EU countries at the time. This multi-level governance initiative has evolved to define European higher education. Bologna has more to do with its origins in the Sorbonne Declaration than with globalization because it was only in 2000 that the EU started to articulate the objectives of the Lisbon Strategy (Amaral 2013). The Lisbon Strategy appropriated the Bologna Process to become part of the strategy for education and economic development. Occasionally, countries use international initiatives to make changes in their own domestic policies (Amaral 2013). Three of the original four Sorbonne Declaration countries (France, Germany, and Italy) used the international reforms to support domestic reforms. The British degree system in the United Kingdom was already consistent with the Bologna Process, which came 1 year later. These four countries signed the Sorbonne Declaration as a reason to implement reforms, which were defined by a system in which two main cycles, undergraduate and graduate, should be recognized for international comparison and equivalence.

The international bureaucratic structure for education has grown exponentially with the Bologna Process and with PISA (Performance of International Student Assessment) for secondary education evaluation by the OECD. This international education initiative started with only several countries in the mid-1990s and today includes more than 70 countries (Martens and Wolf 2009). The leading institutions with an interest in the international educational initiatives are agencies of the EU, the OCED, and UNESCO.

This chapter has considered the three of the five points of qualitative analysis for the case study of Portugal, which are applied to Spain in Chap. 8. The preceding analysis of the national governance background, the political economy context, and higher education governance provides the framing for the following chapter. Chapter 7 discusses the role of stakeholders in the policy process and the modernization of higher education institutions in Portugal.

Notes

1. A method for determining the research design and selected countries for case study analysis comes from John Stuart Mill's logic of comparisons in *A System of Logic* (1843).
2. The Carnation Revolution was mostly peaceful, without bloodshed, culminating in the coup of April 25, 1974 (Anderson 2000: 163). The word "revolution" may not appropriately reflect the relatively peaceful context of the transition. By comparison, revolution did not occur in Spain, where the process of democratic transition occurred following the death of General Francisco Franco on November 20, 1975.
3. In March 2013, there was a significantly large protest against the government of more than one million people in the central plaza Praça do Comércio in Lisbon. The *Diário Notícias* reported "Manifestações: Um milhão e meio protestou contra Governo". March 2, 2013. Available from: http://www.dn.pt/inicio/portugal/interior.aspx?content_id=3084470
4. Since 2010 the three Baltic states joined the euro area: Estonia in January 2011, Latvia in January 2014, and Lithuania in January 2015.

REFERENCES

Amaral, A., & Magalhães, A. (2005). Implementation of higher education policies: A Portuguese example. In Å. Gornitzka et al. (Eds.), *Reform and change in higher education* (pp. 117–134). Dordrecht: Springer.

Amaral, A. (2011). ERA and the Bologna process: Implementation problems and the human resource factor. In S. Avveduto (Ed.). *Convergence or differentiation. Human resources for research in a changing European Scenario* (pp. 13–54). Naples: ScriptaWeb.

Amaral, A. (2013). Founding Director, Centre for Research on Higher Education Policies (CIPES), Matosinhos (Porto) and President of the Administration Council, A3ES Portuguese National Qualifications Agency; May 28, 2013.

Anderson, J. M. (2000). *The history of Portugal.* Westport, CT: Greenwood Press.

Birmingham, D. (2003). *A concise history of Portugal* (2nd ed.). Cambridge: Cambridge University Press.

Bonete Perales, R. (2012, 2013). Associate Professor of Applied Economics, and Assessor for the Vice-Chancellor of Internationalization, University of Salamanca. Counselor for Education to the Permanent Delegations of Spain to OECD, UNESCO and the Council of Europe (July 2010-July 2012). Member of the Bologna Follow Up Group for Spain (2008–2012); June 28, 2012 and May 30, 2013.

Correia Fernandes, M. 2012, 2013. Professor of the Humanities; Former Vice-Rector, University of Porto, Portuguese Member of the Bologna Follow Up Group (2011–2014); July 23, 2012 and May 29, 2013.

Couto, P. A. (2012, 2016). Director of Services of Support to the Network of Higher Education (Direção de Serviços de Suporte à Rede do Ensino Superior). Office of Director General for Higher Education (Direção-Geral do Ensino Superior), Ministry of Education and Science (Ministério da Educação e Ciência), Government of Portugal; July 24, 2012; June 1, 2016.

Dadush, U. (2012). Is the end of the crisis in sight? *Il Sole.* March 28, 2012.

Dobbins, M., & Knill, C. (2009). Higher Education Policies in central and Eastern Europe: Convergence toward a common model? *Governance: An International Journal of Policy Administration, and Institutions, 22*(3), 397–430.

Eurostat. (2012). European Commission statistics historical database.

Eurostat. (2016). European Commission statistics historical database.

Fishman, R. (2004). *Democracy's voices: Social ties and the quality of public life in spain.* Ithaca: Cornell University Press.

Freire, M. R. (2013). Assistant Professor, International Relations in Faculty of Economics. Portugal: University of Coimbra. May 28, 2013.

Freysson, L., & Laura, W. (2013). Economy and Finance: Eurostat Statistics in Focus 12/2013. Brussels: European Commission. April 23, 2013.

Heitor, M., & Hugo, H. (2012). Science and Technology in Portugal: From late awakening to the challenge of integrated communities. In G. Neave & A. Amaral (Eds.). *Higher education in Portugal 1974–2009: A Nation, a Generation* (pp. 179–226). Dordrecht: Springer.

Huntington, S. P. (1991). *The third wave: Democratization in the late twentieth century*. Norman: University of Oklahoma Press.

Lijphart, A. (1999). *Patterns of democracy: Government forms and performance in 36 countries*. New Haven: Yale University Press.

Martens, K., & Wolf, K. D. (2009). Boomerangs and Trojan horses: The unintended consequences of internationalising education policy through the EU and the OECD. In A. Amaral, G. Neave, C. Musselin, & P. Maassen (Eds.), *European integration and the governance of higher education and research* (pp. 81–107). Dordrecht: Springer.

Neave, G., & Amaral, A. (Eds.). (2012). *Higher education in Portugal 1974-2009: A nation, a generation*. Dordrecht: Springer.

O'Donnell, G., & Schmitter, P. C. (1986). *Transitions from authoritarian rule: Tentative conclusions about uncertain democracies*. Washington, DC: Woodrow Wilson Center for International Scholars.

Pereira, Á.S. and Lains, P. (2012). From an Agrarian Society to a Knowledge Economy?: The Rising Importance of Education to the Portuguese Economy, 1950–2009. In Neave, Guy & Alberto Amaral (Eds.). *Higher Education in Portugal 1974–2009: A Nation, a Generation*. Dordrecht: Springer, 109–134.

PORDATA. (2013). Despesas do Estado em educação: execução orçamental em % do PIB—Portugal. Funda Francisco Manuel do Santo.

PORDATA. (2016). Despesas do Estado em educação: execução orçamental em % do PIB—Portugal. Funda Francisco Manuel do Santo. Retrieved from: http://www.pordata.pt/Portugal/Despesas+do+Estado+em+educacao+execu cao+orcamental-866.

Portas, P. (2012). Foreign Minister of Portugal, Speech at Rice University, Houston, Texas. Hosted by Baker Institute for Public Policy; June 7, 2012.

Portugal, Government of. (2010). Ministry of Science, Technology, and Education. The Framework for Higher Education Qualifications in Portugal (FHEQ-Portugal). November 2010.

Royo, S. (Ed.). (2012). *Portugal in the twenty-first century: Politics, society and economics*. Lanham, MD: Lexington Books.

Sabatier, P. A. (1991). Toward Better Theories of the Policy Process. *PS: Political Science and Politics, 24*(2), 147–156.

Sabatier, P. A. (1998). The advocacy coalition framework: Revisions and relevance for Europe. *Journal of European Public Policy, 5*(1), 98–130.

Sabatier, P. A. (Ed.). (2007). *Theories of the policy process.* Cambridge: Westview Press.

Sabatier, P. A., & Weible, C.M. (2007). The advocacy coalition framework. In P. A. Sabatier (Ed.), *Theories of the policy process* (pp. 189–220). Cambridge: Westview Press.

Vasques, I. (2016). Office of Director General for Higher Education (Direção-Geral do Ensino Superior), Ministry of Education and Science (Ministério da Educação e Ciência), Government of Portugal, June 1, 2016.

Veiga, A., & Amaral, A. (2006). The open method of coordination and the implementation of the Bologna process. *Tertiary Education and Management, 12,* 283–295.

Veiga, A., & Amaral, A. (2009a). Policy implementation tools and European governance. In A. Amaral, G. Neave, C. Musselin, & P. Maassen (Eds.), *European Integration and the Governance of Higher Education Research* (pp. 133–157). Dordrecht: Springer.

Veiga, A., & Amaral, A. (2009b). Survey on the implementation of the Bologna process in Portugal. *Higher Education, 57*(1), 57–69.

Wise, P. (2012, April 11). [Portugal] Bailout Agreement Enjoys Support across Party Lines. *Financial Times.*

World Bank Group. (2016). The Worldwide Governance Indicators (WGI) project. Retrieved from: http://info.worldbank.org/governance/wgi/index.aspx.

World federation for medical education and association for medical education in Europe. (2005). Statement on the Bologna process and medical education. February 2005.

CHAPTER 7

The Role of Stakeholders
in Internationalization in Portugal

*Over the past decade we have developed the European Higher Education Area
ensuring that it remains firmly rooted in Europe's intellectual, scientific and
cultural heritage and ambitions; characterised by permanent cooperation between
governments, higher education institutions, students, staff, employers and other
stakeholders.*
Leuven Communiqué (excerpt), April 29, 2009

This chapter considers the roles of the stakeholders from the public, private, and academic sectors in the policy process and the modernization of higher education institutions in Portugal. The neoliberal reforms in Portuguese higher education followed *O Estado Novo* (1933–1974). These reforms included a re-construction of national education that would eventually coincide with a modernization of higher education in Europe. Portugal's commitment to education earned the characterization of "exceptionalism" nationally. This prepared Portugal's path to participate in the Bologna Process, a multi-national system with European institutional architecture in higher education (Neave and Amaral 2012:12). The European dimension in higher education aims to bring about convergence and policy coordination for the national prerogative of education that has been protected by the subsidiarity principle, giving EU Member States policy competency. There are competing theses that the Bologna Process is not the beginning but the end of a

© The Author(s) 2017
B. Barrett, *Globalization and Change in Higher Education*,
DOI 10.1007/978-3-319-52368-2_7

process of neoliberalization in higher education (Neave 2009:51). The transformational nature of this convergence is noted as follows:

> 'Convergence' is not just a watchword. It is, on the contrary, tied in intimately with a very specific policy dynamic which bids fair to change the relationship between the three levels of decision-making—European, national, and institutional. The assumption implicit in the policy of Convergence operates a profound change in the role and status of the national level in the overall process of policymaking in general and very particularly so when the matter in hand concerns the construction of a multi-national system of higher education. Higher education policy, from being an activity of *sovereignty* by the National State, instead sees the National State acting as an *executor* of policy drawn up and agreed at the European level (Neave and Amaral 2012:13).

To distinguish between terms, law that is bound by treaties is "hard law." By comparison "soft law" is not bound by treaties, although it is administered with reputational pressures for compliance among Member States in the EU and participating countries in the region of Europe (Veiga and Amaral 2006). The Open Method of Coordination (OMC) has been the mechanism for countries to implement best practices in soft law. In Europe, soft law is effective in promoting change, but it is not effective in promoting convergence (Amaral 2013). It forces states to change, but in their own way. Each country adapts and applies policies that suit it best. It is not very strict in dictating the way that policies are going to change. Therefore, soft law is weak at promoting convergence, and there remain challenges for some of the countries that are participating in the Bologna Process.

The historical and cultural foundations of policy change are essential to explain why and how policies become implemented. António Nóvoa, former Rector of the University of Lisbon, said that "we still have a national problem with this" and that education is an important, historic problem (Nóvoa 2011). Nóvoa described the divide between Roman Catholic and Protestant countries. In Roman Catholic countries—such as Portugal, Spain, Italy, and France—there has been a problem with the "culture of education" since the sixteenth century. Over the past centuries, there have been low investments in education, compared to northern regions with Protestant countries. The Portuguese dictatorship for the most of the twentieth century had a policy that a minimum level of schooling was sufficient. For example, there were only three to four years of mandatory schooling, between the ages of 6 and 9, during the authoritarian regime (Nóvoa 2011). In 2011, Portugal made education mandatory through the 12th grade of secondary school.

> The state of Portuguese education says a lot about why a rescue is likely to be needed, and why one would be costly and difficult. Put simply, Portugal must generate enough long-term economic growth to pay off its large debts. An unskilled work force makes that hard. Cheap rote labor that once sustained Portugal's textile industry has vanished to Asia. The former Eastern Bloc countries that joined the European Union *en masse* in 2004 offer lower wages and workers with more schooling. They have sucked skilled jobs away. Just 28 percent of the Portuguese population between 25 and 64 has completed high school. The figure is 85 percent in Germany, 91 percent in the Czech Republic and 89 percent in the U.S. (Forelle 2011).

In the *Estado Novo*, universal primary school in Portugal did not come into fruition until the 1950s. This delay of primary education resulted in lower education attainment at multiple levels until the democratic reforms in the last decades of the twentieth century. There were greater inequalities in education in Portugal than in other countries in Europe (Fishman 2013:8). Among the goals of a democratic Portugal were increasing access, to and quality of, higher education reforms. These national initiatives after the 1974 revolution complemented the higher education reforms introduced by the Bologna Process in 1999. Rather than resisting the reforms required to participate in the EHEA, the attitude of Portugal at a national level of governance was to create the laws necessary to reform higher education while maintaining its traditional binary system. At the level of higher education governance, by the year 2008, once the national laws were in place, "higher education institutions immediately made an attempt at the fast implementation of the new system, considering that Bologna-followers would have an advantage over Bologna-laggards in the competition for students" (Veiga and Amaral 2009:58).

There are two main structural challenges, which are continuing to develop the binary system of higher education and the research area in Portugal (Teixeira 2016). The first challenge recognizes the differentiation in the governance and administration of higher education, given the binary system in place since the 1970s. The universities are an older brand, receiving most support traditionally. The emphasis has been to make polytechnics more like universities in quality and in reputation (Teixeira 2016). At the international level, there is differentiated integration in how countries implement reform in the Bologna Process to be part of the EHEA. Countries progress with the reforms at their own pace, with their own priorities (Amaral et al. 2015; Furlong 2010). The second challenge is to continue to develop research systems in Portugal. The impetus from neoliberal reforms of the 1990s followed by the European Commission commitment to the European Research Area (ERA) provides the background for this national priority.

POLICY REFORM: STAKEHOLDERS

The stakeholders, which are the advocacy coalition groups, have had varying influences in shaping higher education over history. This chapter evaluates the role of stakeholders—in the academic, public, and private sectors—for the case studies of Portugal. Given that outcomes take years or generations to become evident, these are limitations to analyzing the role of stakeholders in the policy reform process at the national level. With additional quantitative measures and data, three areas to measure stakeholder influence would be:

1. Number of people mobilized to support policy objective
2. Amount of financial resources dedicated to support policy objective
3. Longevity or duration of support for policy objective

This chapter considers the three stakeholder areas as part of the Advocacy Coalition Framework (ACF) (Jenkins-Smith et al. 2014; Sabatier 1988, 1991, 1998; Weible et al. 2009). The ACF provides a perspective "into the effects of policy-oriented learning on the broader process of policy change by analyzing the manner in which elites from different advocacy coalitions gradually alter their belief systems over time, partially as a result of formal policy analyses and trial and error learning" (Sabatier 1988:130). This is useful as "the ACF predicts that stakeholder beliefs and behavior are embedded within informal networks and that policy-making is structured, in part, by networks among important policy participants" (Sabatier and Christopher 2007:196). There are three layers of individual beliefs that shape participation on advocacy coalitions. Beginning with the most foundational and unlikely to change, these three types of beliefs are: deep core, policy core, and secondary aspects (Sabatier and Weible 2007:194–196; Sabatier 1998:112–113). Stakeholders, as external sources acting on the policy process, influence institutional change. Change to the policy process comes from these external sources rather than from the policy sub-system (Sabatier and Weible 2007:198).

The ACF states that a minimum of 10 years is a suitable time frame for understanding coalition or stakeholder pressures on the policy process (Sabatier 1991, 1998, 2007). The Bologna Process since 1999 is appropriate in this framework, considering that policy-oriented learning may take a decade or more (Sabatier and Christopher 2007:198). This time frame indicates that policy change is a medium-term outcome. In anticipation for outcomes in social change given higher education reform, the time to see results is at least a decade in duration. As a greater number of students become graduates under the Bologna Process, there will be a larger cohort available for assessing the impact of the policy reforms.

Applying the ACF to the Portuguese case is useful, as it identifies factors that affect the resources and behavior of stakeholders or advocacy coalitions. The "degree of consensus" and the "openness of the political system" are appropriate measures for stakeholder influence (Sabatier and Weible 2007:200; Lijphart 1999). Spain's quasi-federal system provides more openings to influence the policy process, making implementation more complicated, as Chaps. 8 and 9 explain. The ACF's premise that "policy subsystems are the most useful unit of analysis for understanding and explaining policy change" makes the policy subsystem a critical focus for analyzing the policy process (Sabatier and Weible 2007:204). In this subsystem, the three coalitions of interest in the Bologna Process reforms are the academic, private, and public sector stakeholders. The dominant coalition is the public sector government coalition, given that it has driven the reform process. Each coalition's policy beliefs and resources are invested in a strategy, which is the guiding instrument leading to decisions by governmental and higher education institutional authorities. In Portugal and Spain, the decisions by governmental authorities are the laws in the form of decrees, *decretos,* passed by the legislative body and signed by the executive. They are *Decreto-Lei* in Portugal and *Real Decreto* in Spain. These decisions have created "institutional rules, resource allocations, and appointments," which result in policy outputs and policy impacts (Sabatier and Weible 2007:202).

Public Sector

Each of the governments in the 48 countries in the EHEA appoints its representative to participate in the Bologna Follow Up Group (BFUG) meetings. There are periodic semi-annual meetings that take place between the EHEA ministerial meetings. The BFUG meetings are hosted by the (six-month rotating) EU Presidency country and by a non-EU country on a rotating semi-annual basis. As a partner alongside the EHEA countries, the European Commission plays a coordinating role in the BFUG meetings, aligned with its oversight in educational and vocational training since the Treaty of Maastrich in 1992 (Neave and Amaral 2012:12). Between 2011 and 2014, the BFUG member for Portugal was Maria de Lurdes Correia Fernandes, former Vice Rector of the University of Porto. Dr. Correia indicated that in the second decade of the Bologna Process, government-led policies have had three central areas of concern (Correia 2012):

1. *Student-centric learning*: This has been emphasized by the Bologna Process guidelines. A contribution of the Bologna Process is to bring the student to the forefront of learning and academic curriculum delivery.
2. *Understanding of the NQF at the Portuguese universities*: The universities are to use the NQF, which is the FHEQ-Portugal, for guidelines in the credit and degree structure application of the Bologna Process criteria.
3. *Using a reliable method to evaluate and to measure* "learning outcomes": During the years 2012–2013, this is an objective for the Bologna Process that has not been completely transferred to the national and institutional levels.

The *Licenciatura* was the traditional degree offered by both Portugal and Spain, which reflected the extent of a Master degree, until the Bologna Process degree cycles were implemented. The recent reforms in Portugal offer a *Licenciatura* degree (three to four years for a Bachelor degree) and a separate Master degree. In special cases, such as Medicine, a combined *Licenciatura* and Master (five or six years in total) is a possibility. This has been met with some resistance, as students want to be certain that they are receiving a complete education, rather than exiting the university prematurely at the end of the current, relatively short *Licenciatura* degree. Many students think that the Master degree is necessary to be competitive in the work place (Freire 2013). Some job opening positions specify in the criteria "pre-Bologna *Licenciatura* or Bologna second-cycle (Master)". Others specify when the Bologna first-cycle (*Licenciatura*) degree is sufficient. The European Credit and Transfer System (ECTS) degree requirements for the three cycles are as follows for Portugal:

1. Bachelor/*Licenciatura* 1st cycle: 180–240 ECTS
2. Master 2nd cycle: 90–120 ECTS
3. Doctorate 3rd cycle: 180–240 ECTS

These three-cycle degrees have come to be known as "3 + 2 + 3" indicating the number of years spent at each level. In Portugal, there is some variation in the *Licenciatura*, Master and Doctorate, which are the first, second, and third cycles. The *Licenciatura* is three to four years, the Master is one and a half to two years, and Doctorate is three to four years. Prior to the reforms, polytechnics offered a three-year Bachelor's, and universities offered a longer 4–6-year *Licenciatura*. After the reforms, both universities and polytechnics offer a first degree of *Licenciatura,* since the previous Bachelor's designation was eliminated. Currently, the *Licenciatura* duration is three years, most often at polytechnics, or four years at universities. Spain's EHEA reform was different in that its first-cycle Bachelor degree was four years in general, until a February 2015 Royal Decree (*Real Decreto*) 84/2015, implementing the June 2014 law on educational credits, approved the duration of three years. The rationale for these decisions, as a response to reforming the Spanish *Licenciatura*, is presented in Chaps. 8 and 9. The appropriate first-cycle duration continues to be debated across Europe, and it may be changed through future national policy.

The timeline for approving key legislation took pace accordingly. In the academic year 2005–2006, there were changes to general laws for education and laws about degree structure. Changing the national legal framework was necessary in order for institutions to be able to reform legally. All changes were to be made formally by the academic year 2009–2010. The preceding academic year of 2008–2009 was when most higher education institutions implemented the new degree structure. The University of Porto (founded in 1911) is the largest public university, and the University of Coimbra is the oldest university (founded in 1290). In both universities, the policy reforms have proceeded relatively well, since the universities were prepared by their leadership (Correia

2013; Freire 2013). The attitude of most stakeholders across the three sectors in Portugal has been of acceptance in the absence of organized resistance to the reforms (Vasques 2016).

Academic Sector

The Bologna Process, with its student-centered approach, brings the potential for recognition of credits and degrees from across universities in Portugal and across the EHEA. This reciprocity of credits and degrees, and mobility of students within the EHEA framework, has been in effect broadly at higher education institutions in Portugal since the academic year 2008–2009. Portuguese students remain active in the Erasmus study-abroad programs. Spain is the country with the most sending and receiving of students in Europe. In Erasmus, there have been challenges with recognition of study accreditation beyond the home institutions (European Students' Union 2012:108). The recognition component is an objective of the EHEA, which is "willing to work together toward the automatic recognition of comparable academic degrees" (EHEA Ministerial Conference 2012).

The students and the faculty are the most active stakeholders within the academic sector. Since the 2005 EHEA Ministerial Conference in Bergen, Norway, the European Commission has published *Bologna through Student Eyes* for each subsequent ministerial meeting. This reflects the student-centered focus of the EHEA at the supranational level. As Portugal implements reforms, updates are made to become more student-centered (Correia 2012). These reforms may be reflected in institutional changes, such as increasing the number of computer lab terminals available and offering more study spaces on campus (Freire 2013). There are student unions and professors' unions that organize to share interests. The number of academic unions is larger in Spain, given the larger population. The greater number of union organizations in Spain may represent the greater divisions in opinions on the Bologna Process. Overall, in Portugal the national reforms have been well received at the university institutional level (Amaro de Matos 2012; Correia 2012, 2013; Freire 2013).

NOVA (Universidade Nova de Lisboa)

Following are two examples of policy implementation at the institutional level: NOVA and the University of Coimbra. NOVA is a relatively new public university (*"nova"* means new in Portuguese). Coimbra, as the oldest university in Portugal, established in 1290, is traditionally selective. NOVA (*Universidade Nova de Lisboa*, New University of Lisbon), founded in 1973, is a public university and is specialized in the fields of Business, Engineering, and Medicine. According to João Amaro de Matos, Associate Dean for International Development in Business, the implementation of the Bologna Process went very well and has been exemplary for other academic programs in Portugal. In the academic year 2007–2008, NOVA's Business academic program was among the first academic programs in the Iberian Peninsula to implement the Bologna Process degree structure criteria (Amaro de Matos 2012). This was one year ahead of the majority of the Portuguese universities that implemented the reforms in the academic year 2008–2009. Although Portugal's national reforms were implemented in a later year, NOVA's rapid implementation of the Bologna Process credit and degree structure reforms made it an example for European higher education institutions (Amaro de Matos 2012). Although it is an example of efficiency in implementation, there are some instances in implementation remain at a discursive level of governance for an extended period until the reforms take place in actuality (Magalhães et al. 2013).

NOVA spent approximately six years reconsidering the new degree curriculum prior to implementation in the college of business (Amaro de Matos 2012). This was simultaneous with national laws being made for the country to implement the Bologna Process. NOVA anticipated and prepared as legislation was being made, rather than responding to laws once they were made. The 2006 national legislation Decree-Law 74/2006 of March 24, 2006, addressed the university degree structure in Portugal. At NOVA, the first cycle for the Bachelor, or *Licenciatura*, degree coursework consists of core curriculum in economics and management. The second-cycle degree Master is designed to include students who completed their first-cycle degree in related fields in the social sciences. Dual degrees, offered by universities collaborating internationally, have brought international institutions together in cooperation. A positive outcome of the Bologna Process is that dual degrees could be offered as a Master degree in one and a half years following the *Licenciatura*. As a member of CEMS: The Global Alliance in Management Education, a challenge is for NOVA to coordinate curriculum requirements with those of fellow institutional members (Amaro de Matos 2012).

In 1995 the English-only curriculum was implemented at NOVA for the Master of Business Administration (MBA) second-cycle degree. At the *Licenciatura*-level, first-cycle degree, there are still basic courses offered in Portuguese. The languages in which courses and degrees are offered affect the extent of the internationalization of that institution. The English-only MBA has provided consistency throughout the curriculum, and it has attracted foreign students to Portugal (Amaro de Matos 2012). Furthermore, the exclusively English-language MBA has made the degree more attractive to Portuguese students who seek an international career and to international students. The English-only MBA program, which was offered before the Bologna Process started in 1999, is an example of internationalization taking effect as a pre-existing initiative in Portugal independent of the EHEA. This is an example of Portugal's driving the higher education reforms by its national interests (intergovernmentalism) rather than by a response to supranational European policy (Europeanization). By comparison, when the English-language MBA was started in 1995 in Portugal, the MBA curriculum in Spain was still in Spanish for the most part (Amaro de Matos 2012).

As a business school, NOVA has a concentrated competency in management, and that competency has been a tangible advantage for its becoming a leader in designing academic curricula for the Bologna Process degree systems. NOVA has been very supportive of the common framework to make degree systems compatible. Several comparative advantages, including internationalization through the English-language coursework, have made NOVA an especially attractive university for Portuguese and international students in these initial years of the Bologna Process. Higher education institutions in Portugal remain connected to the former colonies in particular, as there are educational and employment opportunities for students from the former colonial countries in Africa and in Brazil, which are Portuguese-speaking countries.

The Foundation for Science and Technology (FCT, *Fundação para a Ciência e a Tecnologia*) provides scholarships to Portuguese students, and it is supported by EU Structural Funds. On top of academic credibility, the relatively low cost of living and temperate climate in Lisbon are additional draws for students. In 2012, 50 percent of NOVA applications came from abroad, and 42 percent of applicants enrolled from abroad. The rise in geographic mobility complements the rise in international study through Erasmus. After the Bologna Process, the Master program is stronger and better. "The level of internationalization has increased," commented Amaro de Matos. In Portugal most universities, including the University of Coimbra, implemented the Bologna Process degree structure reforms in the academic year 2008–2009. As the oldest public university in Portugal, and one of the oldest higher education institutions in the world, the University of Coimbra remains exemplary across academic fields.

Universidade de Coimbra
At the University of Coimbra, in the academic year 2006–2007, there were extended discussions among faculty regarding the implementation of the Bologna Process. The academic year 2008–2009 was "the revolutionary year in terms of the Bologna Process" and Coimbra cooperated quickly (Freire 2013). Maria Raquel Freire, a professor since 2005, has served as the coordinator for the International Relations degree program together with her colleague Paula Duarte Lopes. There has been close involvement of the whole International relations team during the Bologna Process degree structure changes at the university, she commented. Freire echoed NOVA Dean Amaro de Matos's perspective that the internationalization of teaching and learning is a valued incentive for implementing the Bologna Process.

The positive aspects of the Bologna process are the degree-structure compatibility and student-centered learning:

> The ideas and rationale of the Bologna Process are really interesting. Providing this mobility idea within Portugal and around Europe is really interesting. It will be much easier for them to have recognition for their first cycle of studies, and enroll easily into a Master or then into Ph.D. We like this idea. We also liked it very much regarding the details of how it works. The students have much more responsibility, and they are more active in their own education. (Freire 2013)

In some academics' opinions, the "student-centered" pedagogical approach to learning, advanced by the Bologna Process EHEA declarations over subsequent years, is attractive in higher education. There are other opinions, particularly, of more senior academics, that have rejected the institutional changes in degree structure and pedagogical approaches. The shift from a teaching-centered paradigm to a learning-centered paradigm reflects the Bologna Process policy reforms in Portugal. The emphasis on the learning-centered paradigm, which is the essence of the student-centered approach, was set as a priority university leadership alongside mobility of students and employability (Veiga and Amaral 2009:61).

Implementing this student-centered approach may be costly for institutions, and, in some respects, remains at the discursive level until implementation. For example, enhancing library services, increasing information technology access, and updating student center spaces requires funds that are limited by university administration. An academic example of being student-centered is the practice of combining traditional theoretical and contemporary practical elements of teaching. This takes place alongside offering the option for students to decide between "continuous evaluation" or "final examination" to assess learning in their course. Continuous evaluation offers a classroom assessment as an option in place of a traditional final exam, and there might be a combination of assessment methodologies. These two options represent the combination of two aspects of education, practical and theoretical. The practical and theoretical aspects of education are combined in continuous evaluation with periodic coursework assignments. In student-centered learning, those students who have limitations to participation in continuous evaluation still have the opportunity for a final examination that combines practical and theoretical elements. The choice that students are empowered to make regarding the type of assessment is "Bologna at work" (Freire 2013). There have been guidelines at the university level of governance that were shared with departments, considering changes to the curriculum to fit the EHEA degree structure and qualifications. There are three overarching ideas for the rationale of the Bologna Process (Freire 2013):

1. Internationalization: Internationalization of education through mobility of knowledge, students, researches, and academic degrees recognized across countries.
2. Student-centered: Efforts to create student-centered learning.
3. Employability: The Bologna Process presents a path to connect students to the employment market in the knowledge economy.

Employability as a neoliberal concept places responsibility on individuals, rather than on the state, for employment status (Simmons and Elkins 2004). The reforms aim to prepare students for employability, which has become a greater responsibility for individuals in a neoliberal context. Some concern remains about the broadly used 3 + 2 formula for the two-cycle degree structure in the EHEA. Many professionals in higher education think that the three-year first-cycle degree may not be sufficient to be prepared for employment. Others support the Bologna Process rationale that a shorter first-cycle degree makes the graduate ready for employment without the greater opportunity cost of staying at the university for a longer period, as was required prior to reforms. The preference to extend time on the academic degree is combined with preference for the greater maturity of students that would result from a longer period in the university (Freire 2013). The Bologna Process is a political and economic issue. Reducing the first-cycle degree to three years has economic advantages for the state. The time and cost to educate students for the first-cycle degree is less.

Although there is an advantage for the state in terms of financing higher education with a shorter first-cycle degree, the employment market takes some time to adjust to the new wave of graduates. In 2013, five years after the universities have reformed, employers post open positions asking applicants to distinguish if their first-cycle degree is post- or pre-Bologna Process reforms (Freire 2013). The Bologna Process reinvented the academic content for five years of study that includes a Master degree. Previously, the *Licenciatura* was four to six years. Given that the pre–Bologna Process degree (*Licenciatura*) was a longer degree, there is the understanding this was a more extensive education than the new first-cycle degree implemented with reforms. As a result, the second-cycle "Master degree has become massified, as nearly everyone does the Master" (Freire 2013). The need to continue to the second cycle may be seen as a shortcoming of the policy reforms if stakeholders are not confident that the first-cycle degree will be sufficient for employment opportunities.

Some professional associations require a minimum number of years in higher education; for example, engineers have been required to have a minimum of five years of higher education.[1] An incentive to complete the Master degree is to have additional training qualifications for a greater number of opportunities in the employment market. In some technical and trade positions, graduates may excel after earning the first-cycle degree. The Master degree is valuable to strengthen critical thinking skills, to cultivate the maturity of the student, and to offer the opportunity to subspecialize. For example, at the University of Coimbra, following a *Licenciatura* degree in International Relations, it is possible to specialize the Master degree in International Political Economy or Journalism. This specialization adds value for graduates when they enter the employment market. Candidates for jobs involving knowledge analysis, such as in the Social Sciences, may benefit from completing the additional education of the Master degree (Freire 2013).

A greater offering of interdisciplinary studies is a result of the degree structure changes in Management, Economics, International Relations, and Sociology. These fields compose the Department of Economics at the University of Coimbra. Students may participate in classes across disciplines while concentrating their degree requirements in a specific field. This emphasis on the value of interdisciplinary studies may reflect a global trend in Social Sciences research that coincides with the Bologna Process reforms, rather than being a result of the latter's direct influence. Nevertheless, the Bologna Process raises awareness about the value of interdisciplinary study (Freire 2013).

Perhaps not unique to Portugal, in the international dimension of higher education there are language limitations for professors. To become a professor at public universities in Portugal, it is necessary to know the Portuguese language. Given the curriculum in Portuguese language, most foreign students in Portugal come from lusophone countries. Portuguese students have an incentive to spend a period of study abroad to learn a foreign language, to diversify their language skills and to gain more global knowledge. Although there is an international market for talent in higher education, this national language requirement limits the market for suitable professors in Portugal. As a result of internationalization and Bologna Process reform in quality assurance, professors are more rigorously evaluated according to the qualifications of the national agency (A3ES). Correspondingly, there are increasing numbers in Erasmus participation each year, as students spend an academic semester or year abroad when coming to, or studying away from, Portugal. Scholarships are more readily available for Erasmus+ (launched in 2014) that includes study beyond the EU countries. This builds upon the previous program, Erasmus Mundus, that was in effect during 2009–2013 to support students and researchers across academic disciplines.

Private Sector Stakeholders

After the 1974 revolution in Portugal, when the higher education participation rate was relatively low, there followed an expansion in demand that the public sector could not accommodate. Allowing for the development of a private sector in higher education was the way to resolve this concern, with the additional advantage that it did not use public money (Amaral 2013). In a country of approximately 11 million people, the majority of businesses are small- and medium-size enterprises (SMEs). The interest and collaboration of the private sector in higher education is noted in the following section on modernizing higher education. Accompanying the neoliberal marketization of higher education in recent decades, the private sector has emerged as a meaningful stakeholder (Slaughter and Rhoades 2004; Cantwell and Kauppinen 2014). The private sector is interested in educational outcomes while seeking graduates who join the workplace. To diversify higher education governance, there have been more opportunities for institutional leadership from the private sector since the implementation of Bologna Process reforms. This participation of external actors in the private sector, who may have limited knowledge of institutional history and higher education governance traditions, has limitations to overcome (Magalhães et al. 2013).

In Europe in particular, given the broad government role in society, the public sector has a history of serving as a dominant investor in research and development (R&D) (Esping-Anderson 1990; Iversen 2005). When public sector budgets reduced with austerity measures, private sector institutions and higher education institutions receive fewer funds (Delicado 2012). The May 2011 economic reform program for Portugal with the troika (EU, ECB, and IMF) resulted in fewer public sector funds available to invest in private businesses. Even though there have been reduced investments in the private sector, the public sector is promoting cooperation with the private sector. The Ministry of Economy and Business (*Ministério de Economia e do Emprego*) presented the "Strategy for growth, employment, and industrial development 2013–2020" in April 2014. An objective of the Strategy is to "strengthen vocational education and dual apprenticeship—reaching 200,000 students." To "make Portugal an international reference centre for entrepreneurs," the strategies for growth plans are the following:

- Promoting a greater coordination and cooperation between educational institutions and companies
- Fostering and funding of investment in R&D with commercial applicability as a way to develop cooperation between educational institutions and companies and to optimize public fund management in this area

Associação Empresarial de Portugal (AEP) is the Portuguese Business Association based in Porto, the second largest city given its industrial profile. *CESAE (Centro de Serviços e Apoio às Empresas)* is affiliated with AEP and is a private, non-profit organization based in Porto with branches throughout Portugal. Among its partners are commercial and industrial associations. Higher education institutions—the University of Porto, the University of Aveiro, and the Polytechnic Institute of Porto—are also partners (AEP 2013). The AEP has not taken a public policy position on higher education as some national business chambers have. Employers' organizations have been conspicuously absent from the policy processes of the Portuguese higher education system. Paradoxically, at a time when the state has used more market-friendly rhetoric and has expressed concern to articulate the connection between higher education and economic activity, Portuguese employers have distanced themselves somewhat from taking on the status of effective political stakeholders involved in higher education policies (Amaral 2013). As a comparison point, the U.S. Chamber of Commerce, the advocate for America's businesses, at the discursive level recognizes the knowledge-based economy, and the key place of education in it:

> In our knowledge-based global marketplace of the 21st Century, a well-educated population is the key to our nation's innovation, economic development, and ability to compete. This need is confirmed by data from the Bureau of Labor Statistics which shows that 90% of the jobs in the fastest growing occupations require some level of postsecondary education and training (U.S. Chamber of Commerce 2013).

The businesses Galp Energia and Bial are two examples of partnerships between the private sector and higher education institutions in Portugal. In 2013, the Portuguese petroleum company Galp Energia started a new partnership for education. Together with the MIT Portugal Program, it is investing in science technology and higher education. Bial is a pharmaceutical business headquartered in Porto that partners with universities in scientific research areas. Energias de Portugal (EDP) is another international Portuguese firm active in supporting science and education through its foundation, Fundação EDP. Competing for EU funds may be easier for Portuguese universities to do in collaboration with a foreign company, rather than a Portuguese company since larger foreign companies may be selected for grants to receive EU funds. The

Portuguese companies have a smaller market in the EU and worldwide, even though historically Portugal is an internationally oriented country (Page 2002).

MODERNIZATION OF HIGHER EDUCATION INSTITUTIONS

There is innovation in the institutional design of the national quality assurance agency in Portugal. A3ES is the official agency that works to accredit higher education institutions and their programs, according to the European Standards and Guidelines, and it was established by Decree-Law 369/2007 in November 2007. Beginning in 2009, it established operations to accredit the higher education institutions in Portugal, and it has a strong measure of independence to operate within the legislative structures.[2] "A3ES is one of the most independent agencies [in Europe] because we are a private institution and private foundation" (Amaral 2013). There is a council of administration that is appointed for a period of four years, and the appointment can be renewed. Over those four years, the council cannot be dismissed. Final decisions are made independently, without political administration interfering in the decision. Not all countries have this autonomy in their national qualifications agencies. For example, it differs in Sweden, where the agency makes a recommendation to the education minister and then the education minister decides (Amaral 2013). The only way the minister can act to influence the quality assurance agency in Portugal is by changing the law. The modernization of higher education aligns with greater investments in R&D. The findings from R&D advance the academic fields in the higher education institutions with which they are affiliated, and they make the institutions world class in rankings value of which advances in research.

Research, Innovation, and the ERA

In the decade from 2000 to 2011, R&D expenditure in Portugal doubled from 0.73 to 1.58 percent of GDP (Eurostat 2012). Many private companies traditionally have been dependent on the state to provide funds for R&D (Delicado 2012). In the initial years since the austerity reforms, there have been fewer funds available from the public sector for private companies. "In Portugal the number of companies large enough to do meaningful research is extremely small" (Amaral 2013). There are mostly SMEs, which do not engage substantively in R&D. The scale of Portuguese companies is smaller. A company that may be relatively large by Portuguese standards is not able to have an R&D impact like a large company in a country with greater population size.

> Growth has been particularly strong in the fields of science and technology, which are growing at 7 to 10 percent per year. The number of PhDs has also increased from fewer than one hundred per year in the 1970s to more than a thousand today; and Portuguese scholars produce more than four thousand scientific papers a year, compared with merely about two hundred in 1981. In 2001, Portugal was included in the list of "countries of excellence" that contribute to the top 1 percent of the world's most highly cited scientific publications. (Royo 2012:204)

Portugal reached 1 percent of GDP allocated to R&D in 2006, which was significant. The 3 percent of GDP target in Europe 2020 is a challenging objective for Portugal and Spain. In Portugal in 2000 R&D was 0.72 percent, and in 2009 peaked at 1.58 percent. In Spain in 2000 R&D was 0.89 percent, and in 2009 peaked at 1.35 percent (Eurostat 2016) (Appendix F). The research and higher education agenda have intersected in recent years. During 2002, the Ministry of Science and the Ministry of Higher Education merged, and they cooperated during the Socialist government in power from 2005 to 2011. During 2011, with the change to Social Democrat government, primary and secondary education functions became incorporated into the new Ministry of Education and Science. Ongoing funding for science has been important at a time when funding for education has been restricted. The researchers in some cases have taken on teaching responsibilities, mitigating the need to hire new professors (Delicado 2012).

Portugal's interest to develop R&D precedes the idea of the ERA advanced by the European Commission (2000). As part of neoliberal reforms advocated by Prime Minister Cavaco Silva and the Washington Consensus, many countries in Europe, including Portugal, pursued investments in R&D for their national economic development. This preceded the Europe 2020 benchmarks for R&D 3 percent of GDP (1 percent from public sector and 2 percent from private sector) established in March 2010. The Foundation for Science and Technology (FCT) (*Fundação para a Ciência e a Tecnologia*) is supported by EU Structural Funds to fund the Ministry of Education and Science, and it provides scholarships to Portuguese students.[3] Approximately half of the funds for the FCT come from the EU (Delicado 2012). Since 2006, the FCT has coordinated a research partnership across Portuguese universities with the Massachusetts Institute of Technology (MIT) in the United States. Recent research from MIT Portugal has centered on biomedical sciences and urban sustainability. There are collaborative research programs with Carnegie Mellon University, Harvard Medical School, and the University of Texas at Austin. The University of Coimbra's Center for Social Studies and the University of Lisbon's ICS Institute of Social Sciences (*Instituto de Ciências Sociais*) are national Social Sciences research centers. These two research centers have the statute as Associated Laboratories, and are among the 26 Associated Laboratories in all scientific disciplines (Delicado 2012). Engineering receives approximately 25 percent of funding, and there has been renewed interest for funding in Medicine since approximately 2012 (Delicado 2012). The President of the FCT and the Secretary of State for Research have medical backgrounds, and this leadership drove the agenda in the year 2012 to advance support for the field of Medicine.

There are various foundations supporting scientific research and higher education. Since 2004, the Champalimaud Foundation is an example of an institute supported by both private and public funds. It conducts innovative research in science and health technologies. The Calouste Gulbenkian Foundation, also in Lisbon, is a private foundation started in the 1950s to support musical training for the fields of Arts and Education. With historical roots in mid-twentieth century authoritarian rule, it promotes internationalization serving educators globally. The Fundação Francisco Manuel dos Santos (FFMS) is a private foundation that supports public debate on policy issues and contributes to research. The Foundation Luso-American Development (FLAD) supports Portuguese companies seeking to internationalize their operations to work in the United States, as well as in the Azores islands and in lusophone Africa.

Summary

The analysis of the roles of stakeholders in the policy process and the modernization of higher education institutions is useful to understand the political economy context that influences Bologna Process reform at the national level. Portugal has become a society that embraces the cultural value of education at every level, which promises that educational access and economic development will follow. In education, patience is necessary to see a return on investment of policy reform, since the beneficial outcomes may take decades or a generation. António Nóvoa, former Rector of the University of Lisbon, believes that Portugal in recent decades has been successful at developing a culture that is stronger across levels of education. This ambition of leaders to create a culture that values education has endured even through years of economic austerity. Across political parties, higher education has been a commitment of political leaders in recent years. This contributes to success in increasing access, quality assurance, and a culture that values education in Portugal.

> You need to create cultural involvement and social involvement and family involvement focusing on learning issues. That's for me the most important thing that we need to do. It was difficult to do it twenty years ago. Twenty years ago our battle, our fight, was to have all the children in school. Now that we have succeeded in this battle, we need to have a second battle that all the children need to learn in school. And we need to fight against dropout rates, and we need to fight against children that are in school that don't get a minimum of learning during their school career (Nóvoa 2011).

Although the culture of education is becoming stronger in Portugal, the national objectives on higher education continue to develop. Portugal has implemented EHEA criteria on credits and degrees with the national and European qualifications frameworks, and it is engaged in continuing efforts toward quality assurance and recognition. Despite these advances through the EHEA, all Bologna Process objectives have not been reached fully. Employability continues to be a concern, given that youth unemployment has been in the range of 40–50 percent in some countries in the south of Europe. The global financial crisis of 2007–2009, followed by the sovereign debt crises of 2010–2011, hampered employability. Concern about student mobility and international recognition recalls the EHEA 2012 "Bucharest Communiqué: Making the Most of Our Potential: Consolidating the European Higher Education Area."

> Fair academic and professional recognition, including recognition of non-formal and informal learning, is at the core of the EHEA. It is a direct benefit for students' academic mobility, it improves graduates' chances of professional mobility and it represents an accurate measure of the degree of convergence and trust attained. We are determined to remove outstanding obstacles hindering effective and proper recognition and are

willing to work together toward the automatic recognition of comparable academic degrees, building on the tools of the Bologna framework,
as a long-term goal of the EHEA. We therefore commit to reviewing our
national legislation to comply with the Lisbon Recognition Convention.
(EHEAMinisterial Conference 2012:4)[4]

Scholars have described the Bologna Process as a neoliberal construct in
higher education and Portugal as being exceptional on its path in higher
education since the end of the *Estado Novo* (Neave and Amaral 2012). To
implement neoliberal policies, it is necessary to have a market. The market
for higher education has expanding concentric circles: National, EHEA,
and global. Neoliberal markets are characterized by convergence, openness, and exchange. A foremost British scholar of higher education argues
that the Bologna Process may be the end, rather than the beginning, of
a neoliberal process that has been ongoing for decades (Neave 2009).
The Bologna Process has advanced as a neoliberal idea further than it has
advanced in implementation. In reality, it is not fully neoliberal—being
open across borders in a cosmopolitan way—since many criteria, such as
automatic recognition of academic degree across countries, remain at the
discursive level and not yet implemented in practice (Kant 1795; Doyle
1983).

The unitary structure of government in Portugal parallels a general
social cohesion, given the ongoing opportunities for cooperation among
government, academic, and private sectors. In democratic Portugal and
Spain, there are opportunities for various stakeholder voices to be heard.
Spain's quasi-federal and pluralistic government of autonomous communities adds another layer of bureaucracy for various voices to be inter-
jected in the process of policy implementation that originates from the
European and national levels.

With the Bologna Process, Portugal has responded to pressures of
globalization with the internationalization of higher education. There
is evidence that the influence of internationalization has permeated
multiple levels of governance: European, national, and university/insti-
tutional. Although the objective of automatic recognition remains at
the discursive level across countries, the degree cycle criteria have been
internationalized with the national legislation to construct the EHEA
degree cycle and the accompanying student-centered focus at higher
education institutions. "Internationalization has become a strategic focus
of the University of Coimbra, in each of its faculties" (Freire 2013).

Accordingly, many institutions maintain internationalization as an incentive in recruiting students, developing student-centered curriculum, making the degrees relevant for employment, and strengthening faculty publications. In the case of Portugal, the Bologna Process reforms coincided with reforms that were underway in the era of neoliberal market growth after the authoritarian regimes of Salazar and Caetano. The initial decade-and-a-half of EHEA reforms correspond with those that were underway to increase access and to improve educational quality since 1974. Portugal participated in the policy convergence of the Bologna Process at the supranational level in a strategic manner that is aligned with its national interests. For this reason, the internationalization of higher education in Portugal corresponds with the liberal intergovernmental policy process in regional integration. "If Portugal embarked late on the drive to massification—late starting did not prevent it from catching up rapidly" (Neave and Amaral 2012:42).

This chapter has considered two of the five points of qualitative analysis for the case study of Portugal: the policy process role of stakeholders and the modernization of higher education. This analysis is useful to understand the political economy context that influences policy reform. The Bologna Process, as an intergovernmental initiative, has provided an opportunity for Portugal to advance its interest to strengthen higher education institutions in the generation after the *Estado Novo*. The liberal intergovernmental and Europeanization policy processes are evident in all participating countries in the EHEA, and the latter is assessed with emphasis on the policy process for institutional change in the case study of Spain discussed in Chaps. 8 and 9.

NOTES

1. There is a distinction between pre-Bologna and post-Bologna first-cycle degrees. Post-Bologna, the classification of engineers with a first-cycle three-year degree is E1. The classification of engineers with a second-cycle Master degree, totaling five years of higher education, is E2.
2. Read about A3ES: http://www.a3es.pt/pt/o-que-e-a3es.
3. Read about the *Fundação para a Ciência e a Tecnologia* (Foundation for Science and Technology) http://www.fct.pt/.
4. Council of Europe. 1997. The Lisbon Convention on the "Recognition of Qualifications concerning Higher Education in the European Region." Available from: http://conventions.coe.int/Treaty/en/Treaties/Html/165.htm.

REFERENCES

AEP: Associação Empresarial de Portugal. (2013). Retrieved from http://www. aeportugal.pt/.

Amaral, A. (2013). Founding Director, Centre for Research on Higher Education Policies (CIPES), Matosinhos (Porto) and President of the Administration Council, A3ES Portuguese National Qualifications Agency, May 28, 2013.

Amaral, A., Magalhães, A., & Veiga, A. (2015). Differentiated integration and the Bologna Process. *Journal of Contemporary European Research, 11*(1), 84–102.

Amaro de Matos, João. (2012). Associate Dean for International Affairs. NOVA University School of Business. Lisboa, Portugal.

Cantwell, B., & Kauppinen, I. (Eds.). (2014). *Academic capitalism in the age of globalization.* Baltimore: Johns Hopkins University Press.

Correia Fernandes, Maria de Lurdes. (2012, 2013). Professor of the Humanities; Former Vice-Rector, University of Porto, Portuguese Member of the Bologna Follow Up Group (2011–2014), July 23, 2012 and May 29, 2013.

Council of Europe. (1997). The Lisbon convention on the recognition of qualifications concerning higher education in the European region. Retrieved from http://conventions.coe.int/Treaty/en/Treaties/Html/165.htm.

Delicado, A. (2012). Researcher, Institute of Social Sciences (ICS-Instituto de Ciências Sociais). University of Lisbon, July 24.

Doyle, M. (1983). Kant, liberal legacies, and foreign affairs. *Philosophy & Public Affairs, 12*(3), 205–235.

Esping-Anderson, G. (1990). *The three worlds of welfare capitalism.* Princeton: Princeton University Press.

EHEA Ministerial Conference. (2012). Bucharest Communiqué: Making the most of our potential: Consolidating the European Higher Education Area. Retrieved from http://www.ehea.info/Uploads/%281%29/Bucharest%20 Communique%202012%281%29.pdf.

European Commission. (2000). Towards a European research area. COM(2000) 6 final. Communication from the Commission to the Council, the European Parliament, the Economic and Social Committee and the Committee of the Regions. January 18, 2000.

European Students' Union. (2012). *Bologna with student eyes 2012.* Brussels: Education and Culture Directorate General.

Eurostat. (2012). European Commission statistics historical database.

Eurostat. (2016). European Commission statistics historical database.

Fishman, R. (2013). *How Civil Society Matters in Democratization: Theorizing Iberian Divergence.* Paper prepared for presentation at the 20th International Conference of Europeanists.

Forelle, C. (2011, March 25). A nation of dropouts shakes Europe. *The Wall Street Journal.*

Freire, M. R. (2013). Assistant Professor, International Relations in Faculty of Economics. Portugal: University of Coimbra, May 28.

Furlong, P. (2010). Bologna's deepening empire: Higher education policy in Europe. In K. Dyson & A. Sepos (Eds.), *Which Europe? The politics of differentiated integration.* Houndmills: Palgrave Macmillan.

Iversen, T. (2005). *Capitalism, democracy, and welfare.* Cambridge: Cambridge University Press.

Jenkins-Smith, H. C., Nohrstedt, D., Weible, C. M., & Sabatier, P. A. (2014). The advocacy coalition framework: Foundations, evolution, and ongoing research. In P. Sabatier & C. M. Weible (Eds.), *Theories of the policy process* (3rd ed.). Boulder, CO: Westview Press.

Kant, I. (1795). *Perpetual peace.* Indianapolis: The Library of Liberal Arts, 1957.

Lijphart, A. (1999). *Patterns of democracy: Government forms and performance in 36 countries.* New Haven: Yale University Press.

Magalhães, A., Veiga, A., Ribeiro, F. M., Sousa, S., & Santiago, R. (2013). Creating a common grammar for European higher education governance. *Higher Education, 65,* 95–112.

Neave, G. (2009). The Bologna Process as alpha or omega, or, on interpreting history and context as inputs to Bologna, Prague, Berlin, and Beyond. In A. Amaral, G. Neave, C. Musselin, & P. Maassen (Eds.), *European integration and the governance of higher education and research* (pp. 17–58). Dordrecht: Springer.

Neave, G., & Amaral, A. (Eds.). (2012). *Higher education in Portugal 1974–2009: A nation, a generation.* Dordrecht: Springer.

Nóvoa, A. (2011, March 25). Video interview. In C. Forelle (Ed.). A nation of dropouts shakes Europe. *The Wall Street Journal.*

Page, M. (2002). *The first global village: How Portugal changed the world.* Lisbon: Casa das Letras.

Royo, S. (Ed.). (2012). *Portugal in the twenty-first century: Politics, society and economics.* Lanham, MD: Lexington Books.

Sabatier, P. A., & Christopher, M. W. (2007). The advocacy coalition framework. In P. A. Sabatier (Ed.), *Theories of the policy process* (pp. 189–220). Cambridge: Westview Press.

Sabatier, P. A. (1998). The advocacy coalition framework: Revisions and relevance for Europe. *Journal of European Public Policy, 5*(1), 98–130.

Sabatier, P. A. (1991). Toward better theories of the policy process. *PS: Political Science and Politics, 24*(2), 147–156.

Sabatier, P. A. (1988). An advocacy coalition framework of policy change and the role of policy-oriented learning therein. *Policy Sciences, 21,* 129–168.

Simmons, B. & Elkins, Z. (2004). The Globalization of Liberalization: Policy Diffusion in the International Political Economy. *American Political Science Review, 98*(1):171–189.

Slaughter, S., & Rhoades, G. (2004). *Academic capitalism and the new economy: Markets, state, and higher education.* Baltimore: Johns Hopkins University Press.

Teixera, P. (2016). Vice-Rector and Professor of Economics. University of Porto, June 14.

U.S. Chamber of Commerce. (2013). Issues: Postsecondary education policy. Retrieved from http://www.uschamber.com/issues/education/postsecondaryed.

Vasques, I. (2016). Office of Director General for Higher Education (Direção-Geral do Ensino Superior), Ministry of Education and Science (Ministério da Educação e Ciência), Government of Portugal, June 1.

Veiga, A., & Amaral, A. (2009). Survey on the implementation of the Bologna Process in Portugal. *Higher Education, 57*(1), 57–69.

Veiga, A., & Amaral, A. (2006). The open method of coordination and the implementation of the Bologna Process. *Tertiary Education and Management, 12,* 283–295.

Weible, C. M., Sabatier, P. A., & McQueen, K. (2009). Themes and variations: Taking stock of the advocacy coalition framework. *The Policy Studies Journal, 37*(1), 121–140.

CHAPTER 8

Spain: Political Economy Explanations for Decentralized Reforms

The public authorities guarantee the right of all to education, through general education programming, with the effective participation of all sectors concerned and the setting-up of educational centres.
The Spanish Constitution of 1978, Section 27.5 (December 1978)

Europeanization is the regional integration framework that is applied to explain the process of higher education reform since the introduction of the Bologna Process in Spain. The preceding chapters demonstrated how the regional integration framework of intergovernmentalism is applied to the process of higher education reform in Portugal. In Portugal, attaining the EHEA objectives has strengthened the trajectory of domestic reforms to increase higher education access and quality that was already on the rise following the Salazar and Caetano era of authoritarian rule in the *Estado Novo*. By comparison, in Spain, the higher education system under the rule of General Francisco Franco (1939–1975), although limited by having fewer institutions, was more broadly accessible. Though higher education in Spain, as in Portugal, primarily served the society's elites during authoritarian rule, it was not as limited with the intent to withhold political challenges (Bonete Perales 2013). In both countries, the Catholic Church played a central societal role, in higher education and in society, in the decades under authoritarian rule. The number of students enrolled in public universities has been higher than those enrolled in private universities, which include Catholic universities,

throughout Spain (Salaburu et al. 2003). The plan for internationalization of Spanish universities presented in late 2014 is the *Strategy for the
Internationalization of Spanish Universities 2015–2020.*

The intergovernmental and Europeanization theories are useful to explain the policy processes of reform in the Bologna Process.
Europeanization, in which policy originates at the supranational level,
is useful to understand Spain's position as a policy-taker in the Bologna
Process (Schmidt 2009). The state influenced by Europeanization may
have a limited voice as a policy-taker in response to European policy initiatives (Börzel and Risse 2000). By comparison, the intergovernmental
policy process is a rational and active position of states pursuing their
interests, bargaining, and pursuing credible commitments (Moravcsik
1998). Alongside the competing theories of intergovernmentalists and
supranationalists is the social constructivist perspective that people and
society are co-constituted (Wendt 1992, 1999). The top-down aspect of
Europeanization parallels that of supranationalism (Bulmer and Radaelli
2004; Radaelli 2008). Europeanization imposes upon traditional state
sovereignty, and the theoretical debate between intergovernmentalism
and supranationalism that has ensued over recent decades remains relevant (Bickerton et al. 2015; Gornitzka 2007; Keohane and Hoffman
1991). State sovereignty is not completely obsolete in Europeanization,
but it is influenced in a top-down direction by norms from European
institutions:

> The analytical discourse has been dominated by an argument between
> theorists who maintain that traditional states ultimately retain sovereignty
> even as they agree to abide by certain norms and rules, and others who
> claim that European integration represents a gradual process by which tra-
> ditional state sovereignty is rendered obsolete. (Marks 1997:154)

In Europeanization, the Bologna Process becomes implemented at
multiple levels of governance originating at the supranational level. As
policy transfer moves from supranational to national to institutional
levels, the institutional shocks become internalized. Ideas, interests,
and knowledge are impacted by internal and external shocks (Marks
1997:158). After the Treaty of Maastricht in 1992, which expanded
the policy competencies of the European Union (EU), the term
"Europeanization" became more fully discussed in the academic literature. Spain's experience of Europeanization in the early 1990s resulted

in formal agreements between the *comunidades autónomas* (autonomous communities) (ACs) and the national government in a quasi-federal arrangement. "The Spanish government and the autonomous communities had to establish a new institutional framework to ensure the effective participation of the ACs in European policymaking" (Börzel 2000:18). Although Europeanization is a significant influence, in higher education policy there is cooperation between the EU and the Member States (Treaty of Lisbon, Article 165, Appendix A). With the Treaty on the Functioning of the European Union (TFEU) subsidiarity principle safeguarding the decisions of Member States for specific competencies, the Member States maintain the prerogative for higher education policy, which has been constructed in a new regional architecture by the Bologna Process.

The acceptance of Europeanization by Spain is part of its complex history, which includes Moorish rule for approximately 700 years between the eighth and fifteenth centuries. Making sense of regionalism, domestic policy, and internationalization is key to identifying political economy influences on policy reform and implementation. Spain is referred to as the *Estado de las Autonomas*, the state of autonomous communities. There exist preferences among some Spaniards to use the term "decentralized" or "quasi-federal" rather than "federal" to explain Spain's governmental structure.[1] Regionalism is a distinctive characteristic of Spanish federal government across the 17 autonomous communities. The autonomous communities of Catalunya, Galicia, and the Basque Country, in particular, have a history of strong regional nationalism, national languages, and overtures toward independence from Spain. This regional nationalism is in tension with the national government seated in Madrid. The word "regionalization" is used together with decentralization to describe the higher education system in post-Franco Spain (Mora and Vidal 2005:140).

Together with regionalization, internationalization is another defining word for Spain in the Bologna Process. Particularly as a driver of the higher education reforms, internationalization is central, given that "the Bologna Process is all about internationalization" (Matilla Vicente 2012). Within the process of internationalization, the government, education, and research sectors have a dynamic relationship. Concerning domestic policy, the original EU treaties lack instruments of direct policy intervention in areas such as education and employment which are national competencies. According to the EU treaties, the Member States have the exclusive oversight of competency in education policy. While the Treaty of Lisbon, in effect since December 1, 2009, defines a role for the EU in supporting the Member States in education and vocational training in Title 12, Articles 165 and 166 (Appendix A). The national identity and propriety attributed to education comes from its strong sociocultural foundations. Another connection from society to education is the economic investments of the people through tax contributions. The national policy domain of education is protected by the EU's subsidiarity principle that is relevant for issues such as education, employment, and environment policies. It has been argued that the process of economic reforms must be a domestic initiative (Royo 2006). Similarly, the process of higher education reforms must be a domestic initiative, given the legal nature and the national engagement necessary to be successful.

GOVERNANCE BACKGROUND: SPAIN AS A CONSTITUTIONAL MONARCHY SINCE 1978

After the death of General Franco on November 20, 1975, the country transitioned from authoritarian rule to a constitutional monarchy and democratic government. Two days later, the monarchy was restored when Juan Carlos I de Borbón was crowned king, as had been planned by General Franco six years prior. As head of state, King Juan Carlos I guided the national process to adopt the democratic Constitution of Spain. With the government in transition, the monarchy was restored in Spain, though not in Portugal, a distinction in historical governance on the Iberian Peninsula. This is an example of how the transition to democracy after authoritarian rule was unique in Spain:

> In Spain, the institutions and legislation of the Franco regime, with roots in previous Spanish experience, were of major importance. The Cortes, its personnel unchanged, committed the extraordinary act of voting its own extinction and opening the way for the establishment of democratic institutions. In addition, the person of the king and the institution of the crown were essential in providing a central focus which consistently supported the transition and was accepted by almost all as being above party, faction, and particular interests. (O'Donnell and Schmitter 1986:22)

Ratified in 1978, the Spanish Constitution gave considerable political power to the regional governments of the 17 autonomous communities.

After the 1977 election, the Spanish Parliament (*Cortes*) drafted the Constitution that was ratified on December 6, 1978. Similar to the Constitution of Germany known as the Basic Law (1949), these democratic countries prioritized decentralizing education and other social services after authoritarian rule. The voice of civil society and democratic development are mutually constitutive (Fishman 2013:3). The Spanish Constitution reorganized the state through simplified decentralization of functions to implement policies. Higher education policies were transferred to the regions in the 1978 Constitution as part of the fundamental principle of decentralization. In addition to the key characteristic of decentralization, the international policy context of Europe has played an ongoing influential role in Spain, particularly since its accession to the EU in 1986 (Roy and Kanner 2001a, b).

Similar to Portugal, Spain delayed for approximately half a decade the implementation of the initial Bologna Process reforms at the national level. It was not until July 2007, after the London EHEA Ministerial Conference on May 17–18, 2007, that Spain established the legal framework for the Spanish Framework of Higher Education Qualifications (MECES) with a Royal Decree, *Real Decreto* 900/2007. Two years prior, in 2005, Spain made legislative changes to the degree structure to establish the EHEA first-cycle Bachelor degree with *Real Decreto* 55/2005. In 2003, a *Real Decreto* 1125/2003, establishing the key elements of the ECTS, was passed. Dissimilar from Portugal, an absent majority in parliament was not the reason for the delay in establishing the National Qualifications Framework (NQF). The Socialist Party government of José Luis Rodríguez Zapatero was in place between 2004 and 2011. Rather, the explanation was that in the initial years of the new millennium, the Spanish higher education system was focused on implementing *Ley Orgánica de Universidades* (LOU) or the Spanish University Act of 2001.

The *Real Decreto 43/2015 de 2 de febrero 2015* (Royal Decree 43/2015 of February 2, 2015) provided for three-year bachelor degree in Spain, in order to be similar to European countries granting the degree over the same time duration. Spain, having offered initially the four-year bachelor degree, may have been perceived as a disadvantage for Spanish students needing to spend more time on their initial degree than their European peers.

Approved in 2001, the LOU was a national initiative, rather than a European initiative, to give the universities more higher education governance autonomy. As an entry point to Bologna Process reforms, the LOU specifically recognized the place for Spanish universities in the EHEA or *EEES* (*Espacio Europeo de Eneseñanza Superior*). Implementing particular criteria of the EHEA was delayed by several years, until the pressures of Europeanization and norms in the region of Europe drove reforms, with most national laws established between 2005 and 2010. These European norms influencing Spanish policy makers are an example of policies that are co-constituted between European and national levels of governance. The stages of international norm dynamics and political change are emergence, cascade, and internalization (Finnemore and Sikkink 1998). The institutions that internalize the reforms are the universities within the autonomous communities. These higher education institutions are impacted by Europeanization, acting upon Spain to drive participation in the EHEA. Europeanization, demonstrated in the case of Spain, is social constructivist, given the social learning from Europe that takes place at the national and institutional levels of governance (Risse 2009).

In Spain a Royal Decree is necessary to change concrete aspects of higher education governance. The Royal Decree is more specific than the resolutions and executive orders, and it is needed to implement the EHEA reforms. The Royal Decree in the field of education is signed by the Minister of Education and the Head of State. A series of key events for higher education reform have taken place in the years since Spain established the National Qualifications Framework (NQF) in 2007. The framework has increased transparency across university institutions, and it is important because the content of degrees is determined within this framework. This content is what is evaluated in quality assurance by the European National Qualifications Association (ENQA) to become comparable across countries (de Micheo 2013). All countries in the EU that participate in the EHEA are required to have a national and a European qualifications framework. Spain established a national framework MECU and an EHEA framework MECES with *Real Decreto* RD 900/2007. These were effective by the year 2014 (see Fig. 8.2):

MECES   *El Marco Español de Cualificaciones para la Educación Superior*
         SQF-HE (Spanish Qualifications Framework for Higher Education EHEA)

MECU   *El Marco Español de Cualificaciones*
         SQF (Spanish Qualifications Framework)

The Ministry of Education has frequently changed leadership in higher education in years before and after the MECU and MECES were created in 2007. The continuously changing leadership in higher education policy at the ministerial and executive levels has presented a challenge for institutional learning of the Bologna Process within Spain (Matilla Vicente 2013). With the government of Mariano Rajoy Brey (since December 2011), there has been a new Minister of Education and Secretary General of Universities. In February 2013, a panel of experts met to give recommendations to the Minister of Education, José Ignacio Wert, between December 2011 and June 2015. This panel of experts, appointed by the Ministry of Education, made its recommendations, which were published in the *Proposal for the Reform and Improvement of the Spanish University System.* Under the previous Minister of Education, Ángel Gabilondo Pujol, the *University Strategy 2010–2015 (Estrategia Universidad 2010–2015)* was published in October 2010. With the leadership changes of education ministers after the national elections, aspects of the *University Strategy 2010–2015* came under review, especially those with budgetary implications. Given national austerity measures, there were limitations in funding after 2011. The *Strategy for the Internationalization of Spanish Universities 2015–2020* was a development from the previous strategy, which emphasized the centrality of internationalization for Spanish universities (Delgado 2016).

Regionalization in Spain in the post-Franco years strengthened the universities in its regions while simultaneously weakening the central government's role. The LOU in 2001 and the Law of University Reform *(Ley de Reforma Universitaria)* (LRU) in 1983 gave a degree of policy autonomy to the regions. The autonomy given to the regions, is challenging for the national government to take back, in higher education policy and across policy areas. There is concern that the autonomous communities have been given too much power, particularly in education and health policies. A professor of finance law at the Universidad Autónoma de Madrid, Álvaro Rodriguez Bereijo, said, "Once political power is given, it is difficult to reclaim by the central government" (Prego 2013). According to his perspective, the 1978 Constitution created a fragmentation of Spain, giving many governance powers to the autonomous communities. As a response to the intense centralization under General Franco, the decentralization was a natural next step to empower citizens in democratic Spain. Today the challenge remains to find the appropriate balance in policy authority between the national and autonomous community-level governance.

The idea of a Europe of Knowledge for higher education cooperation has become commonly accepted across the continent (Corbett 2005). Despite employment and economic growth concerns, acute in recessionary contexts, the idea is an example of a European norm for higher education that has been socially constructed (Risse 2009). As pressures proceeding from the Europeanization to the national level put pressures on autonomous communities, Spain has experienced top-down influence in policy implementation (Mora and Vidal 2005:135). As regionalization has played a defining role in Spain for nearly four decades of democratic governance, internationalization is playing a greater role in public policies in the twenty-first century.

NATIONAL GOVERNANCE HISTORICAL BACKGROUND

Historians have described the story of "Two Spains": the traditional Spain influenced by the Catholic Church and the enlightened Spain open to the ideas of northern Europe (Carr 2000:2). Although contemporary, democratic Spain begins with the Constitution of 1978, democratic governance existed in periods of Spain's history. The power given to the autonomous communities is the foundation of the 1978 Constitution. These 17 *autónomas* have governance prerogative for the administration of education, as well as health and social services. The diversity of population and attitudes in Spain impact economic, political, and social life. The governance background of the country shaped the institution of universities and their legal–political context over time. The universities were led by the Catholic Church during the Middle Ages, when the University of Salamanca was founded in 1218. The early nineteenth century brought the Napoleonic system, in which the state had a central role in the governance of higher education. This state centrality endured throughout the period of rule under General Francisco Franco until the social pressures of the 1970s resulted in major reforms in the 1980s. At that time, the societal sector began to exert more influence on education policy. After the Constitution of 1978, the LRU in 1983 provided some independence from the state for the universities. The LRU gave autonomy to the university community from entities such as the *Consejos Sociales* (Social Councils). The Social Councils are in place at every public university with individuals appointed by the government to serve in a role similar to a board of trustees. The LRU also gave significant power to academic officials at university institutions (Mora and Vidal 2005:138).

Historically, within the autonomous communities or Spain's regions, there has been immense political pressure on universities. Some smaller regions had only one public university, which took on an important regional role in that region's civic life. Starting in the late 1970s, universities within a region were made available in multiple locations to provide the opportunity to increase access (Delgado 2016). For example, there was not only University of Granada in Andalucia, since additional universities such as the University of Almería and the University of Jaén became established in that region, which has 11 universities in 2016. Prior to the Bologna Process, students had a tendency to study within their region in Spain. Though regionalism is characterized by diversity, there had not been diversity across universities in the 1990s (Mora and Vidal 2005:140). The autonomy given to universities by the LOU of 2001 and envisaged by the Bologna Process gives more freedom in curricular design. More freedom for the university institution is intended in the neoliberal higher education market of the EHEA. ANECA is the *Agencia Nacional de Evaluación de la Calidad y Acreditación* (National Agency for Quality Assessment and Accreditation). It has authority in the seven autonomous communities, which are not one of the ten with their own regional qualifications agencies.

Europeanization has made Spain move from a country of competitive regionalism to one of cooperative federalism (Börzel 2000:18). There is a mutual dependence between the autonomous communities and the central government. The autonomous communities rely on the federal government not only for policy funds in some cases, but also for access to the EU and the international level of politics. The federal government relies on the autonomous communities for effective implementation of EU policies. This supports the argument that Europeanization in Spain has advanced cooperative federalism (Börzel 2000:18). Policy issues on which the federal government and the autonomous communities cooperate range from education to health care to transportation. Across policy issues, there is a national–regional tension, as is characteristic of federal states (Lijphart 1999:186). The negotiation of policies across the levels of governance is part of the change and continuity of democratic governance (Olsen 2010). This tension between the central authority and autonomous institutions is characteristic of the ongoing change in political institutions (Olsen 2010:172). The importance of institutions to affect policy change is affirmed by scholars of Spain's economy and politics (Marks 1997; Royo 2008, 2013). In the ongoing assessment of the drivers of change and continuity, change and order are in a balanced, inextricable, and complementary relationship (Olsen 2010:120).

The 1978 Constitution provided the authority for reforms in higher education enacted in 1983 and in 2001. The LRU (1983) was a significant reform that gave the universities some autonomy from the state in administration and governance. The LOU (2001) provided further decentralization of the autonomy of universities and authority to the autonomous communities (Mora and Vidal 2005:136–137). The Bologna Process has entered the policy space where these previous laws had precedents. The challenges of reforming higher education in the Bologna Process's first decade encountered a tumultuous economy in Spain, notably after the financial downturn in the private construction and real estate sector in 2006.

In national political leadership, Mariano Rajoy Brey of the Popular Party (PP, *Partido Popular*) has been Prime Minister of Spain since December 2011. The year 2016 was unusual, given that it took until November to form an election, following the December 2015 national elections. Previously, Rajoy was Minister of Education and Culture during 1999–2000. The Socialist government (PSOE, *Partido Socialista Obrero Español*) of José Luis Rodríguez Zapatero came to power in 2004, just weeks after the terrorist attacks on Madrid's subway system on March 11.[2] A financial crisis developed during Zapatero's tenure, lasting from 2006 nationally to 2008 globally. Subsequently, the Spanish electorate returned to the leadership of the Popular Party with the election of Rajoy in 2011 (Torreblanca and Mark 2011). The alternating leadership between the Popular Party and Socialist Party has been a pattern since Felipe González of the Socialist Party held the longest position of Prime Minister in post-Franco Spain, for 14 years (1982–1996).

The September 7, 2011, constitutional amendment for central control of the regional governments' budget was encouraged by the EU leaders who exerted indirect pressure for reforms (Molina 2016). This was significant because it was only the second constitutional reform to which the two main Spanish political parties, the PSOE and the PP, had agreed since 1978. They agreed to this reform in the weeks following the ECB initial purchases of Spanish bonds, as part of the Securities Market Program to reduce high yields. At this time, the German Chancellor Angela Merkel and French President Nicolas Sarkozy had voiced concern regarding national debt limits (Abad and Galante 2011). The reform places budget control firmly in the hands of the national government.

This was contrary to the 1978 Constitution that had granted budget prerogatives to the 17 autonomous regions.

POLITICAL ECONOMY CONTEXT: OPPORTUNITIES AND CHALLENGES

In comparing Portugal and Spain's path to democratization and international capital markets, it is important to note that civil society has a role in political transformation. "In the context of regime change, civil society's role and the broader nature of democratization pathways are mutually constitutive, developing in a dynamic and iterative series of interactions" (Fishman 2013:3). The unitary government in Portugal and quasi-federal government in Spain shaped the local government that civil society would influence over decades of democratic transitions. The societal influences on democratization and the development of capital markets were unique in Portugal and Spain.

There are competing narratives to explain the crisis of the monetary union and Spain's place in it (Royo 2013:2). One narrative sees the country as unable to maintain its current account balances and sovereign debt. With this predicament, other countries in the euro zone area came to the rescue with the European Financial Stability Mechanism (EFSM) that established the European Financial Stability Facility (EFSF). Another narrative sees the country as having been encouraged by leaders in Europe to join the EMU, which was imperfectly designed. The EMU does not have an exit strategy option to minimize national and regional economic losses should a country choose to leave the currency union. After remarkable growth in the early 2000s, by the end of the decade the private sector and public sector had experienced financial crisis. Spain saw strong economic growth in the initial 5 years of the new millennium, with more than 3 percent average annual GDP growth (World Bank Group 2016). This endured until the real estate market crash of 2006–2007 and the global financial recession of 2008–2009 followed soon after. The weakening of the real estate and construction sectors added to high private-sector debt, which climbed above 200 percent by the end of 2010 (Royo 2013:3). The government of Prime Minister Zapatero experienced falling revenues in conjunction with its spending of €8 billion for a public works stimulus that strained government accounts (Royo 2013:3). In June of 2012 Spain, under the new government of Prime Minister Rajoy, made a formal request to receive financial assistance from the EFSF.

Approximately €100 billion was used, primarily to recapitalize the banking system. Since private banks are not forced to lend capital broadly, the support that banks have received has been limited in its dissemination throughout the economy. Broader economic growth relies on sound lending policies, which have been slow to be put into practice, along with ameliorating the 25 percent rate of unemployment (*The Economist* 2012). Spain became the fourth country in the EU to receive euro-zone financial assistance, following Portugal in May 2011 and Greece and Ireland in 2010.

Adding to the economic strain was the eroding currency competitiveness since Spain joined the euro currency that was born in 1999. The theories from the Varieties of Capitalism literature are useful to provide the political economy context for Spain. Countries excel by doing what they do best and by being unique rather than converging on a particular model of the economy (Royo 2008:20). Spain is a mixed case, given that it does not fit squarely into either of the two traditional categories of Liberal Market Economies (LMEs) or Coordinated Market Economics (CMEs) (Hall and Soskice 2001). Given the importance of the autonomous communities, Spain may be said to be a decentralized state in economy and in politics. There is a relative weakness of labor coordination for the unique typology of Spain that is described as a State-influenced Mixed Market Economy (SMME) (Royo 2008:28, 182).

Low productivity growth on the Iberian Peninsula in the years since the financial crisis has been cause for concern; future economic growth is necessary to alleviate the economic constraints. Between 2009 and 2013, Portugal and Spain's GDP growth has been negative, except for in 2011 (World Bank Group 2016). As a general rule, investing in education broadly across a population can lead to economic growth (Hanushek and Woessmann 2009). The ideational notion of the Bologna Process and EHEA reforms, as related to the larger economic growth strategy of Europe 2020, appeal to proponents of the reforms. Higher education reforms, with the intention to enhance regional and national competitiveness, are drivers of change at multiple levels of governance.

The Bologna Process is a coordinated response to economic globalization, and the impact of globalization is uneven, both across countries and within countries. Particularly within Spain, there are sharp divisions in economic productivity across the 17 autonomous communities. Assessing the impact of globalization on labor markets, institutions, and domestic structures is key to understanding the political economy

(Royo 2008:16). The Lisbon Strategy of 2000 and Europe 2020 have advanced ideas of competitiveness in Europe to respond to the pressures of economic globalization. They, like the Bologna Process, are an international response to globalization.

Higher education access, innovation, and internationalization are opportunities for policy reform across Europe. In Spain, the 40 percent access target has been achieved in 2005, and innovation investment remains in progress (Eurostat 2016). Mobility, complementary to internationalization, is a competitive arena for Spain. Within Erasmus, the European Commission's flagship program, it is the number-one country in Europe for sending and receiving students to study abroad (European Commission 2013). Spain's higher education system is among those with the greatest levels of attainment in Europe. Under Franco there were fewer universities and fewer students, and there was less sociocultural influence on higher education before massification of universities took place in Spain in the 1970s. Currently, there are approximately 1.5 million university students in Spain (ECA 2016). By comparison, in 1979, there were 600,000 university students (Gálvez 2006:210). Prior to that there was less funding available from the state for higher education, and the distance to travel to a given university was longer, given fewer rural universities.

To increase access for students beyond traditional university age, there is the "*Prueba de Aceso Mayores*" exam for students over 25 years of age in Spain. This is similar to the "Over-23" years of age university entrance exam in Portugal. In 1983, the LRU reforms paved the way for the mass education system, characterized by generalized access. The number of professorships and academic degrees offered increased in the years following. In Spain, for the higher education attainment rates in the decade since the launch of the Bologna Process, the average rate has been in the 30 percent range and reached approximately 40 percent starting in 2005 (Fig. 8.1). The higher education attainment level is taken together with a fall in the birth rate since the 1980s. Figure 8.1 shows that Spain has greater higher education attainment and lower employment, whereas Portugal has lower higher education attainment and greater employment between the years 2000 and 2015. Statistical analysis shows that these two variables broadly have an inverse relationship.

Higher education has multiple purposes—to develop civic knowledge for social cohesion nationally and across Europe and to provide preparation for employability. The objectives for employability remain contentious, since many leaders perceive education more traditionally

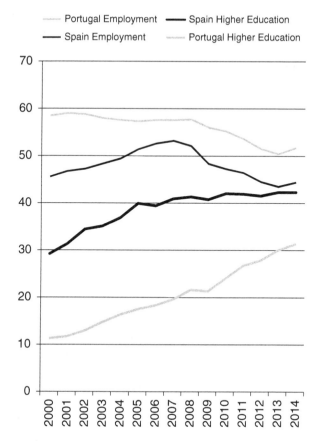

Fig. 8.1 Employment and Higher Education Attainment (%) in Portugal and Spain. *Source* Eurostat, 2016. Higher education attainment (30–34-year-olds) and Employment Data

to be for the exclusive purpose of academic learning. Without intending to compromise learning in an academic field, a practical approach for employability has been an important aspect of the Bologna Process. In order to prepare graduates to participate in the workforce, the objective for students to be well prepared is matched with the objective for the economy to have opportunities for employment. There are various traditions in higher education in Europe, and the EU has provided "flexicurity" to offer flexibility in employment and social arrangements

(Prats-Monné 2010). Flexicurity is a combination of flexibility and security in employment policy that, similar to higher education policy, uses the Open Method of Coordination (OMC) at the national level. The flight of human resource talent has resulted from limited employment opportunities in Spain (Alderman 2013). The financial crisis has exacerbated concerns about brain drain in academic and professional sectors and has caused Spaniards to move to other countries for employment opportunities (Lorca-Susino 2011). There has been an emigration of professionals to neighboring countries in Europe, particularly Germany, which has a need for professionals with engineering and technical education. Given the historical and linguistic ties to Latin America, there have also been waves of migrants from Spain to South America seeking employment opportunities (Stargardter and Day 2012).

Primary challenges to the implementation of the Bologna Process are the scarcity of funding resources and EU political uncertainty. Additionally, changes in political leadership may cause an intermittent vacuum of leadership for organizational development. Scholars have identified a resource dependence of the autonomous communities on funding from the federal government (Börzer 2000:19). Across most federal systems, the states are not uniform in economic productivity or domestic politics. At the national level, the federal government is supported by Structural Funds from the EU. These funds are then dispersed to the regions in a resource-dependent relationship. Since Spain has proximity to the EU in a complex political and economic relationship, uncertainty about the future of the EU is not a meaningful challenge.

There remain concerns about absence of comprehensive funding policies for higher education in Spain (Bonete Perales 2013). Despite the limited resources available for professors' salaries and student scholarships since the financial crisis, in recent decades Spain's investment in higher education had increased exponentially. In 1985, total spending on education was 0.54 percent of GDP (Mora and Vidal 2005:142). Spain's growth in spending on higher education in the 1990s was focused on investment in infrastructure for education, such as buildings and equipment. Over the 12 years, 2000–2011, the EU average was 5.4 percent spending at all levels of education as part of GDP. During those 12 years Spain's average spending was 4.5 percent, whereas Portugal's was 5.4 percent (Eurostat 2012).

The university system, which like extensive bureaucracies is slow to change, has the challenge to remain attractive to students and to offer students an internationally competitive degree. None of the Spanish universities have been among the top 200 internationally in a United Kingdom survey of the *Times Higher Education* World University Rankings in 2013 (Grove 2013). By 2016, six universities made the list for the "100 Under 50 [Years-Old Universities] Rankings" as follows (Times Higher Education 2016):

Pompeu Frau University (Barcelona), 12
Autonomous University (*Autónoma*) of Barcelona, 29
Autonomous University (*Autónoma*) of Madrid, 46
University of Rovira, 80
University of Vigo, 88
Polytechnic University of Valencia, 97

Improving the rankings of Spanish universities remained a policy focus in the Ministry of Education led by Minister José Ignacio Wert between December 2011 and June 2015 (Matilla Vicente 2013). The August 2013 University of Shanghai Jiao Tong Academic Ranking of World Universities (ARWU) showed four Spanish universities approaching the top-200 level. In 2013, their rankings were University of Barcelona (203), Autónoma of Madrid (248), Autónoma of Barcelona (272), and Complutense University of Madrid (292) (Grau i Vidal 2013). The August 2016 ARWU showed positive movement for Barcelona (150–200). While Autónoma of Madrid (200–300), and both the Autónoma of Barcelona and the Complutense University of Madrid slipped to (300–400). There is "differentiated integration" across Spain in implementing higher education reforms across institutions (Cruz-Castro and Sanz-Menéndez 2015). As new legislation becomes developed at the national level and implemented at the university level, leaders will endeavor to overcome challenges from domestic politics and economic constraints in order to enhance the global standing of Spanish universities (Bonete Perales 2013).

HIGHER EDUCATION GOVERNANCE

Higher education policy reform fatigue has been a challenge to Spain's commitments to the Bologna Process and the EHEA. After the LRU in 1983 and the LOU in 2001, university administrators and academics alike are weary of institutional reforms (Matilla Vicente 2013). Initial reforms gave more autonomy to the regions and to the universities, some of which is now being reclaimed by the national government to implement the EHEA criteria. The guidelines and standards provided by ANECA, for the seven autonomous communities that it oversees, and by the additional ten regional agencies require new institutional reporting procedures. Recommendations are made on pedagogical style, as the Bologna Process emphasizes a shift from a teaching to a learning paradigm. Given concerns about the global competitiveness of the Spanish University System, improving the international rankings remains a focus area of the Ministry of Education. With the new government of Prime Minister Rajoy (in late 2011), the Minister of Education, the Secretary General of Universities, and the Bologna Follow-Up Group members each changed The higher education reforms in the *Estrategia Universidad 2000–2015* took place with the Minister of Education Ángel Gabilondo Pujol (2009–2011).

> One of the objectives of future reforms is to improve the governance to make the universities more internationally competitive. The government would like to have more internationalized universities, and to be among the top 200 universities in the world. The most basic reform that the government wants has a lot to do with governance. The Ministry would like to have more expert management areas in how the universities are running (Bonete Perales 2013).

The LOU of 2001 gave further autonomy to the regions for university governance. Introduced two years after the launch of the Bologna Process, it captured the attention of higher education policy makers at the time. Rather than focus on the Bologna Process implementation from its start in 1999, Spain focused instead on implementing the LOU (Matilla Vicente 2013). However, the LOU was a foundation for the Bologna Process because it gave autonomy to the universities, and it supported the student-centered approach that emphasizes learning. Importantly, it also recognized the EHEA (*EEES, Espacio Europeo de Eneseñanza Superior*). Relatively later in the decade, the country took up legislation to implement EHEA criteria.

Between the years 2005 and 2008, there were more than 60 items of national legislation addressing higher education reform (Ministry of Education 2010:215–221). These legislative items included *Real*

Decretos (Royal Decrees), resolutions, and executive orders. In the mid-decade, the *Real Decreto 55/2005* of January 21, 2005, was the initial national legislation that addressed the EHEA higher education reforms. This established the structure for university teaching and Bachelor first-cycle studies, according to the EHEA criteria. It was not until *Real Decreto 900/20007* of July 6, 2007, that the legal framework for the Spanish Framework of Higher Education Qualifications (*MECES:El Marco Español de Cualificaciones para la Educación Superior*) was established (see Fig. 8.2).

Another reform law followed in 2007 to provide modification to the LOU. The *Ley Orgánica de Modificación de la Ley Orgánica de Universidades* (LOMLOU), or the Organic Law of Modification of the Law of the Universities, introduced concepts of the Bologna Process for the Spanish universities to implement EHEA criteria. The appropriate autonomy for the decentralized actors, the universities and the regions, in relation to the central government, continues to be debated as the EHEA reforms become implemented. University governance issues

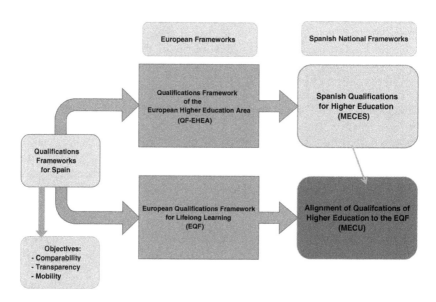

Fig. 8.2 Spanish and European Qualification Frameworks for Higher Education. *Source* Ministry of Education, Culture, and Sport. Government of Spain, 2012

include the selection of institutional leaders and academic staff, the content of academic degrees, and the quality assurance administration. As part of three governing bodies listed below, the *Consejo de Universidades* (Council of Universities) includes the rectors and five members appointed by the President of the Council. The *Consejo de Universidades* was established by the LOU in 2001 together with the *Consejo Sociales de las Universidades* (Social Council of the Universities) that are represented at each public university in Spain.

Within the LOMLOU (*Ley Orgánica 4/2007, de 12 de abril, por la que se modifica la Ley Orgánica 6/2001, de 21 de diciembre, de Universidades*) Original Law of April 2007, Articles 27–30 are particularly relevant to higher education governance. Article 28 focuses on the Council of Universities and its roles for the University Rectors and the Ministry of Education. The primary role is to be the academic coordinating body for the country. Article 29 specifies the composition of the Council of University Rectors, and Article 30 specifies the organization of the Council of Universities. The Council of Universities is composed of the university rectors and representatives from the Ministry of Education designated by the President of the Council. In the Spanish University System, governance is organized with the counsel of three primary governing bodies:

1. The Council of University Rectors
   (Conferencia de Rectores de las Universidades Españolas)
2. The Council of the Regional Ministers of Education
   (Conferencia General de Política Universitaria)
3. The Council of Students
   (Conferencia Social delos Estudiantes)

The Council of University Rectors' professional association is titled CRUE (*Conferencia de Rectores de las Universidades Españolas*), which includes rectors from private and public universities. The Council of the Regional Ministers of Education is composed of the Ministers of Education from the 17 autonomous communities and the Ministry of Education, and it oversees financing of higher education. The Council of University Students of the State (*Consejo de Estudiantes Universitario del Estado*) was established in 2010 with Real Decreto 1791/2010. This Council is evidence of the centrality of students in the Spanish University System influenced by the EHEA. The students have a key role in debating the politics and modernization of the higher education system. There are at least 20 student associations represented in this Council (Matilla Vicente 2012). The Council of the Students, as one of the main consulting governance groups in recent years, recognizes the influence of the student-centered orientation of the Bologna Process. Student-centered learning is an essential component of the periodic declarations of the education ministers (EHEA Ministerial Conference 2012).

Some stakeholders in the Spanish higher education system would like the university rector to have less power, and they would like to change how the rector is elected (Bonete Perales 2013). Since the LOU law was enacted in 2001, the rector is elected by the university community. Currently this is an institutionally closed election process. Bringing in external management expertise may be beneficial for university leadership. Although the LOU of 2001 gave autonomy to the regions, that autonomy was challenged later in the decade when the government and the Ministry of Education gave directives to the universities in the Bologna Process. The LOU legislation raised a public debate on the definition of university autonomy and the role of government in higher education (Mora and Vidal 2005:139).

In 2016, there were 85 universities in Spain: 50 public and 35 private. Universality in curriculum was characteristic of the Spanish University System prior to the LRU in 1983 because the centralized system of higher education had fixed curriculum across regions. In the 1970s, when Spain had its transition from authoritarian rule, there was a societal shift to support mass education in Spain. This wave of massification had taken place throughout Europe and the United States since the end of World War II (Burrage 2010; Trow 2005). The national laws since the LRU have attempted to weaken the power granted to the academic sector in higher education in order to return some instrumental power to the state to support the EHEA.

The Spanish University Act (LOU) of 2001 established the Spanish national qualifications agency ANECA. ANECA, like its counterpart in Portugal, A3ES, works with the European National Qualifications Association (ENQA) to enforce the quality assurance components of the Bologna Process. Through the standards that it sets for Spanish universities and the quality programs, ANECA contributes to quality improvement in higher education by providing evaluation, assessment, and certification for academic degrees and university leadership. ANECA maintains the registry of universities, higher education institutions, and academic degrees known as RUCT (*Registro de Universidades, Centros y Títulos*).

ANECA is organized as a public foundation officially funded through the State Budget Act which is annually passed by the Spanish Parliament. Its directive bodies are twofold: the Board of Trustees chaired by the Ministry of Education which appoints the director or ANECA and the Board of Directors steered by the Director and consisted of four other directors in charge of different programmes conducted by ANECA (ANECA 2013).

Public finances and the existence of an education policy financing gap are challenging areas for Spain. Since March 2012, each region may offer a unique tuition price, which can range from more or less than 3 percent of the national tuition level (Delgado 2016; Matilla Vicente 2013). There are fewer polytechnic institutions in Spain than in Portugal, whereas Spain has a unitary higher education system that combines universities and polytechnic institutions under the same governance. In Portugal, the binary system separating the governance of university and polytechnic institutions developed in the socioeconomic context in which students would benefit from an emphasis on technical training and shorter degree cycles. To accommodate students with additional course offerings, engineering has become widely offered within research universities and polytechnic universities in Spain. This is increasing the types of degrees available across higher education institutions. The influence of the Bologna Process has resulted in examinations in the fields of natural sciences and engineering which are more applied and practical rather than abstract and theoretical (Matilla Vicente 2013).

There exists tension between the regional and federal levels of governance. An example concerns personnel matters. The regional governments are responsible for financing the academic personnel that are evaluated by the national qualifications agency ANECA, in the absence of the region's own qualifications agency.[3] This demonstrates an overlap in regional and national functions in a cooperative federalist system. Since the LOU, there had been gradually more opportunity for professors to be appointed from the regional as well as from the traditional national level. Though with austerity measures since 2012, salaries of some faculty have been reduced and hiring of new professors has slowed. This regional and federal tension leads to the question of where is the authority of higher education policy in contemporary policy in Spain (Mora and Vidal 2005:151). Although the LRU and LOU gave increasing autonomy for higher education to the regions, in the Bologna Process national reforms have been reclaiming more authority for the federal government.

SUMMARY

In Spain, since the launch of the Bologna Process, there have been two changes of government, one in 2004 (to Socialist party) and the second in 2011 (to Popular Party). The initial decade and ensuing years were challenging politically and economically. In the course of these years there were domestic and international political economic pressures. Following the December 2015 national elections, the year 2016 took nearly 11 months to form a government, in which the PP and Prime Minister Rajoy maintained leadership. Commenting on the value of the reforms over the past years, "I have no doubt that it has been positive for us, but at the same time we have had the financial crises where some things are not good" (Bonete Perales 2013). There have been some benefits from the Bologna Process in that the EHEA criteria are a guidepost for reforms that Spain would need to make to compete in higher education in Europe and globally. The greatest tests for Spain's higher education sector are how to overcome the challenges of the economic crisis and how to continue to reform (Fundación CYD 2012:20).

In the 1978 Constitution, the national government of Spain gave significant powers of governance to the regions of 17 autonomous communities. Formed in response to the highly centralized government of General Francisco Franco, the government that has resulted is one of the most decentralized in Europe. There exists an overlapping governance of the regional and national authority in higher education policy. Although Spain started relatively late on the NQF reforms for the EHEA, higher education governance at the national level continues to evolve with anticipated reforms. The *University Strategy 2010–2015* that was completed in October 2010 (under a previous Minister of Education) had been suspended while a commission of experts provided guidance on higher education policy in Spain in a report from February 2013. As the public sector has responded to the financial crises, public opinion has varied regarding support for the government. Globalization-related factors, such as the influence of economic crises from other countries, rather than the action of the domestic governments, are more to blame for economic crises, according to voters with partisan bias in Spain (Fernández-Albertos et al. 2013).

The Bologna Process has supported the initiative of internationalization for the universities. The objective for improving in the rankings goes together with developing the internationalization of higher education in Spain. Since the Lisbon Convention in 1997, "recognition" for the Bologna Process is a sacred word. It remains a challenge to apply recognition for all incoming credits and degrees, depending on the quality of the incoming standards (Delgado 2016). Beyond the EHEA countries that have signed the 1997 "Lisbon Recognition Convention" (Convention on the Recognition on Qualifications concerning Higher Education in the European Region), the United States, Canada, Australia, and New Zealand have signed this document. Before this convention, Spain participated in the process of *amolación* (a Spanish word that means "to make similar") to ensure quality standards in comparing degrees across countries. Compared to 10 years ago, through the Bologna Process, the Bachelor's degree at the universities has been modernized and the offerings in education are better (Bonete Perales 2013). Table 8.1 outlines the Spanish Higher Education Qualifications Framework for degree structure that has come into effect with the Bologna Process.

Improving Spain's position in the international rankings remains a focus, as Spain seeks to compete internationally in higher education. The European University Association's 2007 *Trends V* survey confirmed that an increasing number of universities expect that "the competitive institutions will benefit from the Bologna process, thus indicating that competition is more firmly a part of institutional reality than four years previously" (Crosier et al. 2007:45). The European Commission–sponsored U-Multirank considers teaching and learning to a greater degree than do the Times and Shanghai ranking structures. The U.S. systems of ranking, which emphasize the value of research and external engagement, have served as a model for some global ranking initiatives. The Department of International Relations at the Ministry of Education is promoting the value of internationalization to prepare students to compete internationally and to attract international students to Spain. The process of Europeanization is ongoing in the twenty-first century. More than a century ago, it was recognized by the Spanish philosopher José Ortega y Gasset:

> Regeneration is inseparable from Europeanization: therefore as soon as one feels the reconstructive emotion, anguish, shame, and longing, one thinks of Europeanizing the idea. Regeneration is the desire: Europeanization is the means to satisfy the desire. Truly one thinks clearly from the principle that Spain is the problem, and Europe is the solution (Ortega y Gasset 1910).

In the second decade of the twenty-first century, Spain is regenerating its economy and its national identity. Spain is a serious partner of the EU in southern Europe, and it may be considered the Germany of the south (Molina 2012). The political challenges from the autonomous communities remain fierce, with ongoing calls for successive referendums on independence Economically, Spain seeks to regain its competitiveness as a member of the euro currency and the fifth largest country by population in Europe. As Spain regenerates economically and politically over time, Europe is an important guide for its past and its future. This chapter has considered the historical background, political economy context, and higher education governance in Spain. Chapter 9 assesses the role of

Table 8.1 Spanish Higher Education Qualifications Framework

Levels		*Degrees awarded*
1.	Superior Technical	**Superior Technical Professional Training Degree** (as in Royal Decree 1538/2006, December 15, 2006) **Superior Technical Degree in Art and Design** (as in Royal Decree 596/2007, May 4, 2007 Superior Technical Degree, as in Royal Decree 1363/2007, October 24, 2007)
2.	Undergraduate (Bachelor)	**Bachelor's Degree** (as in Royal Decree 1393/2007, October 29, 2007, which establishes the regulations pursuant to university instruction) **Bachelor's Degree in Higher Education in the Arts**: Music, Dance, Drama, Conservation and Restoration of Cultural Artefacts, Design, and Art (as in Royal Decree 1614/2009, October 26, 2009, which establishes the regulations pursuant to Higher Education in the Arts, as determined by Organic Law 2/2006 Education, May 3, 2006)
3.	Graduate (Master)	**Master's Degree** (as in Royal Decree 1393/2007, October 29, 2007, which establishes the regulations pursuant to official university instruction) **Master's Degree** in Higher Education in the Arts (as in Royal Decree 1614/2009, October 26, 2009, which establishes the regulations pursuant to Higher Education in the Arts, as determined by Organic Law 2/2006 Education, May 3, 2006)
4.	Graduate (Doctorate)	**Doctorate Degree** (as in Royal Decree 1393/2007, October 29, 2007, which establishes the regulations pursuant to university instruction)

Source Ministry of Education. Government of Spain. *Estrategia Universidad 2015*, Table 2, page 37

stakeholders in the policy process and the modernization of the higher education institutions in Spain.

NOTES

1. Using the term "federal" may be perceived as discounting the importance of the 17 autonomous communities. The 1978 Constitution granted them specific political powers that are in tension with the national government in Madrid. For the purposes of this research, the term "federal" is used in a functional manner.
2. Political analysts attribute the election results to a political crisis three days ahead of the general election. Prime Minister José Aznar's Popular Party suffered after Spanish Interior Minister Ángel Acebes initially had stated that the Basque terrorist organization ETA (Euskadi Ta Askatasuna) was responsible for the bombings on March 11, 2004. Later evidence confirmed the international terrorist group Al-Qaeda as responsible.
Carvajal, Doreen. 2004. "Socialists gain amid massive rejection of Aznar's party: Voters reshape Spanish politics after terror strikes." *The New York Times*. March 15, 2004 (Carvajal 2004).
3. During 2016 there were 11 qualifications agencies in Spain, including ANECA.

REFERENCES

Abad, J. M., & Galante, J. H. (2011, September). Spanish constitutional reform: What is seen and not seen. Center for European Policy Studies. No. 253.

Alderman, L. (2013, November 15). Young and educated in Europe, but desperate for jobs. *New York Times*. Retrieved from http://www.nytimes.com/2013/11/16/world/europe/youth-unemployement-in-europe.html.

ANECA. (2013). Fact Sheet. National Agency for Quality Assessment and Accreditation of Spain (ANECA). Madrid.

Bickerton, C. J., Hodson, D., & Puetter, U. (2015). *The new intergovernmentalism: States and supranational actors in a post-Maastricht era*. Oxford: Oxford University Press.

Bonete Perales, R. (2012, 2013). Associate Professor of Applied Economics, and Assessor for the Vice-Chancellor of Internationalization, University of Salamanca. Counselor for Education to the Permanent Delegations of Spain to OECD, UNESCO and the Council of Europe (July 2010–July 2012). Member of the Bologna Follow Up Group for Spain (2008–2012); June 28, 2012 and May 30, 2013.

Börzel, T. A. (2000). From competitive regionalism to cooperative federalism: The Europeanization of the Spanish state of the autonomies. *The Journal of Federalism, 30*(2), 17–42.

Börzel, T. A., & Risse, T. (2000). When Europe hits home: Europeanization and domestic change. *European Integration online Papers (EIoP), 4*(15). Retrieved from http://eiop.or.at/eiop/texte/2000-015a.htm.

Bulmer, S. J., & Radaelli, C. M. (2004). The Europeanisation of national policy? Queen's University Belfast Papers on Europeanisation. No. 1/2004. Retrieved from http://www.qub.ac.uk/schools/SchoolofPoliticsInternationalStudies and-Philosophy/FileStore/EuropeanisationFiles/Filetoupload,38405,en.pdf.

Burrage, J. (Ed.). (2010). *Martin Trow: Twentieth-century higher education: Elite to mass to universal.* Baltimore: Johns Hopkins University Press.

Carr, S. R. (Ed.). (2000). *Spain: A history.* Oxford: Oxford University Press.

Carvajal, D. (2004, March 15). Socialists gain amid massive rejection of Aznar's party: Voters reshape Spanish politics after terror strikes. *The New York Times.* Retrieved from http://www.nytimes.com/2004/03/15/news/15iht-spain_ed3__1.html.

Corbett, A. (2005). *Universities and the Europe of knowledge: Ideas, institutions and policy entrepreneurship in European Union Higher Education 1955–2005.* New York: Palgrave Macmillan.

Crosier, D., Purser, L., & Smidt, H. (2007). *Trends V: Universities shaping the European higher education area.* Brussels: European Universities Association.

Cruz-Castro, L., & Sanz-Menéndez, L. (2015). Policy change and differentiated integration: Implementing Spanish higher education reforms. *Journal of Contemporary European Research, 11*(1), 103–123.

Delgado, L. (2016, May 27). Asesor, Secretaría General de Universidades Ministerio de Educaciòn, Cultura, y Deporte (MECD). Government of Spain.

The Economist. (2012). Going to extra time. June 16, 2012, 26–28.

de Micheo R. L. (2013, 2016). Director of International Relations ANECA (National Agency for Quality Assessment and Accreditation of Spain) and Board Member, ENQA (European Association for Quality Assurance in Higher Education); May 24, 2013; November 16, 2016.

ECA: European Consortium for Accreditation ECA. (2016). Higher education system in Spain. Retrieved from http://ecahe.eu/w/index.php/Higher_education_system_in_Spain.

EHEA Ministerial Conference. (2012). Bucharest communiqué: making the most of our potential: Consolidating the European Higher Education Area. Retrieved from http://www.ehea.info/Uploads/%281%29/Bucharest%20Communique%202012%281%29.pdf.

European Commission. (2013). Erasmus+ is the new EU programme for education, training, youth and sport for 2014–2020, starting in January 2014. Retrieved from http://ec.europa.eu/education/erasmus-plus/index_en.htm.

Eurostat. (2012). European Commission statistics historical database.

Eurostat. (2016). European Commission statistics historical database.

Fernández-Albertos, J., Kuo, A., & Balcells, L. (2013). Economic crisis, globalization, and partisan bias: Evidence from Spain. *International Studies Quarterly, 57*(2), 804–816.

Finnemore, M., & Sikkink, K. (1998). International norm dynamics and political change. *International Organization, 52*(4), 887–917.

Fishman, R. (2013). *How civil society matters in democratization: Theorizing Iberian Divergence.* Paper prepared for presentation at the 20th International Conference of Europeanists.

Fundación CYD (Fundación Conocimiento y Desarrollo). 2012. Resume Ejecutivo. *Informe CYD 2012.* Barcelona, Spain.

Gálvez, I. E. (2006). La política universitaria en la España democrática: logros y carencias después de treinta años. *Tendencias Pedagógicas, 11,* 207–222.

Germany, Federal Republic of. (1949). Basic Law for the Federal Republic of Germany. Constitution of the Federal Republic of Germany. Approved on May 8, 1949.

Gornitzka, Å. (2007). The Lisbon process: A supranational policy perspective: Institutionalizing the open method of coordination. In P. Maassen & J. P. Olsen (Eds.), *University dynamics and European integration.* Dordrecht: Springer.

Grau i Vidal, F. X. (2013, September 2). El 'ranking' de Shanghái: excelencia y especialización. *El País.*

Grove, J. (2013, August 1). Spain tries to keep higher ed moving in a time of austerity. *Times Higher Education* and *Inside Higher Ed.* Retrieved from http://www.insidehighered.com/news/2013/08/01/spain-tries-keep-higher-ed-reform-moving-time-austerity.

Hall, P. A., & Soskice, D. (2001). *Varieties of capitalism: The institutional foundations of comparative advantage.* Oxford: Oxford University Press.

Hanushek, E. A., & Woessmann, L. (2009, November). Do better schools lead to more growth? Cognitive skills, economic outcomes, and causation. IZA Discussion Papers, No. 4575.

Keohane, R. O., & Hoffmann, S. (Eds.). (1991). *The new European Community: Decisionmaking and institutional change.* Boulder: Westview Press.

Lijphart, A. (1999). *Patterns of Democracy: Government forms and performance in 36 countries.* New Haven: Yale University Press.

LOMLOU. (2007). *Ley Orgánica de Universidades* 4/2007, de 12 de abril, por la que se modifica la Ley Orgánica 6/2001, de 21 de diciembre. Modifying the University Act in Spain.

LOU. (2001). *Ley de Ordinación Universitaria*, Ley Orgánica 6/2001, de 21 de diciembre, de Universidades. The University Act in Spain.

Lorca-Susino, M. (2011). Spain and the Brain Drain in the 21st Century. In Roy, J. & Lorca-Susino, M. (Eds.). *Spain in the European Union the First Twenty-Five Years (1986-2011)*, (pp. 211–228). Miami: Miami-Florida European Union Center of Excellence.

LRU. (1983). *Ley de Reforma Universitaria*. University Reform Law in Spain.

Marks, M. P. (1997). *The formation of European policy in post-Franco Spain*. Aldershot: Avebury.

Matilla Vicente, C. (2012, 2013). Director of International Relations, Secretary General of Universities, Ministry of Education, Spain; July 20, 2012 and May 23, 2013.

Ministry of Education, Culture, and Sport. (2010). *Estrategia Universidad 2015 (University Strategy 2015): The Contribution of Spanish Universities to Socio-Economic Progress 2010–2015*. Ministry of Education: Secretary General of Universities. October, 2010. Retrieved from http://www.educacion.gob.es/docroot/universidad2015/flash/eu2015-ingles/index.html.

Molina, I. (2012, 2016). Senior Analyst, Europe, Elcano Royal Institute of International and Strategic Studies, Spain; July 20, 2012; June 3, 2016.

Mora, J.-G., & Vidal, J. (2005). Two decades of change in Spanish Universities: Learning the hard way. In Åse Gornitzka et al. (Eds.), *Reform and change in higher education* (pp. 135–152). Dordrecht: Springer.

Moravcsik, A. (1998). *The choice for Europe: Social purpose and state power from Messina to Maastricht*. Ithaca: Cornell University Press.

O'Donnell, G., & Schmitter, P. C. (1986). *Transitions from authoritarian rule: Tentative conclusions about uncertain democracies*. Washington, DC: Woodrow Wilson Center for International Scholars.

Olsen, J. P. (2010). *Governing through institution building: Institutional theory and recent European experiments in democratic organization*. Oxford: Oxford University Press.

Ortega y Gasset, J. (1910). La pedagogía social como programa político. Lecture given to the 'El Sitio' Society in Bilbao, on March 12, 1910, (1), p. 503–521.

Prats-Monné, X. (2010, November 19). The future of work and the welfare state in Europe. Rutgers University Center for European Studies: John J. Heldrich Center for Workforce Development conference *Responding to the Great Recession: Labor Market Policies in the U.S. and Europe*.

Prego, V. (2013, May 19). Interview with Álvaro Rodríguez Bereijo, Catedrático de Derecho Financiero de la Universidad Autónoma de Madrid, "Conversaciones sobre España 4." Orbyt Press. Retrieved from www.orbyt.es.

Radaelli, C. M. (2008, September). Europeanization, policy learning, and new modes of governance. *Journal of Comparative Policy Analysis, 10*(3), 239–254.

Risse, T. (2009). Social constructivism and European integration. In A. Wiener & T. Diez (Eds.), *European integration theory* (2nd ed., pp. 144–169). Oxford: Oxford University Press.

Roy, J., & Kanner, A. (2001a). *España y Portugal en la Unión Europea*. Cuidad Universitaria, México: Universidad Nacional Autónoma de México.

Roy, J., & Kanner, A. (2001b). Spain and Portugal: Betting on Europe. In E. E. Zeff & E. B. Pirro (Eds.), *The European Union and the member states: Cooperation, coordination and compromise* (pp. 236–263). London: Boulder.

Royo, S. (2006, March). The EU and economic reforms: The case of Spain. Jean Monnet EUMA Paper Series 2. Miami: Miami-Florida European Union Center of Excellence.

Royo, S. (2008). *Varieties of capitalism in Spain: Remaking the Spanish economy for the new century*. New York: Palgrave Macmillan.

Royo, S. (2013). *Lessons from the economic crisis in Spain*. New York: Palgrave Macmillan.

Salaburu, P., Mees, L., & Pérez, J. I. (2003). *Academia Europea de Ciencias y Artes, España: Sistemas Universitarios en Europa y EEUU*. Madrid: Sociedad Anónima de Fotocomposición.

Schmidt, V. A. (2009). The EU and its member states: From bottom up to top down. In D. Phinnemore & A. Warleigh-Lack (Eds.), *Reflections on European integration: 50 years of the treaty of Rome* (pp. 194–211). London: Palgrave Macmillan.

Stargardter, G., & Day, P. (2012, October 31). Reversal of fortunes sends Spaniards to Latin America. *Reuters*. Retrieved from http://www.reuters.com/article/2012/10/31/us-spain-emigration-idUSBRE89U1C820121031.

Times Higher Education. (2016). 100 Under 50 [Years Old] Rankings. Rankings Table Information. London: Times Higher Education World University Rankings.

Torreblanca, J. I., & Mark L. (2011, November). Spain after the elections: The 'Germany of the South?' *European Council on Foreign Policy*.

Trow, M. (2005). *Reflections on the transition from elite to mass to universal access: Forms and phases of higher education in modern societies since WWII* (Working Papers). Institute of Governmental Studies, University of California-Berkeley.

Wendt, A. (1992). Anarchy is what states make of it: The social construction of power politics. *International Organization, 46*(2), 391–425.

Wendt, A. (1999). *Social theory of international politics*. Cambridge: Cambridge University Press.

World Bank Group. (2016). The Worldwide Governance Indicators (WGI) project. Retrieved from http://info.worldbank.org/governance/wgi/index.aspx.

CHAPTER 9

The Role of Stakeholders in Internationalization in Spain

We acknowledge the key role of the academic community—institutional leaders, teachers, researchers, administrative staff and students—in making the European Higher Education Area a reality, providing the learners with the opportunity to acquire knowledge, skills and competences furthering their careers and lives as democratic citizens as well as their personal development.
Budapest–Vienna Communiqué (excerpt), March 12, 2010

The preceding explanations of the recent history, the political economy context, and higher education governance provide a background to understanding the role of stakeholders in the policy process and the modernization of higher education institutions in Spain. The Bologna Process can be understood as an external shock acting on the policy process of higher education governance in Spain, where the competency for higher education is at the sub-national level of the 17 autonomous regions. With an external shock, "the relevance of the core policy beliefs" is less clear than if developed within the internal policy process (Sabatier and Weible 2007:205). This book's qualitative analysis of Portugal and Spain applies the Advocacy Coalition Framework (ACF) to understand the role of stakeholders or coalitions acting on the policy process. In the ACF, "policy-oriented learning" is a path to policy change (Sabatier and Weible 2007:198). Spain has learned from other countries in Europe in implementing the European Higher Education Area (EHEA) criteria. The deep core beliefs and policy core beliefs

© The Author(s) 2017
B. Barrett, *Globalization and Change in Higher Education*,
DOI 10.1007/978-3-319-52368-2_9

change more slowly than the secondary beliefs. It may be said of the Bologna Process in Spain that, like Portugal, Spain is a policy taker. A characteristic of the ACF is that it has macro, meso, and micro levels affecting the dependent variables of belief and policy change (Sabatier and Weible 2007:192). Considering the quasi-federal system in Spain, the autonomous communities of the regions may act as a meso level of public sector stakeholders between the micro-level institutions and macro-level national government in Spain.

The Bologna Process aims for a student-centered approach to learning, compared to the traditional style that is dominated by lecture teaching in which students may be less actively engaged in the educational process. Complementarily, there has been more of an emphasis on research and innovation at universities (Matilla 2012). The International Campus of Excellence, *Campus de Excelencia International* (CEI), program that started in 2005 has focused on creating infrastructure to promote research at universities. After its initial years, funds have become limited on some campuses due to austerity measures in Spain following the financial crisis between 2007 and 2009 (Matilla 2013). The academic and public sectors are the traditional stakeholders in higher education, and the market represented by the private sector is the newer actor in higher education policy (Regini 2011). The cooperation with the European level of governance has ambiguous authority, since the competency for education remains rooted at the national level in the EU treaties. Spain's governance is a unique case, being one of the most decentralized countries in Europe. Spain's 1978 Constitution granted to the autonomous region the authority over education policy. The lead coordinator for internationalization at the Ministry of Education, Culture, and Sports, and a Bologna Follow-Up Group member for Spain explained the multi-level governance for higher education policy:

> The competencies are at the national—and in this country, regional—level. The Commission has no [legal] competencies at all. They can push the process and support the process, but using the Open Method of Coordination, meaning soft governance. Because the real competencies are here [in Madrid] or in the regions, and not in Brussels (Delgado 2016).

The European Commission has been a partner in this intergovernmental process from the start. The challenge is that Europe is a partner in this policy process, but the competency is at the national level. Nevertheless, the Bologna Process has continued to expand in national participation, demonstrating the influence of Europe—through Europeanization—at the national level of governance.

POLICY REFORM: STAKEHOLDERS

After establishing the European Credit and Transfer System (ECTS) and diploma supplement legislation in 2003, the remaining Bologna Process reforms continued relatively late in Spain. Similar to the timing in Portugal, policy reform of the legal framework for the National Qualifications Framework (NQF) took place in 2007, and implementation at the university level began in earnest in the academic year 2008–2009. The ECTS and diploma supplement criteria for the EHEA were reformed earlier in September 2003 with the Royal Decree 1125/2003. The ECTS works as a currency in the market for higher education (de Micheo Llavori 2013). The diploma supplement is powerful for the graduate in terms of employability throughout Europe. The institutions are obliged to issue this document, which explains the learning objectives and information about the degree to employers, in order to enhance access. It was conceived for employability and supports transparency in higher education. There has been greater emphasis on employability and entrepreneurship in Spain in recent years, with the addition of related curriculum. This emphasis on entrepreneurship has been a national priority that advances the objectives of the Bologna Process (Sáinz González 2016).

The first-cycle and second-cycle degree structure in Spain has been 4 + 1, until the February 2, 2015, Royal Decree 43/2015 permitting Spanish universities to modify the degree structure. This previous structure has been less prominent in the EHEA, where most countries have designed the Bachelor's and Master's degrees to have the degree structure 3 + 2. The Spanish higher education system before the Bologna Process included a two-tier system for the length of the degree: the *Diplomatura* and *Arquitectura Técnica,* or *Ingenierías Técnica* (Technical Architecture or Technical Engineering), were 3-year degree programs, and the *Licenciaturas* or *Ingenierías Superiores* (Engineering Higher Degree) were 5-year degree programs. Prior to the *Ley de Reforma Universitaria* (LRU, Law for University Reform) in 1983, the shorter of the technical degrees, *Técnicos*, were called *Peritos* in the case of engineering programs or *Aparejadores* in the case of *Arquitecto Técnico*. A professor at the University of Salamanca and former Bologna Follow-Up

Group representative for Spain, Rafael Bonete Perales offers these explanations for why the former Licenciatura degree became transformed initially (before modification in February 2015 to a 3-year first-cycle) to a 4-year first-cycle Bachelor's degree + 1-year second-cycle Master's degree in Spain as part of the EHEA reforms:

- Since some students arrive to the university at 18 years of age, which is earlier than in other countries in Europe, graduation at less than 22 years of age may be earlier than the international standard. The 4-year Bachelor's degree provides the students the opportunity to assimilate toward the international standard.
- This 4-year Bachelor's degree is compatible with countries outside of Europe, such as the US and the UK.
- The previous degrees, *Licenciatura* (five-years) and *Diplomatura* (three-years), were offered prior to the Bologna Process degrees (*Grados* or *Títulos*). The Bologna Process first-cycle Bachelor's degree of four years offers a distinction in duration from the two previous degrees.

The group of higher education experts, who met in February 2013 at the Ministry of Education, recommended that in some cases three years would be suitable. Considering quality, there have been concerns three years is not a sufficient duration for the first-cycle degree. Considering budget expenditures, the state would pay less over three years as compared to four years. There has not been consensus in Spain on the appropriate duration for the first-cycle Bachelor's degree, between either three or four years (Bonete 2013). Although there are benefits of extended time in higher education study, the 4 + 1 structure for the two-cycle Bachelor's and Master's degrees made student mobility more complicated. "It has made it more difficult to be together with the rest of Europe" (Matilla 2013). Prior to the policy change in February 2015, Spain was the only country in Western Europe with the 4-year, rather than the 3-year, first-cycle degree.

As in Portugal, the public sector is the most influential stakeholder in Spain. A top-down implementation approach has been recognized by some scholars of higher education policy, though there exists uncertainty as to whether the top is the regional or the national level in Spain (Mora and Vidal 2005:135). At the National Agency for Quality Assessment and Accreditation (*Agencia Nacional de Evaluación de la Calidad y Acreditación*) known as ANECA, the Director for International

Relations, Rafael Llavori de Micheo has stated, "The Bologna Process is a bottom-up process in Spain, though it may not look like it is" (2013). This reflects Spain's national character—reforms are ultimately bottom-up, though they take the shape of ministerial top-down reforms. The rationale is that institutions and students have wanted to modernize, and the faculty and students collectively are very interested in reform (de Micheo Llavori 2013). The fact that there are 11 qualifications and accreditation public agencies in Spain, including ANECA, demonstrates the engagement of the regions in education policy in Spain.[1]

Considering the ACF applied to Europe, it is recognized that "the extent that EU directives are 'soft' law allow[s] considerable discretion to implementing officials" (Sabatier 1998:121). The ACF recognizes that there are core and secondary aspects of policy change and that subsystems are often nested within each other. In the case of Spain, the ACF is useful to identify the autonomous communities as providing openness of political system for stakeholders or advocacy coalitions (Sabatier and Weible 2007:200). Spain's quasi-federal system provides more opportunities for the coalitions from the academic, public, and private sectors to influence the policy process, making implementation more complicated. In Spain, compared to in Portugal, there are a greater number of people, divided in their opinions on the Bologna Process, together with the *autónomas* level of governance influencing the policy process. The extent of the organization of the stakeholders, and of their effective communication to influence policy makers, is a critical aspect that influences reform and institutional processes (Scott 2014:181).

Public Sector

In Spain and in Portugal, the public sector of the government is the dominant sector in the ACF. Together with the academic and private sectors, these are the three major stakeholder coalitions across countries in the Bologna Process. As in Portugal, the exam for university access, *Pruebas de Acceso a la Universidad* (PAU, Exam for University Access), is administered by the Ministry of Education, which determines student placement in public universities. The *Consejos Sociales de Universidades* was created to include stakeholders' contributions to higher education governance. Over the past decades, their influence has been relatively weak in comparison to the political power of the university leaders known as rectors. The public sector has a role in administering quality assurance, as designed by the EHEA and the European Quality Assurance Register for Higher Education (EQAR). Quality assurance and internationalization are mutually supportive, and both contribute to improvement in international rankings. In quality assurance, the accreditation and evaluation procedures of ANECA have three stages: ex-ante, follow-up, and ex-post. At each stage, the Council of Universities is present to determine if the university is ready for accreditation. Quality assurance builds trust among countries and institutions within countries (Bonete Perales 2012; de Micheo Llavori 2013).

Spain's decentralized structure provides for the regional governments' role as key public stakeholders. The national legislative system has been the primary mechanism for higher education reforms, which have confronted the resistance of regional governments.

> In the decentralization process the central government has attempted to recoup some of its lost power using legal reforms, rather than consensus. This strategy is not an isolated case—it is not only a problem for higher education, but is an aspect of a larger debate concerning the organization of the new decentralized state. In the end, most of the conflict comes from an unresolved tension among the three main groups of actors: universities, regional governments, and central government. (Mora and Vidal 2005:151)

Given ongoing political tension in a quasi-federal state, the Ministry of Education recognizes the central place of the autonomous communities in higher education governance. The regions are joined with the Ministry of Education in university governance that is influenced by the missions, people, capacity-building, and environment (Fig. 9.1). The former Director of International Relations at the Ministry of Education commented on the strong presence of the regions in education policy "It is very difficult to mitigate the representation of the autonomous communities. This is our concern in Spain" (Matilla Vicente 2013). The presence of the regions in higher education policy is a result of the powers given to the autonomous communities in the democratic constitution in 1978, as well as the subsequent LRU and LOU reform laws. Changing these foundational documents that grant powers to the regions would present a political challenge, given the domestic policy preferences for strong regional identification across Spain.

Seeking to improve in the rankings is a calculated strategy of the Ministry of Education in response to pressures of economic globalization. Driving policy is the external influence of global rankings, such as the Times Higher

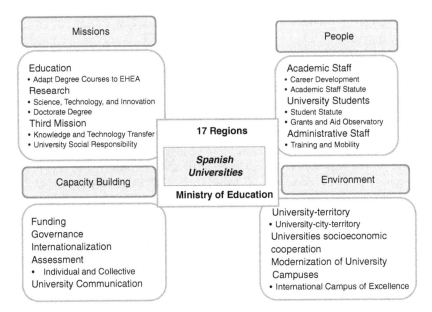

Fig. 9.1 University Governance: Collaboration of the Regions and Ministry of Education *Source* Ministry of education. *Estrategia Universidad 2015*, Graph 1 "Ambits, axes, and lines of action," p. 20

Education World University Rankings, the Shanghai Academic Ranking of World Universities, and the EU's U-Multirank. U-Multirank, funded by the European Commission, was introduced in 2012 and produced the initial report ranking 500 universities in Europe in 2014. The influence of globalization, beyond the regional pressures of Europeanization, has pushed Spain's intentions to reform and to excel in higher education rankings. To make universities more internationally competitive, the government has supported the program *Campus de Excelencia International* (CEI) (International Campus of Excellence), which, when launched in 2005, was inspired by the EU Lisbon Strategy. After the financial crisis, the national funds for the program, from the national level to the autonomous communities, were reduced in size. The left-leaning *Partido Socialista Obrero Español* (PSOE) government of José Luis Rodríguez Zapatero that was in power between 2004 and 2011 had over-spent the education budget. After the right-leaning *Partido Popular* (PP) government of Mariano Rajoy took power in December 2011, these funds became further constricted with the austerity budget reforms of 2012 (Matilla Vicente 2013).

Changes in political leadership and the Ministry of Education leadership, together with limited budgetary funds since the new government's austerity programs launched in 2012, have altered the course of higher education policy in Spain. There were limitations on implementing *Estrategia Universidad 2015* because of this shortage of funds (Matilla Vicente 2013). National legislation may amend the governance of the universities regarding the *Consejo de Universidades*, the *Consejos Sociales de Universidades*, and nearly all aspects of higher education administration and governance (Bonete Perales 2013). In 2013, reforms took place at the secondary school level, with the intention to improve the Organization for Economic Co-operation and Development (OECD) international testing results in the Programme for International Student Assessment (PISA) (Popp 2014). As changes in governance take place with public sector decisions, the influence of the Bologna Process and Europeanization will continue to drive domestic policy decisions.

Academic Sector

The academic sector of stakeholders includes students, professors, and administrators. The *Ley Orgánica de Universidades* (LOU), or Spanish University Act of 2001 gave political power to academic leadership to decide curriculum and management issues. It has been a challenge to build consensus within the academic sector regarding Bologna Process reforms (Bonete Perales 2013; Matilla Vicente 2013). As may be characteristic across institutions, established senior academics have been those most opposed to higher education policy change. The Bologna Process has brought an additional European layer of governance to complete the quality assurance administered by ANECA and 10 additional regional qualifications agencies. Although the focus of this research is at the national level, there are following examples of academic stakeholders' interests at the University of Salamanca in the region of Castilla y León and at the University of Barcelona in the region of Catalunya.

Across Spain, the support for, or opposition to, the Bologna Process reforms among faculty has been generally balanced, given that approximately one-third are supportive, one-third are indifferent, and one-third are opposed (Bonete Perales 2013). The financial crisis, between 2007 and 2009, has resulted in compromises to incentivize higher education quality. Professors have had their salaries cut, and professors who have retired have not had their positions replaced due to budget limitations.

Consequently, a reduced number of professors have been asked to do more, which has made for a stressful atmosphere at the universities. Likewise, students are concerned with having funds to pay the fees, which are higher at the Master level of studies as a result of the degree-cycle reforms. Since after 2007, when the financial crises in Spain began, the students have had to pay more to cover tuition costs at higher degree levels. There is not a strong student loan and student grant program in Spain as in the United States.

The periodic European Students' Union publication, *Bologna with Student Eyes,* discusses the social dimension across Europe. The EHEA ministerial declarations aim to strengthen the social dimension through discourse at the supranational level, with the intention of implementation through Europeanization at the national level. Among the approximately 85 universities in Spain, the University of Salamanca is the oldest and the University of Barcelona is the most competitive, ranking highest on the Shanghai Academic Ranking of World Universities (ARWU) (ARWU 2016; Grau i Vidal 2013). Beyond the national level, as the focus of this research in policy implementation, these are two examples of ongoing institutional change at the university level.

University of Salamanca
Salamanca is the oldest university in Spain, dating from 1218. Seated in the heart of the autonomous community of Castilla y León, north-west of Madrid, it is rooted in Spanish tradition.[2] In Spain, the Bologna Process reforms have blended some aspects of higher education that are traditionally Spanish with European attributes for learning in the context of the Europe of Knowledge (European Commission 1997). Reflective of the contemporary presence and support of Europe at the supranational level, the Faculty of Economics and Business' newest buildings have been built with funds from the EU. Across the EHEA, the European Commission offers curriculum ideas, and the adaptation of these ideas is voluntary. An example of recommended curriculum is the *Tuning*program, which has been adopted by countries and regions worldwide. In the Department of Applied Economics, *Tuning Educational Structures: Reference Points for the Design and Delivery of Degree Programmes in Business in Europe* has been a useful guide for curriculum. The *Tuning* program is separate from, though complementary to, the Bologna Process. It is another area in which the European Commission a partner in the Bologna Process, has influence in higher

education. *Tuning* has been adapted by countries in other world regions such as Africa, Latin America, and North America. Its usefulness demonstrates creativity and innovation in curriculum, and its availability as a curriculum guide that provides common reference points supports the autonomy of universities advanced by the EHEA reforms (Bonete Perales 2013).

Perspectives from professors and students, as academic stakeholders, are valuable for learning about the institutional impacts of the Bologna Process. Across Spain, the *claustro*—annual or biannual meeting that determines the political leadership of the university—is led by the rector and vice-rector at each university. The *Consejo del Gobierno* (governing council) at the university constitutes the level of governance below the level of the *claustro*, and it meets once a month. Members of the governing council include nominated students alongside professors, administrative staff, the vice-rector, and the rector. A student leader at the University of Salamanca who is a member of the university governing council said that the EHEA model of education has brought change together with problems. In the eyes of this student leader, Rashid Mohamed Vázquez, there are positive and negative aspects of the reforms. Positive aspects are more practical and less theoretical learning, the model of assessment that is called "continuous evaluation", and more individualized attention for students from professors attentive to practical learning. As in Portugal, part of the EHEA student-centered reforms focus on a learning paradigm, and there is an optional continuous evaluation administered through ongoing practical coursework. The continuous evaluation is offered to students as an option to the traditional course final exam. Negative aspects of the reforms are the higher student tuitions costs for Master studies, potential inequalities for access to higher education at the Master level and beyond, and concerns about quality of teaching. Tuition costs vary across the country, depending on the decisions of the regions, which can assess fees more or less than 3 percent of the fee recommendation by the national government (Delgado 2016). The more the funds that the national and regional governments provide, the lower the cost is for students at public institutions.

University of Barcelona

The University of Barcelona, founded in 1450, is in the capital city of the nationalistic and most economically productive autonomous community of Catalunya. Barcelona has the largest geographic concentration of universities in Spain, including the Autonomous University of Barcelona, the Polytechnical University of Catalunya, and the internationally recognized Pompeu Fabra alongside additional private universities. A professor and researcher in the field of business organization at the University of Barcelona, Xavier M. Triadó Ivernhas voiced concerns about limited funds for university administration that are similar to those concerns noted at the University of Salamanca. The financial crisis environment has limited the national funds, whereas autonomous communities are limited in their funding position. This has forced additional universities in Catalunya to cut their budgets as well, limiting some practical aspects of Bologna Process reforms. Across regions, from Barcelona to Salamanca, the impacts of the financial crisis have been at the forefront of concerns for universities and their ability to implement the EHEA objectives and to advance research. Professors who are stakeholders in the academic sector have contributed to the dialogue on appropriate competencies for the Master-level degree (Triadó et al. 2013).

The unique quasi-federal structure of Spain's government has enabled autonomous communities, or regions, to have their own quality assurance agencies, which may apply to be reviewed against the European Standards and Guidelines (ESG). The competencies that students are to learn, or the content of each degree as defined in the NQF, are accredited by the quality assurance agency. The Catalan University Quality Assurance Agency, AQU-Catalunya, is one of the ten quality agencies in the autonomous community regional governments that have been accepted for external review against the ESG administered by European Association for Quality Assurance (ENQA) in Brussels, Belgium. Three regions that were accepted by 2013 for external review against the ESG are Andalucía (AAC), Castilla y León (ACSUCYL), and Galicia (ACSUG). In addition to the four noted above, these are six newer quality assurance agencies that are also reviewed against the ESG: The Basque Country (UNIBASQ), Balearic Islands (AQUIB), Aragón (ACPUA), Madrid (ACAP), Comunidad Valenciana (AVAP), and Canary Islands (ACCUEE). Regions without their own qualifications agency providing a formal relationship to the ESG, operate the quality assurance review through the national agency, ANECA, located in the capital city Madrid.

Based in Barcelona, the *Fundación Conocimiento y Desarrollo* (CYD, Foundation for Knowledge and Development) is a higher education research foundation that is independent of the government of Spain. It has an executive committee that provides guidance based on its research and publications on higher education administration and policies. Since 2004, it has published the annual report, *Informe CYD*, on higher education governance challenges and opportunities in Spain, which identifies important trends and developments countrywide. The Minister of Education and the Council of University Rectors (CRUE) support its initiatives, including the presentation of the annual reports. The CYD Foundation, as a private institution, provides a bridge to the private sector and research industries with interests in higher education.

Private Sector

Since the early years of democracy in the late 1970s, public life in Spain has been marked with protests about institutional change that have been politically driven (Carr 2000:270). The nationalism present in some regions of Spain has precipitated public criticism of the Bologna Process and EHEA reforms driven by the national level of governance. A similar critique of the perceived corporatization of universities, potentially resulting in less emphasis on the tradition of education as a public good, has been voiced about universities beyond Europe, in the United States, and worldwide (Dale and Robertson 2009; Slaughter and Rhoades 2004). Private higher education institutions are private sector stakeholders as well as academic stakeholders. There are public–private partnerships and private stakeholders from the business sector that influence higher education. During the 1990s, the share of private sector funding for higher education increased to nearly 26 percent by 1999. Although Spain was on an upward trajectory in private funding in the 1990s, the EU countries' average for private funding was comparably lower at around 14 percent (Mora and Vidal 2005:142).

The Modernization Agenda for Universities: Education, Research and Innovation in the *Estrategia Universidad 2010–2015* makes explicit the importance of the relationship with the private sector, advocating a partnership with the twin goals of "addressing weaknesses in European universities and fulfilling the objectives laid out in the broader Lisbon Strategy" (2010:27). This is an example of policy intentions in national higher education being influenced by Europeanization. In Spain, the chambers of commerce, *las Cámaras de Comercio*, are organized by the *Consejo Superior de Cámaras de Comercio, Industria y Navegación de España* (High Council of Chambers of Commerce,

Industry, and Navigation of Spain). Although the chambers have not taken an active position on higher education collectively, there are private firms that have been committed to improving higher education in Spain.

There are four main categories of organizations in the private sector that support higher education:

1. Public–private partnerships and foundations
2. Multinational businesses
3. Spanish banks and financial institutions
4. Autonomous communities' investment in innovation and development

An example of a public–private partnership is the *Fundación Española para la Ciencia y la Tecnología* (FECYT), the Spanish Foundation for Science and Technology. FECYT is a private foundation within the Ministry for Economy and Competition that supports higher education. The *Centro para el Desarrollo Tecnológico Industrial* (CDTI, Center for the Development of Technological Industry) supports the development of SMEs and has partnership with universities. The *Fundación Universidad Empresa* (FUE, the Foundation for University Business) has served to link universities with business opportunities since the 1970s.

Among the multinational businesses investing in higher education is the Spanish multinational energy firm Repsol. Repsol supports higher education and professional development training as a pathway to joining its international workforce. The Repsol Foundation and the Education and Development (*Educación y Formación*) programs are active in Spain at all levels of education. Another leader in the energy industry, Endesa, has a foundation that supports education. Endesa is the largest company in the Spanish electricity sector and the largest private electricity multinational firm in Latin America.

Many private sector businesses, particularly in the finance sector, have their own foundations that support education. BBVA (Banco Bilbao Vizcaya Argentaria), La Caixa, Sabadell, and Santander are among them. The IVIE (Valencian Institute of Economic Research) is an example of a research institute run by an autonomous community. The autonomous community of Valencia's public agencies in the Generalitat Valenciana supports its research at universities. The IVIE receives funds from private businesses, including the association FUNCAS, *Fundación de las Cajas de Ahorros*, the Foundation of the Savings Banks. The private banks Bankia and BBVA and the private foundation Cañada Blanch are among the diverse investors in the IVIE. The BBVA Foundation and IVIE partnered in 2012 to produce the report *Universidad, universitarios y productividad en España* (University, about Universities, and Productivity in Spain). Other autonomous community institutes investing in higher education and scientific innovation are the IKER Basque Foundation for Science and the Comunidad de Madrid. Despite the quantity of private entities engaged in supporting higher education and research, there remain limited funds for the administration of universities and the tuition support of students.

MODERNIZATION OF HIGHER EDUCATION INSTITUTIONS

The emphasis on internationalization and research are defining aspects in the modernization of higher education institutions in Spain. In defining internationalization, it is more than mobility of students or offering courses in the English language. There is attention given to meaningful curriculum for "internationalization at home" to serve the great majority of students, since an average of only 10 percent may have the opportunity to study abroad (Delgado 2016).

> Knowledge—in other words, education, research, and innovation—has become a pivotal driving force in terms of growth and prosperity…One of the main consequences of the adaptation process for the economy to the demands of a global society and knowledge acquisition is that it has placed the spotlight on education. Strategy for the Internationalization of Spanish Universities, 2015–2020 (Ministry of Education 2014)

In the political economy context, investing in innovation is an opportunity to advance the EHEA and the European Research Area (ERA) objectives, given the assumption that innovation will lead to economic growth and competitiveness. The EHEA includes the 48 participating countries in the Bologna Process. By comparison, the ERA was established by the EU for its 28 Member States and is not inclusive of all EHEA members (European Commission 2000). Like the Europe 2020 economic growth strategy, the objectives for the ERA may provide standards as reference points for the non-EU countries in the EHEA. In higher education, innovation through international mobility and research are priorities for Spain. Research is administered separately from teaching in the national agency, the *Consejo Superior de Investigaciones Científicas* (CSIC),[3] the Advisory Council of Scientific Research. Although independent from teaching, it collaborates with universities and industry as part of a research triangle. Spain has an innovation strategy for 2013–2020 administered by the Ministry of Economy and Competition. A Humboldtian model, valuing scientific discovery in education, inspires the relationship between industry and universities, which supports the idea of a Europe of Knowledge (Matilla Vicente 2012).

With the greatest number of incoming and outgoing students nationally in Europe since at least 2012 as measured by Erasmus), the mobility of university students for Spain is leading in this internationalization aspect of higher education innovation (European Commission 2012). Although higher education mobility is a strength supporting the diffusion of knowledge, there are limitations on outgoing students, given the limitations of funds. The regional and national levels of government have provided funds for mobility when there are funds available. Without regional and national funds, students depend primarily on Erasmus program funds from the European Commission for public support. The European Commission memo of July 8, 2013 titled "Erasmus programme in 2011–2012: the figures explained" called Spain the Erasmus champion:

> Spain sent out the most Erasmus students for both studies and placements (39,545), followed by Germany (33,363) and France (33,269).
>
> Spain was also the most popular destination country with 39,300 incoming students, followed by France (28,964) and Germany (27,872) (European Commission 2013:3).

Spain is the number-one country in Europe for students who would like to spend a time period studying abroad. Spain is a choice for many graduate students from South America, where there are linguistic and historic colonial ties.

Research, Innovation, and the ERA

The Europe 2020 research and development (R&D) target of 3 percent of GDP is relatively high for Spain and for Portugal, given their economic constraints in public and private investments during their years of post-crisis austerity. When the public sector is a stakeholder, the CSIC agency coordinates research on a particular theme. To address the post-crisis context for economic development, the Ministry of Economy and Competition published the *Spanish Strategy of Science, Technology and Innovation 2013–2020*, which states the following objectives (Ministry of Economy and Competition 2013):

> To recognize and promote talent in Research, Development, and Innovation (R&D&I) and the employability of that talent; To provide impetus for business leadership in R&D&I; To promote excellence in scientific and technical research and to foster R&D&I activities that address the global challenges facing society.

To reach these objectives the *Strategy* will:

1. Improve the quality of human resources at all levels.
2. Maintain support for R&D and innovation despite difficult budgetary conditions.
3. Help small innovative companies to grow and increase the innovativeness of larger firms.
4. Build on the dynamism in emerging technologies and improve the connection between Spanish research and global innovation networks.

The improvement in human resources noted above implies investment in Higher education. Despite limitations on funding for higher education and research budgets, higher education and research strategic objectives are complementary. EU Framework Programme budgetary funds have been a source of funding for Spain, which remains committed to the ERA and Horizon 2020. The European Commission's Horizon 2020 program was launched in 2014, and its goals overlap with the Europe 2020 objectives, including the national target of 3 percent of GDP investment in R&D. The European Commission collaborates with each country to identify research projects of interest for future investment. There is collaboration among research networks across countries in the EU on shared research models. The Spanish *Oficinas de Transferencia de Resultados de Investigación* (OTRI, Transfer Office of Research Results) was created in 1980 to coordinate financing and to serve as a liaison between researchers and industry (Perotti 2011:194).

The region of Catalunya is advanced in its pursuit of innovative research. At the University of Barcelona, the University of Barcelona Group (UB Group) works to promote innovation knowledge and transfer. The agencies that compose the group represent the collaboration of public and private stakeholders: the Bosch i Gimpera Foundation, the Patents Centre, the Science and Technology Centres, and the Barcelona Science Park. The UB Group undertakes research and engages in technology transfer between the group and external public and private institutions. To address decreasing public budgets in higher education and research, Royal Decree 14/2012 was issued in April 2012. In the same month, a commission of experts made recommendations to elevate university research to a more advanced scientific level and to strengthen scientific research in universities across Spain (*El País* 2012).

SUMMARY

Spain, like Portugal, is a policy taker rather than a policy maker in the Bologna Process. Initially, these Bologna Process reforms were not a democratic process originating with the people at the national level. They followed the lead taken by the Sorbonne Declaration of May 25, 1998, with the ministers of education from France, Germany, Italy, and the United Kingdom meeting at the historic university in Paris. Over time some Spaniards have come to value the modernity that the EHEA reforms have facilitated in the Spanish University System. Others have resisted the reforms at the regional level of government of the autonomous communities and at the institutional level of universities. This university level of governance has had instances of resistance from the academic community. Administrators and professors who had reformed policies for the LRU and LOU, in recent decades, were confronted with additional reforms with the Bologna Process. Reform fatigue may explain the delay in implementing reforms at the national, regional, and university institutional levels. Higher education policy issues for future consideration have to do with governance, hiring of professors, and decisions on the length of the first and second cycles. Given the decentralized nature of these reforms, they will involve negotiations between the autonomous regions and the national government in Madrid. The ACF explains the influence of the Portuguese and Spanish stakeholders in the Bologna Process at the national level.

Regarding private political perspectives on the Bologna Process, Spaniards' views fall along the spectrum from socialist-left to capitalist-right positions. There is a range of attitudes on the Bologna Process that reflects diverse voices of the stakeholders. Those who see policy reform negatively see it as a corporatization of universities and criticize the conditions of uniformity that are imposed on language and other pedagogical principles (García de Cortazar 2013). Those who see policy reform positively say it supports internationalization of universities, which is an important trend in the twenty-first century that is characterized by globalization. Chapter 10 discusses of the conclusions of my research together with the application of cooperative integration in higher education to other world regions. There are historical, cultural, and commercial ties between Portugal and Spain with the Ibero-American countries where there have been attempts to establish similar regional qualifications framework in higher education. This chapter has considered the role of coalitions or stakeholders from the academic, public, and private sectors. Internationalization and research innovation remain central to modernizing higher education institutions in Portugal and Spain, across Europe, and worldwide.

NOTES

1. ANECA. 2016. Agencias de las Comunidades Autónomas. Available from: http://www.aneca.es/Agencias-de-las-Comunidades-Autonomas.
2. As one particularly graphic example of this traditionalism, in the *Facultad de Economía y Empresa* (Department of Economics and Business), is the names of the doctoral candidate graduates from recent decades written in bull's blood on a wall of honor. Over centuries the bull has had a symbolic meaning for Spain's identity and nationhood.
3. Ministry of Economy and Competition. Government of Spain. 2013. Available from: http://www.csic.es/web/guest/home.

REFERENCES

Academic Ranking of World Universities (ARWU). (2016). World University Rankings for Spain. Shanghai Ranking Consultancy. Retrieved from http://www.shanghairanking.com/World-University-Rankings-2016/Spain.html.

Bonete Perales, R. (2012, 2013). Associate Professor of Applied Economics, and Assessor for the Vice-Chancellor of Internationalization, University of Salamanca. Counselor for Education to the Permanent Delegations of Spain to OECD, UNESCO and the Council of Europe (July 2010–July 2012). Member of the Bologna Follow Up Group for Spain (2008–2012); June 28 and May 30.

Carr, S. R. (Ed.). (2000). *Spain: A history.* Oxford: Oxford University Press.

Dale, R., & Robertson, S. (2009). *Globalisation and Europeanisation in education.* Cambridge: Symposium Press.

Llavori de Micheo, R. (2013, 2016). Director of International Relations ANECA (National Agency for Quality Assessment and Accreditation of Spain) and Board Member, ENQA (European Association for Quality Assurance in Higher Education); May 24; November 16.

Delgado, L. (2016). Asesor, Secretaría General de Universidades Ministerio de Educaciön, Cultura, y Deporte (MECD). Government of Spain. May 27, 2016.

El País, Agencias Madrid. (2012). El Gobierno pone a una científica al frente de la reforma universitaria. April 13.

European Commission. (1997). Towards a Europe of Knowledge. COM(97) 563 final. Communication from the Commission to the Council, the European Parliament, the Economic and Social Committee and the Committee of the Regions. November 12, 1997.

European Commission. (2000). Towards a European research area. COM (2000) 6 final. Communication from the Commission to the Council, the European Parliament, the Economic and Social Committee and the Committee of the Regions. January 18.

European Commission. (2012). Erasmus hits new record with 8.5% increase in student exchanges. Press Release IP-12-454_EN. August 5.

European Commission. (2013). Erasmus+ is the new EU programme for education, training, youth and sport for 2014–2020, starting in January 2014. Retrieved from http://ec.europa.eu/education/erasmus-plus/index_en.htm.

García de Cortázar, F. (2013). La destrucción de la enseñanza. Director, Fundación Dos de Mayo, Nación y Libertad, ABC. May 19, 2013.

Grau i Vidal, Francesc Xavier. (2013). El 'ranking' de Shanghái: excelencia y especialización, *El País.* September 2.

Matilla Vicente, C. (2012, 2013). Director of International Relations, Secretary General of Universities, Ministry of Education, Spain; July 20 and May 23.

Ministry of Education, Culture, and Sport. (2014). *Strategy for the internationalization of Spanish universities 2015–2020.* Ministry of Education, Internationalisation Working Group. Secretary General of Universities. October.

Mora, J.-G., & Vidal, J. (2005). Two decades of change in Spanish universities: Learning the hard way. In Å. Gornitzka et al. (Eds.), *Reform and change in higher education* (pp. 135–152). The Netherlands: Springer.

Perotti, L. (2011). Spain: Major reforms and mixed performance. In M. Regini (Ed.), *European universities and the challenge of the market: A comparative analysis*. Cheltenham: Edward Elgar.
Popp, M. (2014). New culture, old system—Reactions to internationalization n Spanish education policy. In Kerstin Martens, Philipp Knodel, and Michael Windzio. (2014). *Internationalization of education policy: A new constellation of statehood in education?* (pp. 163–178). London: Palgrave Macmillan.
Regini, M. (2011). *European universities and the challenge of the market: A comparative analysis*. Cheltenham: Edward Elgar.
Sabatier, P. A. (1998). The advocacy coalition framework: revisions and relevance for Europe. *Journal of European Public Policy*, *5*(1), 98–130.
Sabatier, P. A., & Christopher M. Weible. (2007). The advocacy coalition framework. In P. A. Sabatier (Ed.). *Theories of the policy process* (pp. 189–220). Cambridge: Westview Press.
Sáinz González, J. (2016). Secretario General de Universidades. Ministerio de Educación, Cultura, y Deporte (MECD). Government of Spain. May 30, 2016.
Scott, W. R. (2014). *Institutions and organizations: Ideas, interests, and identities* (4th ed.). Los Angeles: SAGE.
Slaughter, S., & Rhoades, G. (2004). *Academic capitalism and the new economy: Markets, state, and higher education*. Baltimore: Johns Hopkins University Press.
Triadó Ivern, X. M., Aparicio-Chueca, P., & Elasri-Ejjaberi, A. (2013). La evaluación de competencias en la Educación Superior: el caso de un máster Universitario. *Revista d'Innovació Recerca en Educació*. Barcelona: Universitat de Barcelona, Institut de Ciències de l'Educació.

CHAPTER 10

Lessons for the Future of the Bologna Process and the Internationalization of Higher Education

The Bologna Process, an unprecedented voluntary initiative that has garnered the participation of 48 countries, has resulted in institutional reform in the higher education space in Europe. This institutional reform at multiple levels of governance—European, national, and university/institutional—has taken place through soft law, which is not legally binding through treaties. It has created the European Higher Education Area (EHEA) for the recognition of higher education qualifications across these countries. As an initiative in regional integration, it builds upon the historical institutional structures of economic and political agreements in the years following World War II. Over time a greater number of national issues areas, such as education, have been confronted to gain the support and cooperation of these European countries, nearly 25 percent of the countries in the world (Pierson 2004; Dinan 2014; Wiener and Diez 2009).

The conclusions in this chapter address the implementation of the Bologna Process objectives at the national level, how this complements the Europe 2020 economic growth strategy, and how it may be a model for integration in higher education in other regions of the world. The research done to write this book has related the political economy context, as the independent variable, to the Bologna Process policy reform, as the dependent variable. The theoretical paradigms and policy processes of intergovernmentalism and Europeanization explain the reforms and progress on outcomes thus far.

© The Author(s) 2017
B. Barrett, *Globalization and Change in Higher Education*,
DOI 10.1007/978-3-319-52368-2_10

This chapter presents the research findings, comparing the qualitative points of analysis in case studies on Portugal and Spain. Along with ongoing qualitative process tracing, it reviews the hypothesis tested with quantitative analysis of the European Union (EU) countries in Chap. 5. Assessing qualitative and quantitative aspects together, it considers the EHEA and the Europe 2020 economic growth strategy as guidelines for the regional investment in higher education. The example for regional integration in the Bologna Process is explained in relation to burgeoning regional integration schemes across world regions, with an emphasis on the Ibero-American region that has ties to the Iberian countries. Last, this chapter discusses the second decade of the Bologna Process and beyond. The book discusses three dynamics related to the political economy and policy processes that influence the Bologna Process:

1. Competitive economic pressures: globalization
2. Domestic politics at the level of the state: intergovernmentalism
3. Leadership from the supranational European Union that socially engages stakeholders and constructs regional norms: Europeanization

Given the breadth and complexity of the Bologna Process, the main focus of this book is the degree structure and National Qualifications Frameworks (NQF) aspect for national-level policy implementation in the case-study countries Portugal and Spain. The quality assurance and international degree recognition aspects are still developing at varying rates across countries. The internationalization of higher education and the pursuit of competitiveness in the region, guided by the European Commission's Europe 2020 economic growth strategy, are drivers for reform (Martens et al. 2014). The structure of government, the Political leadership, and the funding available are variables that influence policy implementation. The cases of Portugal and Spain are the most similar for research design, and they have diverged on the dependent variable of reforms toward higher education attainment. With the Bologna Process criteria and with the Europe 2020 target for higher education attainment, Portugal has proceeded at a faster pace than Spain (European Commission 2015; Rauhvargers et al. 2009).

Although Portugal and Spain are similar countries as members of the European Union (EU), they vary in government and higher education system structures, but the countries share a similar timeframe for the national legislation to legally establish the NQF in 2007. The drivers of this similar timeframe are the policy processes of intergovernmentalism and Europeanization.

RESEARCH FINDINGS IN QUALITATIVE CASE STUDIES

History matters because it determines the trajectory that institutions take (Pierson 1996, 2000, 2004). The temporal dimension provides the necessary context that is critical for evaluating politics in time: "Placing social analysis in time implies recognizing that any particular moment is situated in some sort of temporal context—is part of an unfolding social process" (Pierson 2004:167). A parallel comparison of the two Iberian countries as they have implemented policy reforms in the Bologna Process at the national level examines the five areas of qualitative analysis: (1) national governance background, (2) policy economy context, (3) higher education governance, (4) policy implementation, and (5) modernization of higher education institutions.

National Governance Background

In the mid-twentieth century, generally there was more freedom for political expression and participation in higher education under authoritarian rule in Spain than in Portugal. In Spain, there were a lesser number of universities and longer distances to travel to attend, resulting in lower levels of higher education attainment when education was an elite system. Between the 1930s and the 1970s, the countries shared the notion of higher education as a privileged system to serve the elites, and the Catholic Church continued to run some private universities. In the 1978 Spanish Constitution, the quasi-federal system gave meaningful political power for governance to the 17 autonomous communities. Once granted, this autonomy became strongly embedded in the national culture; leadership in policy areas is shared between the autonomous communities and the national government in Madrid. Portugal's unitary structure, compared to Spain's quasi-federal governmental structure, provides for a process of policy reform that may be more direct in design (Lijphart 1999). In practice, there have been institutional challenges and opportunities, and stakeholder coalitions act upon the policy process in both countries.

Political Economy Context

In the financial crises, Spain's crisis was initially a private sector debt crisis. Property and asset prices declined steadily from 2007, prior to the global financial crisis. Portugal, on the other hand, had a sovereign debt crisis caused by public sector indebtedness, which became unsustainable after the global financial crisis in 2008–2009. The opportunities for higher education reform—attainment, innovation, and internationalization—are shared. The challenges of limitations on funding affect each country differently. There have been austerity measures in both countries, causing a reduction in spending in Portuguese and Spanish education systems in 2013 (Spain Ministry of Education, Culture, and Sport 2015:10; PORDATA 2016). The spending reported is across every level of educational—primary, secondary, and tertiary for higher—without specific details for higher education in focus. In Portugal, the reduction has not limited the progress to expand higher education attainment. In Spain, the reduction has limited public funding for the International Campus of Excellence initiatives. This has narrowed the resources toward the Spanish objective to increase their universities in international rankings. The University of Lisbon (Portugal) and the University of Barcelona (Spain) are highest ranked globally as top 200 universities (ARWU 2016).

The quantitative analysis informs that the impact of a reduction in education spending has been an inverse relationship with higher education attainment, which continued on an upward trajectory. In these two countries, education spending had a significant, negative relationship with higher education attainment (between 2000 and 2011) (see statistical analysis in Chap. 5, Table 5.4). The wealth of a country, measured by GDP per capita, did not have a significant relationship with higher education attainment for these two countries during this time period, even though there was a statistically significant relationship with the EU countries taken together during the years 2000–2014. The quasi-federal structure in Spain adds a layer of complexity for tax revenues taken from, and funds granted to, the autonomous communities. They have shared some limitations in funding private and public research initiatives, although a number of public research institutions remain supported by EU Structural Funds. Both countries suffered sovereign debt downgrades in 2011 that were followed by Austerity reform packages negotiated with the troika (ECB, EU, and IMF) in 2011 in Portugal and in 2012 in Spain.

Higher Education Governance

Both the governmental structure and the higher education system structure are different between Portugal and Spain, making these the diverging variables in the most similar cases for comparison in the research methodology. Portugal is unitary, or centralized, and Spain is quasi-federal, or decentralized, in governmental structure. Portugal has a binary higher education system, whereas Spain has a unified higher education system. Portugal's binary system of higher education includes university and polytechnic institutions. Spain's unified system of higher education includes all types of universities within a single higher education governance structure. The quasi-federal system is more complicated for university governance because of the authority granted by the 1978 Spanish Constitution to the regional governments of the 17 autonomous communities. In Spain, despite having a unified higher education system, there is a greater plurality of public sector stakeholders, making policy reform more contentious.

Consistency of leadership matters, which is evident in comparing Portugal and Spain. There has been more consistency in leadership in higher education administration in Portugal than in Spain, even though both countries changed governments in 2011. Although in both countries the legal framework for the NQF was established with legislation in 2007, Spain took two years longer (2011) compared to Portugal (2009) to define the contents of the NQF. Nevertheless, the influences of the explanatory variables in the political economy, alongside the policy processes of intergovernmentalism and Europeanization, drove the similar outcome of the legal framework NQF initial legislation in 2007 in both countries.

The following are future issues that will remain important for Portugal: reform emphasis on teaching and learning, governance, and internationalization (Teixera 2016). Particularly, in light of youth employment and underemployment, making teaching and learning more practical is a primary goal. The governance reform of higher education policy that began in 2007 continues to progress. Financial constraints stem from dependency on funding primarily from the public sector. Internationalization remains a priority, as higher education institutions continue to develop an external orientation beyond the parameters of the country. This has roots in the Bologna Process launched in 1999, which recognizes the policy reform needed in the twenty-first century knowledge economy (European Commission 1997).

Spain has similar concerns that are manifest across the 17 autono-mous communities with regional policies alongside national policies. The Bologna Process has supported the autonomy of the higher education institutions, which parallels the direction of higher education policy in Portugal and Spain in recent decades. Although seemingly an incongru-ity, the state continues to have a central role in oversight (Neave 2012).

Policy Reform: Stakeholders

The public sector is the dominant coalition stakeholder in both Portugal and Spain. The governments, represented by the ministers of educa-tion at the EHEA ministerial conferences, have driven the reforms at the national level. By comparison, in some countries such as the United States, the academic sector may be more important in driving change in higher education because accreditation is granted by associations of peer universities that operate with oversight of the Department of Education. The accrediting quality assurance agencies in Europe are institutions that are created by national legislation, which are required to operate inde-pendent of the state and the higher education institutions. In the aca-demic sector in Spain there is a greater number of faculty, students, and administrators who have diverse attitudes, positive and negative, toward the Bologna Process. In Portugal, there was general cohesion among the academic sector at universities to implement reforms on degree structure by the year 2008 (Correia 2012; Freire 2013).

Because of the differences in the size of their economies measured by GDP, there are more private sector businesses in Spain than in Portugal, resulting in more influence on higher education by private sector actors in Spain. The World Bank reports that in 2013 the GDP of Spain was $1.4 trillion and that of Portugal was $227 billion. The inclusion of a variety of stakeholders in higher education from across sectors has limi-tations; namely the stakeholders beyond the traditional academic sec-tor lack historical institutional knowledge. However, they bring value: from the private sector comes knowledge of market forces, and from the public sector comes a connection to the European level of govern-ance. As higher education institutions grow in partnerships across sec-tors, an appropriate form of engagement may be found for stakeholders' involvement in governance leadership. Their engagement may be in dis-tinct roles depending on the specific country, as influenced by its history and sociocultural values. As soft-law policies, the Bologna Process and the EHEA allow for variations in implementation, allowing countries to develop unique partnerships that are beneficial to attaining their objectives in higher education.

The Modernization of Higher Education Institutions

The European higher education space partly overlaps with the space of the European Research Area (ERA). The EHEA has the participation of the 48 country members in the Bologna Process. The ERA is designed by the European Commission to support the 28 EU Member States through programs such as Europe 2020 (since 2010) and Horizon 2020 (since 2014). To advance research, innovation, and the ERA, both Portugal and Spain's national research agencies benefit from EU structural funds. The primary agency in Portugal is the *Fundação para a Ciência e a Tecnologia* (FCT, Foundation for Science and Technology). The counterpart agency in Spain is the *Consejo Superior de Investigaciones Científicas* (CSIC, Advisory Council of Scientific Research). In Portugal, the FCT is associated with the Ministry of Science, Technology, and Higher Education.[1] In Spain, the CSIC is associated with the Ministry of Economy, Industry, and Competitiveness.

At the national level of governance, both countries have developed innovation strategies for the years 2013–2020 that are promoted by the ministries of economy. The national innovation strategies in Portugal and Spain align with the Europe 2020 objectives for increased employment and investment in research and development (R&D). There are domestic and international incentives for economic growth. At the European level of governance, there are the Horizon 2020 guidelines and research agendas for the innovation program sponsored by the European Commission to develop the ERA. This cross-over of policies and the co-constitutive relationship between the national and European levels of policymaking demonstrate intergovernmentalism and Europeanization in research and innovation policy.

POLICY REFORM OUTCOMES

In the policy reform of the Bologna Process, both Portugal and Spain have been policy-takers (Molina 2012). The policy-makers have been the four countries (France, Germany, Italy, and the United Kingdom) that signed the Sorbonne Declaration on May 25, 1998, which laid the foundation for the Bologna Process. The EU Member States have National Qualifications Frameworks (NQFs) and EHEA qualifications frameworks. The FHEQ-Portugal and the MECES in Spain are the NQFs. The FHEQ-EHEA in Portugal and the MECU in Spain are the EHEA qualifications frameworks. These countries moved forward with their respective legislation to define the content and qualifications of academic degrees, after the overarching European framework for qualifications was adopted at the Bergen EHEA Ministerial Conference in May 2005. The NQF legal frameworks were established in similar timeframe, two years after the EHEA Bergen Ministerial Conference and soon after the London EHEA Ministerial Conference in May 2007. The initial national legislation legally establishing the NQF was adopted in Spain in July and in Portugal in December of 2007. This demonstrates the influences of intergovernmentalism and Europeanization as policy processes in establishing this central component of the EHEA within a similar annual timeframe in these two countries.

Although liberal intergovernmentalism and Europeanization are distinct processes, they are not opposites; they may even be complementary (Schmidt 2009:211). Intergovernmentalism is framed by rational institutionalism; Europeanization is framed by sociological institutionalism; and each has explanatory power in higher education reform. In the case of Portugal, intergovernmentalism has been applied as an explanation of the policy process. Portugal's national interest has been to advance upon the EHEA reforms, since the country has been on a trajectory to widen educational access after the limited higher education attainment during the *Estado Novo*. The regional integration process of intergovernmentalism, where domestic interests are represented at the European level of cooperation, is useful to explain the willingness to participate in reform in Portugal once the 1986 Law for the Education System Act was amended in 2005. Portugal's national interest in reform is strategic instrumentalism to expand educational access coinciding with the Bologna Process initiative. Europeanization is also relevant to understand how European norms influenced Portugal to reform, and in this research it applies directly in the case of Spain.

Europeanization explains the policy process in Spain that built upon the national *Ley de Ordinación Universitaria* (LOU, Law of University Ordinance) reform of 2001. In 2000, a year after the Bologna Process launch, Spain had higher education attainment at 29 percent, compared to Portugal's 11 percent (Eurostat 2016).[2] In Spain, the national incentive to increase higher education attainment was less pressing than in Portugal. Since Spain's autonomous communities exercise the governance granted to them in the 1978 Constitution, the push for reform at a national level is resisted to a certain extent in order to protect regional autonomy. The *Ley de Reforma Universitaria* (LRU, Law of University Reform) in 1983 and the LOU reform that Spain experienced in the post-Franco years were intended to give the autonomous communities and university institutions more autonomy from the state in higher education governance. Since then, Bologna Process reforms have reclaimed some of that independence. When the national level of governance in Spain is influenced by the European level of governance, this Europeanization effect diffuses policy implementation to the regions and to their university institutions (Börzel 2000; Börzel and Risse 2012). It may be argued that, had it not been for the Bologna Process, Spain may not have undertaken these further reforms beyond the changes enacted with the LOU in 2001. The comparisons of qualitative case studies provide country cases that have explanatory value to relate to other national circumstances. Taken together, the qualitative and quantitative research methods reveal the political, economic, and social factors that influence policy reform at the national level (Table 10.1).

Addressing the Hypothesis

Relationships over time call for the analysis of political, economic, and social change in the theoretical perspective of historical institutionalism (Pierson 2004:171). With the social construction of institutions over space and time, concepts of higher education ideas and policy legislation are born of policy discourse (Nokkola 2007, 2012). Placing politics in time has two intentions: to bound political inquiry temporally and to develop theory and methods to address key concepts (Pierson 2004:169–172). The theory of liberal intergovernmentalism claims a rational motivation for participation in the policy process (Moravcsik 1998; Moravcsik and Schimmelfennig 2009). The theory of Europeanization is a process of socially constructing institutions from the European level to the national level (Schmidt 2009; Börzel 2000, Börzel and Risse 2012). These theories describe complementary processes that have changed institutions through policy discourse about an idea of Europe that has national and institutional impacts (Ravinet 2005; Schmidt and Claudio 2004). A combination of quantitative and

Table 10.1 Portugal and Spain Comparisons

National Profile Variables:
Italicized: shared variable of interest that is similar temporally

	Portugal	Spain
Country transition	*1970s to*	*1970s to*
	1986 EU Accession	*1986 EU Accession*
Government structure	Unitary	Quasi-federal
Government style	Republic	Constitutional monarchy
University system	Binary	Unified
Population[a]	10.5 million	47.25 million
GDP[a]	$212 billion	$1.3 trillion
GDP per capita (2000–2014 average)[a]	$27,000	$33,000

[a]*Source* World Bank (2016)

Policy Outcome of Interest (Degree Structure Reform in the Same Year, 2007): Bologna Process Policy Reform at the National Level
NQF (National Qualifications Framework) Legal Establishment of Academic Degrees

	Portugal	Spain
NQF legal framework	12/2007	7/2007
	Decree-Law	Royal Decree
	396/2007	900/2007

Additional outcomes:
Bologna Process Policy Reforms at the National Level

	Portugal	Spain
ECTS	2/2005	9/2003
	Decree-Law	Royal Decree 1125/2003
	42/2005	
NQF defined	7/2009	7/2011
	Ordinance 782/2009	MECES
	2010 Report	Royal Decree
	FHEQ-Portugal	1027/2011
National accreditation agency established	11/2007	6/2001
	A3ES	ANECA
	Decree-Law	Ley Orgánica 6/2001
	369/2007	
Higher education attainment (30–34-year olds)	31.9% in 2015	40.9% in 2015
	(Eurostat)	(Eurostat)

qualitative research methods has been used to investigate the following hypothesis of the political economy context at the national level. Secondary questions concern the extent of globalization through regional integration, namely international trade, and stakeholder coalitions' influence on the process of policy reform of the Bologna Process.

Hypothesis 1 (H1) for Research Question (Political Economy Explanations for Policy Reform) A higher level of economic development, measured by GDP per capita, has a relationship with relative progress on higher education reform—especially higher education attainment. Countries with weaker levels of economic development may have higher opportunity costs and lesser capacities for policy reform.

To address H1 there were applications of statistical analysis in Chap. 5 using linear regression on a dataset with observations from 26 of the 28 EU Members State countries. Luxembourg and Croatia were omitted, due to missing data, and the latter acceded to the EU in July 2013. The countries of Portugal and Spain discussed in Chaps. 6–9 provide the case-study analysis comparing the Iberian countries on the five points of qualitative analysis previously outlined in this chapter. The dependent variable for quantitative analysis is higher education attainment. GDP per capita is presented as the most significant independent variable among the political economy variables tested in this analysis. The panel regression of the 26 EU Member States between the 15 years inclusive, 2000–2014, determined a statistically significant relationship between independent variable GDP per capita and higher education attainment at the highest $***p < 0.01$ level in Model 1 and Model 2, which introduces the variable of time.

Reflecting both sides of the economic average in Europe, the Iberian countries' average GDP per capita for the 15 years falls on each side of the EU average of approximately $31,000 GDP per capita. Over these years, Portugal's average is below and Spain's average is above that of the EU countries (see Chapter Appendix Table 7.3). Over these 15 years, the average GDP per capita for Portugal is approximately $27,000, and that for Spain is approximately $33,000 (World Bank Group 2016). Comparing these two countries, the higher GDP per capita in Spain is associated with higher levels of higher education attainment (38.6 percent average) over 15 years. The lower GDP per capita in Portugal is associated with lower levels of higher education attainment (20.3 percent average) over the same time period. As explained previously, there are countless unquantifiable cultural and historical factors that may be unobserved explanatory variables influencing higher education attainment. According to the statistical analysis, however, overall wealth, measured by GDP per capita, has a positive and significant relationship with higher education attainment. Since per capita values are an average, it is necessary to be cautionary with data analysis, since it is not reflective of individual cases. Qualitative analysis is necessary to provide a more complete assessment: The quality of education matters beyond its mere attainment (Elken and Stensaker 2012; Rosa et al. 2016).

In Portugal and Spain, the influence of Europe, through liberal intergovernmentalism and Europeanization, drove similar timing to adopt the NQF, which defines the content of academic degrees, in the year 2007. The NQF is important for establishing learning outcomes, which is a next step in policy coordination (Sursock and Smidt 2010:7). Testing the hypothesis reveals the relationship of political economy factors on policy reform at the national level. Progress on a period of reforms is represented by the average higher education attainment and average annual change for the years 2011–2014 (See Fig. 5.1). Considering higher education attainment and recent change, Portugal, at 31 percent attainment and nearly 6 percent average annual change between 2011 and 2014, progressed more rapidly than Spain during that period. By comparison, Spain, at 42 percent attainment, has changed less than 0.5 percent in the same period (European Commission 2015:3). However, Spain has already reached the Europe 2020 target for 40 percent average higher education attainment for 30–34-year-olds. These countries continue to strive to reach their national objectives for the year 2020. Portugal's target is the EU average of 40 percent, and Spain's target is 44 percent. By April 2013, eight countries had achieved the Europe 2020 target for 40 percent higher education attainment (EurActiv 2013). By November 2016, 17 countries had achieved the target (European Commission 2016:48). The higher education and research innovation strategies in Portugal and Spain are complementary to Europe 2020 objectives for employment and investment in R&D. The European Commission's Europe 2020 objectives have been exemplary for many of the countries beyond the EU that are part of the European Higher Education Area (EHEA) (Tyson 2016).

In recent decades, Portugal and Spain have experienced important governance transitions from authoritarian rule, where education policies were planned by the state. In Portugal, with a unitary government and a population of approximately 11 million, the pace of higher education reforms has progressed steadily, resulting in its being an EHEA pathfinder country between 2012 and 2015. The pathfinder countries have been committed to finding ways to implement the automatic recognition criteria of the EHEA, and they have represented a variety of higher education systems. The idea and selection of pathfinder countries was introduced at the 2012 EHEA Bucharest Ministerial Conference. With the European Commission as the facilitator, they are Belgium (Flemish and French regions), Croatia, Denmark, Estonia, Germany, Luxembourg, The Netherlands, Portugal, and Slovenia. The pathfinder countries started work soon after the Bucharest Ministerial and, in 2015, reported to the EHEA Yerevan Ministerial Conference with recommendations on automatic recognition (EHEA Pathfinder Group 2015). They made recommendations that are legislative and technical in nature, with the ultimate objective of increasing trust across institutions and across countries in the EHEA.

To advance the change in higher education attainment and related policy reforms, leadership was integral to the success of Portuguese higher education institutions. In response to the public sector as the leading stakeholder, the academic institutional governance experienced a collective undertaking of the new academic degree structure in the year 2008. With consistent leadership at the national level, resulting in less turnover of higher education leadership than in Spain, there was an opportunity to advance higher education policies. As policy-takers in the Bologna Process, Portugal and Spain have changed their national systems of higher education to adapt to the European-level recommendations. This international cooperation in higher education complements efforts to strengthen the regional economy's common market, which is defined by the four freedoms of movement of goods, services, labor, and capital in the EU Single Market.

THE EHEA AND EUROPE 2020

The pressures of economic globalization act on countries oriented to compete in the global economy. Beneficial partnerships provide opportunities for shared learning and a strengthened position in the global market for knowledge and commerce. The research for this book has been framed by the new institutional theoretical frameworks that consider the organization of political life and its impact on the performance of systems in historical, rational, and sociological perspectives (Peters 2012). In the face of institutional change, education policies remain national competencies, as protected by the subsidiarity principle of the EU (Ritzen 2010:32). Although Europeanization has been in effect, it does not preclude education policy continuing as a national competency. The policy processes of liberal intergovernmentalism and Europeanization are evident in each country to varying extents.

Giving an address at a U.S. university, former Italian Prime Minister Matteo Renzi acknowledged the important role that international education has played in Europe (Renzi 2016). Considering Europe's place in the world, Renzi emphasized the dynamism of the Erasmus international student exchange, which, since 1986, has grown to include countries beyond Europe through Erasmus+. The head of government from the country where Bologna is the oldest university city in Europe, dating from 1088, mentioned these achievements in education together with the current opportunity to pursue human travel to Mars.

The history and the opportunity of international cooperation in education make it an area full of possibilities at each level of governance. Universities and all types of higher education institutions have experienced unprecedented institutional change in the knowledge society (Cantwell and Kauppinen 2014). Educational sociologists have concurred that the international convergence of academic degree programs that comes from the Bologna Process is unprecedented (Frank and Meyer 2007:299). The Strategic Framework—Education &Training 2020, provided by the European Commission, provides the rubric to pursue objectives and provide reporting in higher education. The Open Method of Coordination (OMC) among countries, discussed in Chap. 3, has provided a policy tool for countries to share best practices across the soft-law policy areas of education, employment, and environment.

To gauge public opinion, the European Commission has conducted Eurobarometer surveys and reports for the initial 3 years after the launch of the Europe 2020 economic growth strategy. The results for these semi-annual surveys in the years 2011, 2012, and 2013 indicate that public opinion of the higher education attainment objective of 40 percent remained consistently on the positive side. Over these three years, 47–50 percent of participants in the countries surveyed consistently considered the quantifiable objective "about right". However, as the years progressed a greater number of respondents considered the objective "too ambitious". This public opinion of "too ambitious" increased from 20 in 2011 to 38 percent in 2013 (European Commission 2013b). Across the EU there may be various reasons for the growing concern that the higher education objective may be too ambitious, such as limited economic opportunity following sovereign debt crises and austerity reforms. The first decade of the twenty-first century ended with the global financial crisis, which resulted in a retreat from international economic cooperation and a greater focus on domestic political concerns. Since the idea was presented with the Sorbonne Declaration, the Bologna Process has been used as a lever for domestic reforms in higher education (Neave 2009). Although there remains cynicism about globalization efforts, the Bologna Process has been a relative success, given its continuity throughout and after national and global financial crises.

The pedagogical paradigm shift to greater emphasis on teaching and learning, as part of a student-centered approach, has been initiated in the Iberian countries and across the EHEA (EU High Level Group 2013; Matilla 2013; Veiga and Amaral 2009). This emphasis on teaching and student-centered learning is a central component of the report that recommends EU support to establish a European Academy for Teaching and Learning (EU High Level Group 2013:67). The former European Commissioner for Education, Culture, Multilingualism, Youth and Sport, Androulla Vassiliou, wrote in the Foreword of the *Report to the European Commission*, "In such a time of crisis, Europe needs to invest more in higher education, especially in the quality of teaching and learning. Every Member State needs to invest as much as it can afford and to maximise the return on every euro it spends" (European Union: High Level Group 2013:5). Seeing the regional economic challenges as an opportunity rather than an obstacle is further reason to strengthen investment in higher education. This was the same message that was put forward in the Communiqué and Statement on the Bologna Policy Forum at the previous year's EHEA Ministerial Conference in Bucharest. The European Commission Communication on "European higher education in the world" frames the EHEA in the context of the growing demand for higher education. It states that by the year 2030 the number of students worldwide will grow fourfold, from nearly 100 million at present to 414 million (European Commission 2013a:2). The report recognizes the intra-European integration through EHEA transparency tools such as the ECTS and the European Qualifications Framework. Simultaneously it recognizes the global dimension of educational integration. The EU, through the policy-making entity of the European

Commission, which has been a partner alongside the participating countries, has influenced the EHEA countries in the process of policy reform. The influence has extended to other world regions as an example from which to simulate aspects and to take lessons learned.

GLOBAL TRENDS IN REGIONAL INTEGRATION OF HIGHER EDUCATION

The Bologna Process's policy reforms in Europe have been simulated by other regions of the world. Across regions, the degree of integration in higher education varies, from discursive originations as in Latin America to broader extents of cooperation as in Asia. As countries embrace democratic trends that provide opportunities for global citizenship, elites are challenged and there is greater pressure on educational institutions to serve the broader society (Ansell 2008; Kamens 2012:203). The following are some examples of how the international policy convergence, as undertaken by the EHEA, has been applied to other regional integration schemes.

The Bologna Process has provided a model for delivering and evaluating higher education for countries in the EHEA and beyond. In Africa, Asia, Latin America, and North America, there are examples of international cooperation in higher education and research. An Italian diplomat, Consul General explained that EU Member States have been involved in bilateral international development initiatives in higher education, guided by the Bologna Process (Nava 2013). As former head of the Unit for Scholarships in the Directorate General for Development Aid at the Foreign Ministry of Italy in Rome, Fabrizio Nava worked with students from the Balkans and the Middle East beyond the EHEA. Among the initial Erasmus students who studied in Italy, Nava said, "The Bologna Process was and still is the only beacon that all these countries have to orientate the fundamental requirements for studying abroad". Countries and territories in the regional neighborhood, such as Egypt and Palestine, have evaluated curricula for studies abroad within the parameters of the degrees, credits, and quality assurance systems established by the Bologna Process. Nava attributes the end of the Cold War and the political transitions of countries as a central precursor to this initiative of internationalization in higher education. As an accelerator for globalization in the early 1990s, the political transformations across Central and

Eastern Europe provided impetus for globalization of the economy and correspondingly higher education. Working toward academic recognition was among the objectives for bringing Central and Eastern European countries into EU accession (Nava 2013).

The European Commission's curriculum development initiative, *Tuning*, has a program for Africa called "Tuning Africa". The neighborhood policies of the EU extend into North Africa, which has been an area of heightened interest politically since the Arab Spring in early 2011. Supported by the African Union, the African Higher Education Harmonization and Tuning Project (Tuning Africa), is part of the Africa–EU strategic partnership (Tuning Africa 2013). To implement the Plan of Action for the Second Decade of Education for Africa (2006–2015), the African Union Commission has established a framework for policy convergence of Higher Education Programmes in Africa (Woldegiorgis 2013:20). The EU initiative *Tuning* is a template for regional integration in higher education. This policy diffusion has influenced the South African Development Community SADC and MercoSur across policy areas (Lenz 2012).

The Ibero-American countries, which have historic ties to Portugal and Spain, encompass most countries in Latin America. The political will to make regional higher education cooperation a policy priority is needed to elevate the issue and to develop more formal structures of cooperation (Llavori 2016). The Interuniversity Center for Development (*Centro Interuniversitario de Desarollo*), known as CINDA, based in Santiago, Chile is an association of Ibero-American member institutions that shares best practices. The guidance of the Spanish national quality assurance agency, *Agencia Nacional de Evaluación de la Calidad y Acreditación* (ANECA), extends beyond Spain to support quality assurance and accreditation in higher education through involvement with the Ibero-American Network for Quality Assurance in Higher Education (RIACES) based in Asunción, Paraguay.

In South America, there have been efforts historically to cooperate in higher education with MercoSur-Educativo. Both MercoSur-Educativo and the Bologna Process higher education reforms are impacted by economic globalization (Vergera and Hermo 2010). Since its founding in 1991 by the Treaty of Asunción, MercoSur—the common market of the southern cone in South America—has not experienced the deepening of economic integration on par with the EU. However, even prior to the launch of the Bologna Process in 1999, there were efforts in the 1990s to converge higher education policy with MercoSur-Educativo (Vergera and Hermo 2010:112). These preliminary efforts did not formally institutionalize higher education reforms as took place with the Bologna Process. The comparably moderate pace of integration in economics and higher education through MercoSur is even less for the regional trade area of the Andean Community that was established in 1969 with the Cartagena Agreement. Some countries—such as Brazil and Venezuela—have vacillated in their alliances within regional groups in South America, and trade negotiations beyond the region have merited attention. New trends in regional integration in Latin America have emerged in the past decade. The Community of Latin American and Caribbean States (CELAC) was formed in 2010, and it is the second largest group of countries in the region after the Organization of American States. The Union of South American Nations (UNASUR), formed in 2008 among 12 countries, has not taken up higher education cooperation as a policy priority. The primacy of state sovereignty, which may limit regional cooperation in political economy, is a trend observed in international politics to a greater extent in Latin America than in the EU (Gomez-Mera 2013; Malamud 2012).

Potential collaboration in higher education and research were agenda issues covered in the bilateral meeting of the presidents of Mexico and United States in May 2013 (U.S. Department of State 2013). Framed at the discursive level as an "emerging issue", there are opportunities for mobility of higher education, research, and workforce development between the countries (Vassar and Barrett 2014; Wood 2013). The rigidities facing mobility of human capital and labor in North America reflect a decades-long struggle for immigration reform. The regional economic relationship was formalized with the North American Free Trade Agreement (NAFTA) in effect as of 1994, and the resulting economic cooperation has led to opportunities for developing human capital in North America. As is the case to elevate a policy priority across Ibero-American countries, strengthening domestic political will on both sides of this bilateral relationship is necessary to advance international mobility of human capital in higher education, research, and labor markets (Studer 2012a, b).

The Pacific-coast Latin American countries—Chile, Colombia, Costa Rica, Mexico, and Peru—have an orientation toward Asia, which is reflected in their 2011 Pacific Alliance partnership. The Pacific Alliance gives these countries a united position in negotiating trade with Asian countries and the world. An early goal of the alliance has been to "create a joint university system where, much like in Europe, students will be able to get credits for their studies in any of the bloc's member countries" (Oppenheimer 2012). Representatives from the Association of Southeast Asian Nations (ASEAN) were present as observers and participants in the Bologna Policy Forum at the EHEA Ministerial Conferences in Bucharest in 2012 and in Yerevan in 2015. In 2005, the ASEAN ministers of education embarked upon regional higher education collaboration with the decision to hold the ASEAN Education Ministers' Meetings (ASED). The Asia Pacific Quality Network (APQN), similar to the ENQA and EQAR for the EHEA, was established to support the national higher education quality assurance agencies.

The preceding are examples of efforts and ongoing considerations for convergence in higher education policy within world regions. In keeping with the Bologna Process, "a distinguishing feature of policy convergence is that the process is owned by nation-states, but the activities are facilitated by regional institutions", as convergence assumes regional and national policy levels (Woldegiorgis 2013:21). The title of the Sorbonne Declaration emphasizes harmonization of policies in the "Joint declaration on the harmonization of the architecture of the European higher education system." The Bologna Process went further to emphasize convergence, to support the national prerogatives that maintain diversity, while coordinating with participating countries on the criteria of the EHEA. Diversity is a key EHEA asset connected to countries' cultural, linguistic, and historical backgrounds, making the Bologna Process like a symphony. Though each country has its own instrument, they play together in harmony (Lagier 2013). The instruments for institutional change are the degree structure, quality assurance, and international academic recognition, toward which the participating countries have converged with higher education policy reform.

Worldwide, there are examples of regional integration through higher education that have some reference to the Bologna Process and the EHEA (Vögtle 2010). The United Nations Educational, Cultural, and Scientific Organization, a partner in the Bologna Process, will convene the Global Convention on the Recognition of Higher Education Qualifications (UNESCO 2015). In 2018 the UNESCO global convention and the 20th anniversary of the Sorbonne Declaration take place in Paris, France.

THE SECOND DECADE OF THE BOLOGNA PROCESS

The second decade of the Bologna Process, reflecting the institutions and ideas of a Europe of Knowledge, is one with greater emphasis on higher education in policy, economy, and society (Corbett 2005; Bourdan 2012). The number of countries, and the extent of their objectives in the regional integration of higher education, participating in the EHEA are unparalleled in other world regions. As the EHEA continues to be developed to achieve its commitments through the year 2020, the lessons from the Bologna Process are valuable (European Higher Education Area 2012). The European University Association's report *Trends 2010: A Decade of Change in European Higher Education* reviews the progress in the decade that preceded the establishment of the EHEA in 2010. By 2010, 95 percent of the higher education institutions had implemented the degree structure requirements. In comparison by 2003, 53 percent of the countries had implemented the degree structure requirements (Sursock and Smidt 2010:7). There has been continued emphasis on enhancing the quality of teaching and student-centered learning, which has been reaffirmed by the European Commission and the EHEA ministers of education. Concerns about the social dimension and employability are also at the forefront for graduates, and these relate to the dual purposes of education.

The dual purposes of education, for sociocultural development and economic development, are central to the values of stakeholders in the Bologna Process. These dual purposes are intertwined, and the institutional theories that are the basis for the Bologna Process frame each purpose accordingly: sociological institutional theories for sociocultural issues and rational institutional theories for economic development. There are dual roles of higher education institutions as recipients of policy change at the national and European levels, and as agents of policy change in the knowledge economy. The goal for broadened access to higher education attainment is in tandem with the incentives for innovation and internationalization as universities evolve over time (Mazza et al. 2008). There are a greater number of stakeholders in the higher education system today and in the European economic space (Rosamond 2002).

Since the granting of managerial autonomy from the state to European universities in the 1980s and 1990s, universities have become engaged with a third actor in the economic market (Regini 2011:4).

With the growth of globalization and the quest for research programs to support innovation, the private sector of the market has become increasingly attractive as an actor in higher education, gaining strength as globalization intensifies. Higher education institutions have responded with an interest in partnering with the private sector in research initiatives as part of internationalization. For market logic to become potentially relevant in a higher education system, universities must first acquire an identity and the ability to pursue their organizational interests autonomously (Regini 2011:5).

Institutional theories in political economy frame the research done for this book. A historical institutional perspective emphasizes the importance of space and time for understanding social change (Pierson 2004). It bridges the rational and sociological institutional perspectives that explain the motivations and the sociological embeddedness of institutional change (Hall and Taylor 1996). This book examines theories of rational institutionalism that relate to intergovernmentalism and those of sociological institutionalism that relate to Europeanization to explain the processes of international policy convergence in a historical institutional perspective. There is a rational logic of expected consequences and a sociological logic of appropriateness in implementing the Bologna Process. These logics are complementary and are beneficial when seen as a conversation rather than a debate (Fearon and Wendt 2002). A logic of expected consequences from rational theory and a logic of appropriateness from social constructivist and sociological theory, respectively, explain incentives to compete in the economy and to strengthen epistemic communities. A rational choice perspective is useful to explain why institutions continue to exist: "The persistence of institutions depends on the benefits it can deliver" (Hall and Taylor 1996:952). As long as the EHEA continues to deliver benefits to the participating members, such as trust building through quality assurance and facilitating mobility in higher education and employment, it will continue to exist. The European values and the objectives to achieve increased international mobility of students complement the social dimension of higher education. Rational institutionalism and the logic of expected consequences frame the motivations for participation in the EHEA. Sociological institutionalism identifies the co-constitution of agency, stakeholder agents, and structure in higher education reform. The former informs expectations in national and European outcomes, and the latter informs development of national and European identity. In the 1990s, the emergent democracies of Central and Eastern European countries embraced the opportunity to associate with Europe, politically as well as educationally and culturally, part of which led to the Bologna Process. The cultural and sociological dimensions provide a normative influence that is transformative (Powell and DiMaggio 1991). Social learning takes place in European policy making (Radaelli 2008). In higher education, examples of normative influences have been the coordination of policies for quality assessment and the growth in the significance of international rankings (Regini 2011:210). The stakeholders in the academic, public, and private sectors experience change within the constraints of institutional structures.

As a result of decades of regional integration, understandings and commitments develop through the process of cooperation. These take place within a rationally motivated liberal intergovernmentalism and a sociologically diffused Europeanization that are redefined as intertwined:

> A strong liberal of constructivist analysis...would suggest that four decades of cooperation may have transformed a positive interdependence of outcomes into a collective "European identity" in terms of which states increasingly define their self-interests. Even if egoistic reasons were its starting point, the process of cooperating tends to redefine those reasons by reconstituting identities and interests in terms of new intersubjective understandings and commitments. (Wendt 1992:417)

New intersubjective understandings and commitments evolved over the first decade of the Bologna Process. In its second decade, historical institutionalism remains relevant, providing the perspective to understand the institutionally embedded policy change over time (Pierson 2004). Since the post-World War II years, there have been ongoing developments in higher education policy in Europe (Corbett 2005). European politics together with domestic politics and international pressures have influenced each country on its own path-dependent trajectory. In 1968 students made their voices heard in social protests across Europe. This brought the student stakeholders more visibly onto the stage of university governance. Since then, non-state stakeholders in higher education, as from the marketplace of the private sector, have become increasingly interested in educational outcomes for employability. They also have had an increasingly larger presence as potential partners in research and innovation. The countries used as case studies, Portugal and Spain, demonstrated that the public sector advocacy coalition of stakeholders is the dominant stakeholder in the national contexts of policy implementation in the Iberian countries.

Since 1986, Erasmus, the European Commission-sponsored international exchange program, has been one of the most meaningful international initiatives of the EU. The flagship program, Erasmus, captured the spirit of the EU, reflecting its motto "unity in diversity". This inspired the Sorbonne Declaration in 1998 that led to the Bologna Process in 1999, and participating countries made commitments to create the EHEA by 2010. The Bologna Process has been more challenging because it has a greater number of elemental components than Erasmus, encompassing entire academic degree structures and quality assurance. Rather than a beginning, the Bologna Process is the end stage of a process—reform of higher education governance and rules—that has been taking place since the advancement of neoliberal principles in the last decades of the twentieth century (Schmidt and Thatcher 2013). It is a progressive stage in neoliberal cooperation in higher education (Neave 2009). "The Bologna Process should be regarded as means to an end: its main goal is to provide the educational component necessary for the construction of a Europe of knowledge within a broad humanistic vision and in the context of massified higher education systems" (Sursock and Smidt 2010:9).

As a model for regional integration of higher education for other world regions, the Bologna Process and the corresponding Erasmus program continue to expand their reach. Amid contemporary economic and political struggles in the EU, Erasmus and the subsequent Bologna Process are the cultural and educational exchange mechanisms that may be the most positive aspect of the ever-closer union for the Member States and neighboring states in the region of Europe (Ellwood 2013). Higher education policy, like all policy, requires some economic and political negotiation (at multiple levels of governance in the EHEA), for its reforms to go into effect (Musselin 2008). Struggles among stakeholder groups in the Bologna Process take place as they compete for resources in the political economy.

When the EHEA education ministers meet in Paris in the spring of 2018, the meeting will mark 20 years since the Sorbonne Declaration signed by France, Germany, Italy, and the UK, which set the Bologna Process in motion. National cultures and historic traditions provide essential information for a complete understanding of policy reform in a qualitative sense—an understanding that is limited by analysis of quantitative factors alone. Qualitative analysis reveals the influences of history, culture, and tradition on legislative processes at the national levels. Taken together, the multi-method research approach provides a comprehensive analysis (Goertz and Mahoney 2012). Collaboration in higher education has advanced the convergence of higher education policy on academic degrees and complemented the mobility of the four freedoms in the common market, especially the mobility of labor as concerns student graduates. It has not been without challenges and obstacles, including restrictions on funding available to students, professors, and institutions, as well as limited leadership and organizational capacity at various levels of governance. Future studies may assess how public and private universities compare in policy reform within countries and across the EHEA. Of particular relevance is future research on the role of higher education institutions in contributing to tangible socioeconomic outcomes in the knowledge economy and the knowledge society (Temple 2012). The Bologna Declaration of 1999 captured the essence of a "Europe of Knowledge" (European Commission 1997). This terminology, or linguistic discourse, is valuable in a social constructivist perspective that relies upon language shared inter-subjectively to create meaning:

> A Europe of Knowledge is now widely recognised as an irreplaceable factor for social and human growth and as an indispensable component to consolidate and enrich the European citizenship, capable of giving its citizens the necessary competencies to face the challenges of the new millennium, together with an awareness of shared values and belonging to a common social and cultural space. (Bologna Declaration 1999)

The broader context of the EHEA, for the 48 participating countries, and the Europe 2020 economic growth strategy, for the EU Member States, remains relevant to the second decade of the Bologna Process. Taking lessons from regional integration of higher education in Europe, initiatives have begun in other world regions to replicate aspects of the Bologna Process. These lessons are directly related to the political economy context that has influenced the policy reform and implementation at the national level.

The explanatory variables in politics, economics, and sociology have driven institutional change at the national level. Domestically, political and economic conditions influence decisions to serve the state's interests in a rationally motivated manner that leads to liberal inter-governmentalism. The countries participating in the Bologna Process have decided, with varying degrees of interest, to adopt the EHEA criteria by cooperating in intergovernmental efforts of policy coordination (Neave and Maassen 2007). Internationally, influences of Europeanization stemming from the European level of governance act upon national governments that make laws to adopt the EHEA criteria. Europeanization is a sociological institutional influence, given that the European and national levels of policy interactions are co-constituted within the given constraints of social actors (Börzel and Risse 2012; Radaelli 2008). Pressures from domestic and international policy interests influence policy coordination and international relationship strategy (Keohane and Milner 1996; Milner 1997). Framing this analysis throughout decades since the start of the European project for regional integration after World War II, the historical institutional perspective connects rational and sociological institutional policy factors (Hall 2010; Hall and Taylor 1996).

To understand institutional change at a national level, both the higher education institutional system and the country's status in the knowledge economy must be considered. Despite success in higher education attainment, there remains a struggle for sufficient employment opportunities for graduates.[3] Pursuing entrepreneurial activities has been outside the historic cultural norm in Europe, and opportunities vary across countries given national regulations (World Bank Group 2013). The national and societal concerns about employment opportunities after graduation have become a broader regional concern, reflected in the inclusion of employment and higher education as core areas in the economic growth strategy Europe 2020. Assessing the challenges and opportunities in the employment dimension, following higher education, is a potential area for future research.

BEYOND THE SECOND DECADE

The policy outcomes for countries and the region will take years and generations to assess comprehensively. The interaction of the EHEA and the ERA over time will reveal the synergies between higher education and research. As internationalization gains strength in future years, the processes of globalization, intergovernmentalism, and Europeanization that have advanced the Bologna Process may continue to build momentum or may become undermined by national and global influences. It is a challenging time for opening international frontiers, considering the skepticism among some toward globalization and European integration. In the case of higher education, there has been a stronger force to promote spaces of confidence between institutions and between countries through quality assurance and academic recognition through the institutions of the Bologna Process (Llavori 2016).

The Bologna Process has implications for Europe and for other world regions that learn from its example of international cooperation and institutional change. The political economy and policy reform in the EHEA contribute to the evolving conceptions of a society and an economy in which the value placed on knowledge has become more central in Europe and in the world. The Bologna Process is unparalleled, in the number of participating countries and the scope of its policies, enhancing interest in ongoing engagement with it in the second decade of its inception and beyond. The ideas that gave rise to the Bologna Process in 1999 were prescient in discerning that knowledge is more important in the twenty-first century than ever. The institutions that brought to life this new paradigm for international relations in higher education have been constructed to endure for decades. In this century, which coincides with a new millennium, we continue to experience globalization as a compelling force.

NOTES

1. In Portugal, the ministries have changed functions under successive ministers in recent decades. From 2005 to 2011, there was a Ministry of Science, Technology, and Higher Education (Minister Mariano Gago) separate from the Ministry of Education. From 2011 to 2015, there was a unified Ministry of Education and Science (Minister Nuno Crato) as in previous years. From 2015, there has been again a separate Ministry of Science, Technology, and Higher Education (Minister Manuel Heitor).
2. Eurostat. 2016. Tertiary educational attainment by sex, age group 30–34; Tertiary educational attainment—total. Available from: http://epp.eurostat.ec.europa.eu/tgm/table.do?tab=table&init=1&plugin=0&language=en&pcode=t2020_41.
3. Private sector consulting firms such as McKinsey & Co. have addressed this challenge. Under the theme Tackling Youth Unemployment, they have identified the Education to Employment Challenge. Available from: http://mckinseyonsociety.com/education-to-employment/.

REFERENCES

Academic Ranking of World Universities (ARWU). (2016). World university rankings for Spain. Shanghai Ranking Consultancy. Retrieved from http://www.shanghairanking.com/World-University-Rankings-2016/Spain.html.

Ansell, Ben W. (2008). Traders, teachers, and tyrants: Democracy, globalization, and public investment in education. *International Organization, 62*(2), 289–322.

Bologna Process. (1999). The Bologna declaration of 19 June 1999: Joint declaration of the European Ministers of Education.

Börzel, T. A. (2000). From competitive regionalism to cooperative federalism: The Europeanization of the Spanish state of the autonomies. *The Journal of Federalism, 30*(2), 17–42.

Börzel, T. A., & Risse, T. (2012). From Europeanisation to diffusion: Introduction. *West European Politics, 35*(1), 1–19.

Bourdan, M. (2012). *L'Europe des universitaires.* Collection Europa. Grenoble: Presses Universitaires de Grenoble.

Cantwell, B., & Kauppinen, I. (Eds.). (2014). *Academic capitalism in the age of globalization.* Baltimore: Johns Hopkins University Press.

Corbett, A. (2005). *Universities and the Europe of Knowledge: Ideas, institutions and policy entrepreneurship in European union higher education 1955–2005.* New York: Palgrave Macmillan.

Correia Fernandes, Maria de Lurdes. (2012, July 23, 2013, May 29). Professor of the Humanities; Former Vice-Rector, University of Porto, Portuguese Member of the Bologna Follow Up Group (2011–2014).

Dinan, D. (2014). *Origins and evolution of the European union,* 2nd edition. The New European Union Series. Oxford: Oxford University Press.

Ellwood, D. W. (2013, July). Senior Adjunct Professor of European and Eurasian Studies, Johns Hopkins University SAIS Europe. Formerly Associate Professor of Contemporary International History, University of Bologna. Correspondence.

EHEA Pathfinder Group on Automatic Recognition. (2015, January). Report by the EHEA Pathfinder Group on Automatic Recognition. To Present to the Ministers of the Bologna Ministerial in Yerevan, Armenia.

Elken, M., & Stensaker, B. (2012). Policies for quality in higher education coordination and consistency in EU-policy-making 2000–2010. *European Journal of Higher Education, 1*(4), 297–314.

EurActiv. (2013). Eight EU Countries Hit 2020 Education Goals Early: Eurostat. Retrieved April 12, 2013, from http://www.euractiv.com/priorities/eu-countries-hit-2020-education-news-519080.

European Commission. (1997). Towards a Europe of Knowledge. COM(97) 563 final. Communication from the Commission to the Council, the European Parliament, the Economic and Social Committee and the Committee of the Regions. November 12, 1997.

European Commission. (2013a, July 11). *European higher education in the world*. Communication from the Commission to the European Parliament, the European Council, the European Economic and Social Committee and the Committee of the Regions. COM(2013) 499 final.

European Commission. (2013b). Spring 2013 Eurobarometer: A greater dose of optimism. Press Release 23 July 2013, Retrieved from http://ec.europa.eu/public_opinion/archives/eb/eb79/eb79_en.htm.

European Commission. (2015, November 26). European semester thematic fiche: Tertiary education attainment.

European Commission. (2016). Directorate-general for education and culture. *Education and Training Monitor.*

European Higher Education Area. (2012). Ministerial conference and third Bologna policy forum. Retrieved from http://bologna-bucharest2012.ehea.info/background-documents.html.

European Union: High Level Group on the Modernisation of Higher Education. (2013). *Report to the European commission: Improving the quality of teaching and learning in Europe's higher education institutions.* Luxembourg: Publications Office of the European Union.

Fearon, J., & Wendt, A. (2002). Rationalism vs. constructivism: A skeptical view. In W. Carlsnaes, T. Risse, & B. A. Simmons (Eds.), *Handbook of international relations* (pp. 52–72). London: Sage.

Frank, D. J., & Meyer, J. W. (2007). University expansion and the knowledge society. *Theory and Society, 36*(4), 287–311.

Freire, M. R. (2013, May 28). *Assistant Professor, International Relations in Faculty of Economics.* Portugal: University of Coimbra.

Goertz, G., & Mahoney, J. (2012). *A tale of two cultures: Qualitative and quantitative research in the social sciences.* Princeton: Princeton University Press.

Gomez-Mera, L. (2013). *Power and regionalism in Latin America: The politics of MERCOSUR.* Notre Dame, IN: The University of Notre Dame Press.

Hall, P. A. (2010). Historical institutionalism in rational and sociological perspective. In J. Mahoney & K. Thelen (Eds.), *Explaining institutional change: Ambiguity, agency, and power.* Cambridge: Cambridge University Press.

Hall, P. A., & Taylor, R. C. R. (1996). Political science and the three new institutionalisms. *Political Studies, XLIV,* 936–957.

Kamens, D. H. (2012). *Beyond the nation-state: The reconstruction of nationhood and citizenship.* Bingley, UK: Emerald Group Publishing.

Keohane, R. O., & Milner, H. M. (Eds.). (1996). *Internationalization and domestic politics.* New York: Cambridge University Press.

Lagier, H. (2013, February, 2016, September 1). Direction des Relations Européennes et Internationales et de la Coopération (DREIC). Ministère de l'Enseignement supérieur et de la Recherche. Program Officer, European and International Cooperation, Ministry of Higher Education and Research, France. Correspondence.

Lenz, T. (2012). Spurred emulation: The EU and regional integration in Mercosur and SADC. *West European Politics, 35*(1), 155–173.

Lijphart, A. (1999). *Patterns of democracy: Government forms and performance in 36 countries.* New Haven: Yale University Press.

Llavori de Micheo, R. (2013, May 24, 2016, November 16). Director of International Relations ANECA (National Agency for Quality Assessment and Accreditation of Spain) and Board Member, ENQA (European Association for Quality Assurance in Higher Education).

Malamud, A. (2012). Sovereignty in back, integration out: Latin America travails with regionalism. In J. Roy (Ed.), *The state of the union(s): The Eurozone crisis, comparative regional integration and the EU model* (pp. 177–190). Miami: Miami-Florida European Union Center of Excellence.

Martens, K., Knodel, P., & Windzio, M. (2014). *Internationalization of education policy: A new constellation of statehood in education?.* London: Palgrave Macmillan.

Matilla Vicente, C. (2012, July 20, 2013, May 23). Director of International Relations, Secretary General of Universities, Ministry of Education, Spain.

Mazza, C., Quattrone, P., & Riccaboni, A. (Eds.). (2008). *European universities in transition: Issues, models, and cases.* Northampton: Edward Elgar Publishing Limited.

Milner, H. V. (1997). *Interests, institutions, and information: Domestic politics and international relations.* Princeton: Princeton University Press.

Ministry of Education, Culture, and Sport. (2015). *Datos y Cifras del Sistema Universitaria Español, Curso 2015–2016.* Data and Figures of the Spanish University System, School Year 2015-2016.

Molina, I. (2012, July 20, 2016, June 3). Senior Analyst, Europe, Elcano Royal Institute of International and Strategic Studies, Spain.

Moravcsik, A. (1998). *The choice for Europe: Social purpose and state power from Messina to Maastricht.* Ithaca: Cornell University Press.

Moravcsik, A., & Schimmelfennig, F. (2009). Liberal intergovernmentalism. In A. Wiener & T. Diez (Eds.), *European integration theory* (2nd ed.). Oxford: Oxford University Press.

Musselin, C. (2008). Les politiques d'enseignement supérieur. In O. Borraz & V. Guiraudon (Eds.), *Politiques Publiques* (pp. 147–172). Paris: Presses de Sciences Po "Académique".

Nava, F. (2013, January 9). Consul General of Italy in Houston, Texas.

Neave, G. (2009). The Bologna Process as alpha or omega, or, on interpreting history and context as inputs to Bologna, Prague, Berlin, and Beyond. In A. Amaral, G. Neave, C. Musselin, & P. Maassen (Eds.), *European integration and the governance of higher education and research* (pp. 17–58). Dordrecht: Springer.

Neave, G. (2012). *The evaluative state, institutional autonomy and re-engineering higher education in Western Europe: The prince and his pleasure.* London: Palgrave Macmillan.

Neave, G., & Maassen, P. (2007). The Bologna Process: An intergovernmental policy perspective. In P. Maassen & J. P. Olsen (Eds.), *University dynamics and European integration.* Dordrecht: Springer.

Nokkola, T. (2007). The Bologna process and the role of higher education: Discursive construction of the European higher education area. In J. Enders & B. Jongbloed (Eds.), *Public-private dynamics in higher education: Expectations, developments and outcomes* (pp. 221–245). Piscataway: Transaction Publishers.

Nokkola, T. (2012). Institutional autonomy and the attractiveness of the European higher education area—facts or tokenistic discourse. In A. Curaj, P. Scott, L. Vlasceanu, & L. Wilson (Eds.), *European higher education at the crossroad: Between the Bologna Process and national reforms. Parts 1 and 2.* Dordrecht: Springer Science + Business Media.

Oppenheimer, A. (2012, June 11). New 'Pacific Alliance' bloc may have a chance. *Miami Herald.*

Peters, B. G. (2012). *Institutional theory in political science: The new institutionalism* (3rd ed.). New York: Continuum Books.

Pierson, P. (1996). The path to European integration: A historical institutionalist analysis. *Comparative Political Studies, 29*(2), 123–163.

Pierson, P. (2000). Increasing returns, path dependence and the study of politics. *American Political Science Review, 94,* (2).

Pierson, P. (2004). *Politics in time: History, analysis, and social analysis.* Princeton: Princeton University Press.

PORDATA. (2016). Despesas do Estado em educação: execução orçamental em % do PIB—Portugal. Funda Francisco Manuel do Santo. Retrieved from http://www.pordata.pt/Portugal/Despesas+do+Estado+em+educacao+execu cao+orcamental-866.

Radaelli, C. M. (2008, September). Europeanization, policy learning, and new modes of governance. *Journal of Comparative Policy Analysis, 10* (3), 239–254.

Rauhvargers, A., Deane, C., & Pauwels, W. (2009). *Bologna Process stocktaking report 2009: Report from working groups appointed by the Bologna follow-up group to the ministerial conference in Leuven/Louvain-la-Neuve.* Bologna Process Benelux.

Ravinet, P. (2005). The Sorbonne meeting and declaration: Actors, shared vision and Europeanisation. Report for the third conference on *Knowledge and Politics,* University of Bergen.

Regini, M. (2011). *European universities and the challenge of the market: A comparative analysis.* Cheltenham, UK: Edward Elgar.

Renzi, M. (2016, October 19). Speech address at Johns Hopkins university school of advanced international studies (SAIS). Washington, D.C.

Ritzen, J. (2010). *A chance for European universities.* Amsterdam: Amsterdam University Press.

Rosa, M. J., Sarrico, C. S., Tavares, O., & Amaral, A. (2016). *Cross-border higher education and quality assurance: Commerce, the service directive and governing higher education.* London: Palgrave Macmillan.

Rosamond, B. (2002). Imagining the European economy: 'Competitiveness' and the social construction of 'Europe' as an economic space. *New Political Economy, 7*(2), 157–177.

Schmidt, V. A. (2009). The EU and its member states: From bottom up to top down. In D. Phinnemore & A. Warleigh-Lack (Eds.), *Reflections on European integration: 50 years of the treaty of Rome* (pp. 194–211). London: Palgrave Macmillan.

Schmidt, V. A., & Claudio, M. R. (2004). Policy change and discourse in Europe: Conceptual and methodological issues. *West European Politics, 27*(2), 183–210.

Schmidt, V. A., & Thatcher, M. (Eds.). (2013). *Resilient liberalism in Europe's political economy.* Cambridge: Cambridge University Press.

Studer, I. (2012a, December 4). 2012: A New Mexican vision for North American integration. Modern Mexico Task Force, Center for Hemispheric Policy, University of Miami.

Studer, I. (2012b). Mercados de trabajo y capital humano en América del Norte: oportunidades perdidas. *Foro Internacional, 209*(3), 584–627.

Sursock, A., & Smidt, H. (2010). *Trends 2010: A decade of change in European higher education.* Brussels: European Universities Association.

Temple, P. (Ed.). (2012). *Universities in the knowledge economy: Higher education organisation and global change.* London: Routledge.

Teixera, P. (2016, June 14). Vice-Rector and Professor of Economics, University of Porto.

Tuning, Africa. (2013). 2013 year of Pan Africanism and European commission. Retrieved from http://www.tuningafrica.org/.

Tyson, A. (2012, April 25, 2016, September 6). Acting director for strategy and evaluation, former head of UnitC1, higher education and Erasmus, directorate-general education and culture, European commission.

UNESCO. (2015). *Consolidated report on the implementation of the 1993 recommendation on the recognition of studies and qualifications in higher education.* General Conference 38th Session, Paris. 38 C/72 November 2, 2015.

U.S. Department of State. (2013). Fact Sheet. United States-Mexico Bilateral Forum on Higher Education, Innovation, and Research. Retrieved May 2, 2013, from https://2009-2017.state.gov/r/pa/prs/ps/2013/05/208579.htm.

Vassar, D., & Barrett, B. (2014, August 20). U.S.-Mexico academic mobility: Trends, challenges, and opportunities. Mexico Center Issue Brief. Baker Institute for Public Policy, Rice University, Houston, Texas.

Veiga, A., & Amaral, A. (2009). Survey on the implementation of the Bologna Process in Portugal. *Higher Education, 57*(1), 57–69.

Vergera, A., & Javier, P. H. (2010). The governance of higher education regionalisation: Comparative analysis of the Bologna Process and mercosur-educativo. *Globalisation, Societies, and Education, 8*(1), 105–120.

Vögtle, E. M. (2010). Beyond Bologna: The Bologna Process as a global template for higher education reform efforts. Transformation of the State, (Working Papers. No. 129). University of Bremen. Konstanzer Online Publikations System (KOPS).

Wendt, A. (1992). Anarchy is what states make of it: The social construction of power politics. *International Organization, 46*(2), 391–425.

Wiener, A., & Diez, T. (Eds.). (2009). *European integration theory* (2nd ed.). Oxford: Oxford University Press.

Woldegiorgis, E. T. (2013). Conceptualizing harmonization of higher education systems. *Higher Education Studies, 3*(2), 12–23.

Wood, D. (2013). *Educational cooperation and exchanges: An emerging issue.* Washington, D.C.: Wilson Center for International Scholars, Mexico Institute.

World Bank Group. (2013). *Doing business: Measuring business regulation.* Retrieved from http://www.doingbusiness.org/.

World Bank Group. (2016). The Worldwide Governance Indicators (WGI) project. Retrieved from: http://info.worldbank.org/governance/wgi/index.aspx.

Erratum to: Globalization and Change in Higher Education

Erratum to:
B. Barrett, *Globalization and Change in Higher Education*,
https://doi.org/10.1007/978-3-319-52368-2

The original version of the book was inadvertently published with some errors in Appendix, Appendix reference and Index, which have been now corrected.

The updated online version of this book can be found at
https://doi.org/10.1007/978-3-319-52368-2

© The Editor(s) (if applicable) and The Author(s) 2017   E1
B. Barrett, *Globalization and Change in Higher Education*,
https://doi.org/10.1007/978-3-319-52368-2_11

Appendix A:
Treaty of Lisbon, Signed December 17, 2007, Effective December 1, 2009

TITLE XII: Education, Vocational Training, Youth and Sport

Article 165 (ex Article 149 TEC)

1. The Union shall contribute to the development of quality education by encouraging cooperation between Member States and, if necessary, by supporting and supplementing their action, while fully respecting the responsibility of the Member States for the content of teaching and the organization of education systems and their cultural and linguistic diversity. The Union shall contribute to the promotion of European sporting issues, while taking account of the specific nature of sport, its structures based on voluntary activity, and its social and educational function.

2. Union action shall be aimed at:
   - developing the European dimension in education, particularly through the teaching and dissemination of the languages of the Member States,
   - encouraging mobility of students and teachers, by encouraging *inter alia*, the academic recognition of diplomas and periods of study,
   - promoting cooperation between educational establishments,
   - developing exchanges of information and experience on issues common to the education systems of the Member States,

© The Editor(s) (if applicable) and The Author(s) 2017
B. Barrett, *Globalization and Change in Higher Education*,
DOI 10.1007/978-3-319-52368-2

- encouraging the development of youth exchanges and of exchanges of socioeducational instructors, and encouraging the participation of young people in democratic life in Europe,
- encouraging the development of distance education,
- developing the European dimension in sport, by promoting fairness and openness in sporting competitions and cooperation between bodies responsible for sports, and by protecting the physical and moral integrity of sportsmen and sportswomen, especially the youngest sportsmen and sportswomen.

3. The Union and the Member States shall foster cooperation with third countries and the competent international organizations in the field of education and sport, in particular the Council of Europe.

4. In order to contribute to the achievement of the objectives referred to in this Article:
   - the European Parliament and the Council, acting in accordance with the ordinary legislative procedure, after consulting the Economic and Social Committee and the Committee of the Regions, shall adopt incentive measures, excluding any harmonization of the laws and regulations of the Member States,
   - the Council, on a proposal from the Commission, shall adopt recommendations

Article 166 (ex Article 150 TEC)

1. The Union shall implement a vocational training policy which shall support and supplement the action of the Member States, while fully respecting the responsibility of the Member States for the content and organization of vocational training.

2. Union action shall aim to:
   - facilitate adaptation to industrial changes, in particular through vocational training and retraining,
   - improve initial and continuing vocational training in order to facilitate vocational integration and reintegration into the labor market,
   - facilitate access to vocational training and encourage mobility of instructors and trainees and particularly young people,
   - stimulate cooperation on training between educational or training establishments and firms,

- develop exchanges of information and experience on issues common to the training systems of the Member States.
3. The Union and the Member States shall foster cooperation with third countries and the competent international organizations in the sphere of vocational training.
4. The European Parliament and the Council, acting in accordance with the ordinary legislative procedure and after consulting the Economic and Social Committee and the Committee of the Regions, shall adopt measures to contribute to the achievement of the objectives referred to in this Article, excluding any harmonization of the laws and regulations of the Member States.

Appendix B:
The Bologna Declaration, June 19, 1999—Bologna, Italy

Joint declaration of the European Ministers of Education

The European process, thanks to the extraordinary achievements of the past few years, has become an increasingly concrete and relevant reality for the Union and its citizens. Enlargement prospects together with deepening relations with other European countries, provide even wider dimensions to that reality.

Meanwhile, we are witnessing a growing awareness in large parts of the political and academic world and in public opinion of the need to establish a more complete and far-reaching Europe, in particular building upon and strengthening its intellectual, cultural, social, and scientific and technological dimensions.

A Europe of Knowledge is now widely recognized as an irreplaceable factor for social and human growth and as an indispensable component to consolidate and enrich the European citizenship, capable of giving its citizens the necessary competences to face the challenges of the new millennium, together with an awareness of shared values and belonging to a common social and cultural space.

The importance of education and educational cooperation in the development and strengthening of stable, peaceful, and democratic societies is universally acknowledged as paramount, the more so in view of the situation in Southeast Europe.

The Sorbonne declaration of May 25, 1998, which was underpinned by these considerations, stressed the universities' central role in

© The Editor(s) (if applicable) and The Author(s) 2017
B. Barrett, *Globalization and Change in Higher Education*,
DOI 10.1007/978-3-319-52368-2

developing European cultural dimensions. It emphasized the creation of the European area of higher education as a key way to promote citizens' mobility and employability and the continent's overall development.

Several European countries have accepted the invitation to commit themselves to achieving the objectives set out in the declaration, by signing it or expressing their agreement in principle. The direction taken by several higher education reforms launched in the meantime in Europe has proved many governments' determination to act.

European higher education institutions, for their part, have accepted the challenge and taken up a main role in constructing the European area of higher education, also in the wake of the fundamental principles laid down in the Bologna Magna Charta Universitatum of 1988. This is of the highest importance, given that universities' independence and autonomy ensure that higher education and research systems continuously adapt to changing needs, society's demands, and advances in scientific knowledge.

The course has been set in the right direction and with meaningful purpose. The achievement of greater compatibility and comparability of the systems of higher education nevertheless requires continual momentum in order to be fully accomplished. We need to support it through promoting concrete measures to achieve tangible forward steps. The 18 June meeting saw participation by authoritative experts and scholars from all our countries and provides us with very useful suggestions on the initiatives to be taken.

We must in particular look at the objective of increasing the international competitiveness of the European system of higher education. The vitality and efficiency of any civilization can be measured by the appeal that its culture has for other countries. We need to ensure that the European higher education system acquires a worldwide degree of attraction equal to our extraordinary cultural and scientific traditions.

While affirming our support to the general principles laid down in the Sorbonne declaration, we engage in coordinating our policies to reach in the short term, and in any case within the first decade of the third millennium, the following objectives, which we consider to be of primary relevance in order to establish the European area of higher education and to promote the European system of higher education worldwide:

Adoption of a system of **easily readable and comparable degrees**, also through the implementation of the Diploma Supplement, in order to promote European citizens' employability and the international competitiveness of the European higher education system.

Adoption of a system essentially based on **two main cycles**, undergraduate and graduate. Access to the second cycle shall require successful completion of first cycle studies, lasting a minimum of three years. The degree awarded after the first cycle shall also be relevant to the European labor market as an appropriate level of qualification. The second cycle should lead to the master and/or doctorate degree as in many European countries.

Establishment of a **system of credits**—such as in the ECTS system—as a proper means of promoting the most widespread student mobility. Credits could also be acquired in nonhigher educational contexts, including lifelong learning, provided they are recognized by the receiving universities concerned.

Promotion of **mobility** by overcoming obstacles to the effective exercise of free movement with particular attention to:

- for students, access to study and training opportunities and to related services
- for teachers, researchers, and administrative staff, recognition and valorization of periods spent in a European context researching, teaching, and training, without prejudicing their statutory rights.

Promotion of **European cooperation in quality assurance** with a view to developing comparable criteria and methodologies.

Promotion of the **necessary European dimensions in higher education**, particularly with regard to curricular development, interinstitutional cooperation, mobility schemes, and integrated programs of study, training, and research.

We hereby undertake to attain these objectives—within the framework of our institutional competences and taking full respect of the diversity of cultures, languages, national education systems, and of university autonomy—to consolidate the European area of higher education. To that end, we will pursue the ways of intergovernmental cooperation, together with those of nongovernmental European organizations with competence on higher education. We expect universities again to respond promptly and positively and to contribute actively to the success of our endeavor.

Convinced that the establishment of the European area of higher education requires constant support, supervision, and adaptation to the continuously evolving needs, we decide to meet again within two years in order to assess the progress achieved and the new steps to be taken.

Appendix C:
Convention on the Recognition of Qualifications concerning Higher Education in the European Region, Preamble, June 11, 1997—Lisbon, Portugal

The Treaty of Lisbon amending the Treaty on European Union and the Treaty establishing the European Community entered into force on December 1, 2009. As a consequence, as from that date, any reference to the European Community shall be read as the European Union.

The Parties to this Convention:

Conscious of the fact that the right to education is a human right, and that higher education, which is instrumental in the pursuit and advancement of knowledge, constitutes an exceptionally rich cultural and scientific asset for both individuals and society;

Considering that higher education should play a vital role in promoting peace, mutual understanding and tolerance, and in creating mutual confidence among peoples and nations;

Considering that the great diversity of education systems in the European region reflects its cultural, social, political, philosophical, religious, and economic diversity, an exceptional asset which should be fully respected;

Desiring to enable all people of the region to benefit fully from this rich asset of diversity by facilitating access by the inhabitants of each State and by the students of each Party's educational institutions to the educational resources of the other Parties, more specifically by facilitating their efforts to continue their education or to complete a period of studies in higher education institutions in those other Parties;

© The Editor(s) (if applicable) and The Author(s) 2017
B. Barrett, *Globalization and Change in Higher Education,*
DOI 10.1007/978-3-319-52368-2

Considering that the recognition of studies, certificates, diplomas, and degrees obtained in another country of the European region represents an important measure for promoting academic mobility between the Parties;

Attaching great importance to the principle of institutional autonomy, and conscious of the need to uphold and protect this principle;

Convinced that a fair recognition of qualifications is a key element of the right to education and a responsibility of society;

Having regard to the Council of Europe and UNESCO Conventions covering academic recognition in Europe:

- European Convention on the Equivalence of Diplomas leading to Admission to Universities (1953, CETS No. 15), and its Protocol (1964, CETS No. 49);
- European Convention on the Equivalence of Periods of University Study (1956, CETS No. 21);
- European Convention on the Academic Recognition of University Qualifications (1959, CETS No. 32);
- Convention on the Recognition of Studies, Diplomas, and Degrees concerning Higher Education in the States belonging to the Europe Region (1979);
- European Convention on the General Equivalence of Periods of University Study (1990, CETS No. 138);

Having regard also to the International Convention on the Recognition of Studies, Diplomas and Degrees in Higher Education in the Arab and European States bordering on the Mediterranean (1976), adopted within the framework of UNESCO and partially covering academic recognition in Europe;

Mindful that this Convention should also be considered in the context of the UNESCO conventions and the international recommendation covering other Regions of the world, and of the need for an improved exchange of information between these Regions;

Conscious of the wide ranging changes in higher education in the European region since these conventions were adopted, resulting in considerably increased diversification within and between national higher education systems, and of the need to adapt the legal instruments and practice to reflect these developments;

Conscious of the need to find common solutions to practical recognition problems in the European region;

Conscious of the need to improve current recognition practice and to make it more transparent and better adapted to the current situation of higher education in the European region;

Confident of the positive significance of a convention elaborated and adopted under the joint auspices of the Council of Europe and UNESCO providing a framework for the further development of recognition practices in the European region;

Conscious of the importance of providing permanent implementation mechanisms in order to put the principles and provisions of the current Convention into practice.

Appendix D:
Treaty of Maastricht, Signed February 7, 1992, Effective November 1, 1993

CHAPTER 3
EDUCATION, VOCATIONAL TRAINING, AND YOUTH
ARTICLE 126

1. The Community shall contribute to the development of quality education by encouraging cooperation between Member States and, if necessary, by supporting and supplementing their action, while fully respecting the responsibility of the Member States for the content of teaching and the organization of education systems and their cultural and linguistic diversity.

2. Community action shall be aimed at:
   - developing the European dimension in education, particularly through the teaching and dissemination of the languages of the Member States;
   - encouraging mobility of students and teachers, *inter alia* by encouraging the academic recognition of diplomas and periods of study;
   - promoting cooperation between educational establishments;
   - developing exchanges of information and experience on issues common to
   - the education systems of the Member States;
   - encouraging the development of youth exchanges and of exchanges of socioeducational

© The Editor(s) (if applicable) and The Author(s) 2017   255
B. Barrett, *Globalization and Change in Higher Education*,
DOI 10.1007/978-3-319-52368-2

- instructors;
- encouraging the development of distance education.

3. The Community and the Member States shall foster cooperation with third countries and the competent international organizations in the field of education, in particular the Council of Europe.

4. In order to contribute to the achievement of the objectives referred to in this Article, the Council:

- acting in accordance with the procedure referred to in Article 189b, after consulting the Economic and Social Committee and the Committee of the Regions, shall adopt incentive measures, excluding any harmonization of the laws and regulations of the Member States;
- acting by a qualified majority on a proposal from the Commission, shall adopt recommendations.

Appendix E:
European Cultural Convention,
December 19, 1954—Paris, France

The governments signatory hereto, being members of the Council of Europe,

Considering that the aim of the Council of Europe is to achieve a greater unity between its members for the purpose, among others, of safeguarding and realizing the ideals and principles which are their common heritage;

Considering that the achievement of this aim would be furthered by a greater understanding of one another among the peoples of Europe;

Considering that for these purposes it is desirable not only to conclude bilateral cultural conventions between members of the Council but also to pursue a policy of common action designed to safeguard and encourage the development of European culture;

Having resolved to conclude a general European Cultural Convention designed to foster among the nationals of all members, and of such other European States as may accede thereto, the study of the languages, history and civilization of the others and of the civilization which is common to them all,

Have agreed as follows:

© The Editor(s) (if applicable) and The Author(s) 2017
B. Barrett, *Globalization and Change in Higher Education*,
DOI 10.1007/978-3-319-52368-2

Article 1

Each Contracting Party shall take appropriate measures to safeguard and to encourage the development of its national contribution to the common cultural heritage of Europe.

Article 2

Each Contracting Party shall, insofar as may be possible:

a. encourage the study by its own nationals of the languages, history, and civilization of the other Contracting Parties and grant facilities to those Parties to promote such studies in its territory; and
b. endeavor to promote the study of its language or languages, history and civilization in the territory of the other Contracting Parties and grant facilities to the nationals of those Parties to pursue such studies in its territory.

Article 3

The Contracting Parties shall consult with one another within the framework of the Council of Europe with a view to concerted action in promoting cultural activities of European interest.

Article 4

Each Contracting Party shall, insofar as may be possible, facilitate the movement and exchange of persons as well as of objects of cultural value so that Articles 2 and 3 may be implemented.

Article 5

Each Contracting Party shall regard the objects of European cultural value placed under its control as integral parts of the common cultural heritage of Europe, shall take appropriate measures to safeguard them and shall ensure reasonable access thereto.

Article 6

1. Proposals for the application of the provisions of the present Convention and questions relating to the interpretation thereof shall be considered at meetings of the Committee of Cultural Experts of the Council of Europe.
2. Any State not a member of the Council of Europe which has acceded to the present Convention in accordance with the provisions of paragraph 4 of Article 9 may appoint a representative or representatives to participate in the meetings provided for in the preceding paragraph.
3. The conclusions reached at the meetings provided for in paragraph 1 of this article shall be submitted in the form of recommendations to the Committee of Ministers of the Council of Europe, unless they are decisions which are within the competence of the Committee of Cultural Experts as relating to matters of an administrative nature which do not entail additional expenditure.
4. The Secretary General of the Council of Europe shall communicate to the members of the Council and to the government of any State which has acceded to the present Convention any decisions relevant thereto which may be taken by the Committee of Ministers or by the Committee of Cultural Experts.
5. Each Contracting Party shall notify the Secretary General of the Council of Europe in due course of any action which may be taken by it for the application of the provisions of the present Convention consequent on the decisions of the Committee of Ministers or of the Committee of Cultural Experts.
6. In the event of certain proposals for the application of the present Convention being found to interest only a limited number of the Contracting Parties, such proposals may be further considered in accordance with the provisions of Article 7, provided that their implementation entails no expenditure by the Council of Europe.

Article 7

If, in order to further the aims of the present Convention, two or more Contracting Parties desire to arrange meetings at the seat of the Council of Europe other than those specified in paragraph 1 of Article 6, the Secretary General of the Council shall afford them such administrative assistance as they may require.

Article 8

Nothing in the present Convention shall be deemed to affect:

a. the provisions of any existing bilateral cultural convention to which any of the Contracting Parties may be signatory or to render less desirable the conclusion of any further such convention by any of the Contracting Parties, or
b. the obligation of any person to comply with the laws and regulations in force in the territory of any Contracting Party concerning the entry, residence and departure of foreigners.

Article 9

1. The present Convention shall be open to the signature of the members of the Council of Europe. It shall be ratified, and the instruments of ratification shall be deposited with the Secretary General of the Council of Europe.
2. As soon as three signatory governments have deposited their instruments of ratification, the present Convention shall enter into force as between those governments.
3. With respect to each signatory government ratifying subsequently, the Convention shall enter into force on the date of deposit of its instrument of ratification.
4. The Committee of Ministers of the Council of Europe may decide, by a unanimous vote, to invite, upon such terms and conditions as it deems appropriate, any European State which is not a member of the Council to accede to the present Convention. Any State so invited may accede by depositing its instrument of accession with the Secretary General of the Council of Europe. Such accession shall take effect on the date of receipt of the said instrument.
5. The Secretary General of the Council of Europe shall notify all members of the Council and any acceding States of the deposit of all instruments of ratification and accession.

Article 10

Any Contracting Party may specify the territories to which the provisions of the present Convention shall apply by addressing to the Secretary General of the Council of Europe a declaration which shall be communicated by the latter to all the other Contracting Parties.

Article 11

1. Any Contracting Party may denounce the present Convention at any time after it has been in force for a period of five years by means of a notification in writing addressed to the Secretary General of the Council of Europe, who shall inform the other Contracting Parties.
2. Such denunciation shall take effect for the Contracting Party concerned six months after the date on which it is received by the Secretary General of the Council of Europe.

In witness whereof the undersigned, duly authorized thereto by their respective governments, have signed the present Convention.

Done at Paris this 19th day of December 1954, in the English and French languages, both texts being equally authoritative, in a single copy which shall remain deposited in the archives of the Council of Europe. The Secretary General shall transmit certified copies to each of the signatory and acceding governments.

Appendix F: Iberia Data: Key Variables Trends for Portugal and Spain (2000–2014)

© The Editor(s) (if applicable) and The Author(s) 2017
B. Barrett, *Globalization and Change in Higher Education*,
DOI 10.1007/978-3-319-52368-2

Table A.1 Data: economic and education variables of interest (2000–2015)

	2000	2001	2002	2003	2004	2005	2006	2007	2008
Higher education attainment									
Portugal	11.3	11.7	12.9	14.7	16.3	17.5	18.3	19.5	21.6
Spain	29.2	31.3	34.4	35.1	36.9	39.9	39.4	40.9	41.3
GDP per capita									
Portugal	26,147	26,468	26,526	26,180	26,590	26,744	27,111	27,732	27,747
Spain	30,630	31,470	31,848	32,275	32,727	33,377	34,187	34,825	34,657
R&D/GDP									
Portugal	0.72	0.76	0.72	0.7	0.73	0.76	0.95	1.12	1.45
Spain	0.89	0.89	0.96	1.02	1.04	1.1	1.17	1.23	1.32
trade/GDP									
Portugal	67.42	65.06	62.16	60.44	62.76	62.57	68.07	69.65	71.96
Spain	60.24	58.07	54.98	53.11	54.21	54.34	55.66	57.41	55.76
population									
Portugal	10,289,898	10,362,722	10,419,631	10,458,821	10,483,861	10,503,330	10,522,288	10,542,964	10,558,177
Spain	40,263,216	40,756,001	41,431,558	42,187,645	42,921,895	43,653,155	44,397,319	45,226,803	45,954,106
employment									
Portugal	58.5	59	58.8	58	57.6	57.3	57.6	57.6	57.7
Spain	45.5	46.7	47.2	48.3	49.4	51.4	52.6	53.2	52.1
GDP growth									
Portugal	3.79	1.94	0.77	-0.93	1.81	0.77	1.55	2.49	0.2
Spain	5.29	4	2.88	3.19	3.17	3.72	4.17	3.77	1.12

(continued)

Table A.1 (continued)

	2009	2010	2011	2012	2013	2014	2015	Average
Higher education attainment								
Portugal	21.3	24	26.7	27.8	30	31.3		20.3
Spain	40.7	42	41.9	41.5	42.3	42.3		38.6
GDP per capita								
Portugal	26,895	27,393	26,932	25,953	25,800	26,175		26,693
Spain	33,123	32,976	32,530	31,657	31,230	31,750		32,617
R&D/GDP								
Portugal	1.58	1.53	1.46	1.38	1.33	1.29		1.1
Spain	1.35	1.35	1.33	1.28	1.26	1.23		1.16
trade/GDP								
Portugal	61.08	67.3	72.86	75.93	78.03	79.71		68.34
Spain	46.5	52.34	58.09	59.76	60.7	62.6		56.25
population								
Portugal	10,568,247	10,573,100	10,557,560	10,514,844	10,457,295	10,401,062		10,480,920
Spain	46,362,946	46,576,897	46,742,697	46,773,055	46,620,045	46,480,882		44,423,215
employment								
Portugal	56	55.2	53.6	51.5	50.4	51.7		56
Spain	48.3	47.2	46.4	44.5	43.5	44.4		48
GDP growth								
Portugal	-2.98	1.9	-1.83	-4.03	-1.13	0.91	1.45	0.42
Spain	-3.57	0.01	-1	-2.62	-1.67	1.36	3.21	1.69

Data Sources:
Eurostat.2016. Tertiary Education Attainment, R&D Spending as Percentage of GDP, and Employment as a Percentage of the Population
World Bank. 2016. Trade as Percentage of GDP, GDP Growth, GDP Per Capita, and Population
See Quantitative Data Sources (References)

APPENDIX G:
PRIMARY SOURCES OF RESEARCH

Interviews and/or correspondence:

Amaral, Alberto. Founding Director, Centre for Research on Higher Education Policies (CIPES), Matosinhos (Porto) and President of the Administration Council, A3ES Portuguese National Qualifications Agency; July 23, 2012; May 28, 2013; and June 1, 2016.

Amaro de Matos, João. 2012. Associate Dean for International Affairs. NOVA University School of Business. Lisboa, Portugal. July 24, 2012.

Bonete Perales, Rafael. Associate Professor of Applied Economics, and Assessor for the Vice-Chancellor of Internationalization, University of Salamanca. Counselor for Education to the Permanent Delegations of Spain to OECD, UNESCO and the Council of Europe (July 2010-July 2012). Member of the Bologna Follow Up Group for Spain (2008-2012); June 28, 2012 and May 30, 2013.

Corbett, Anne. 2017. Senior Associate, LSE Enterprise. London School of Economics and Political Science. Correspondence. February 27, 2017.

Correia Fernandes, Maria de Lurdes. Professor of the Humanities; Former Vice-Rector, University of Porto, Portuguese Member of the Bologna Follow Up Group (2011-2014); July 23, 2012 and May 29, 2013.

Couto, Priscila Alexandra. Director of Services of Support to the Network of Higher Education (Direção de Serviços de Suporte à Rede do Ensino Superior). Office of Director General for Higher Education (Direção-Geral do Ensino Superior), Ministry of Education and Science (Ministério da Educação e Ciência), Government of Portugal; July 24, 2012; June 1, 2016.

Dale, Roger. Professor of Education, University of Bristol and Founding Editor, *Globalisation Societies, and Education*; July 9, 2012.

Delgado. Luis. Asesor, Secretaría General de Universidades Ministerio de Educaciön, Cultura, y Deporte (MECD). Government of Spain. May 27, 2016.

Delicado, Ana. Researcher, Institute of Social Sciences (ICS-Instituto de Ciências Sociais), University of Lisbon; July 24, 2012.

Ellwood, David William. Senior Adjunct Professor of European and Eurasian Studies, Johns Hopkins University SAIS Europe. Formerly Associate Professor of Contemporary International History, University of Bologna. Correspondence July 2013.

Freire, Maria Raquel. Assistant Professor, International Relations in Faculty of Economics, University of Coimbra, Portugal; May 28, 2013.

Kania, Krzysztof. European Commission, Policy Officer, Directorate General for Education and Culture (DG EAC). Directorate A - Lifelong learning: horizontal policy issues and 2020 strategy, Unit A1 - Education and Training in Europe 2020; country analysis. Correspondence December 2012; September 7, 2016.

Lagier, Hélène. Direction des Relations Européennes et Internationales et de la Coopération (DREIC). Ministère de l'Enseignement supérieur et de la Recherche. Program Officer, European and International Cooperation, Ministry of Higher Education and Research, France. Correspondence February 2013; September 1, 2016.

Llavori de Micheo, Rafael. Director of International Relations ANECA (National Agency for Quality Assessment and Accreditation of Spain) and Board Member, ENQA (European Association for Quality Assurance in Higher Education); May 24, 2013; November 16, 2016.

Malamud, Andrés. Researcher, Institute of Social Sciences (ICS-Instituto de Ciências Sociais), University of Lisbon; July 24, 2012.

Magalhães, António. Professor, Universidade do Porto and Researcher, Centre for Research in Higher Education Policies (CIPES). Matosinhos (Porto), Portugal; May 29, 2013; June 2, 2016.

Matei, Liviu. Chief Operating Officer and Professor of Public Policy, Central European University, Budapest, Hungary. July 18, 2012. (2012a)

Matilla Vicente, Carmen. Director of International Relations, Secretary General of Universities, Ministry of Education, Spain; July 20, 2012 and May 23, 2013.

Molina, Ignacio. Senior Analyst, Europe, Elcano Royal Institute of International and Strategic Studies, Spain; July 20, 2012; June 3, 2016.

Nava, Fabrizio. Consul General of Italy in Houston, Texas. January 9, 2013.

Neave, Guy. Scientific Director, Centre for Research in Higher Education Policies (CIPES), Matosinhos (Porto), Portugal; July 23, 2012. (2012a)

Perez-Gomez, Patricia. 2016. Policy Officer for Portugal and Spain, Directorate General for Education and Culture, European Commission. September 22, 2016.

Prats-Monné, Xavier. 2012, 2016. Director-General for Heath and Food Safety; Former Director General for Education and Culture. European Commission; Correspondence April 2012; September 6, 2016.

Robertson, Susan. Professor of Education, Cambridge University and Founding Editor, *Globalisation Societies, and Education*; July 9, 2012.

Sáinz González, Jorge. Secretario General de Universidades. Ministerio de Educación, Cultura, y Deporte (MECD). Government of Spain. May 30, 2016.

Teixera, Pedro. Vice-Rector and Professor of Economics, University of Porto. June 14, 2016.

Temesi, József. Director, Center for International Higher Education Studies and Vice Rector 1995-2004, Corvinus University of Budapest, Hungary; July 12, 2012.

Tyson, Adam. Acting Director for Strategy and Evaluation, Former Head of UnitC1, Higher Education and Erasmus, Directorate-General Education and Culture. European Commission; April 25, 2012; September 6, 2016.

Vasques, Inês. Office of Director General for Higher Education (Direção-Geral do Ensino Superior), Ministry of Education and Science (Ministério da Educação e Ciência), Government of Portugal, June 1, 2016.

Vázquez, Rashid Mohamed. University Student, Governing Council Member. Universidad de Salamanca, Spain. Correspondence July 2013.

Veiga, Amélia. Researcher, Centre for Research in Higher Education Policies (CIPES). Matosinhos (Porto), Portugal; July 23, 2012; May 29, 2013; June 2, 2016.

Vilén, Jari. EU Ambassador to the Council of Europe (2014-). Ambassador of Finland to Hungary (2007-2012) and to Poland (2012-2014), Member of Finnish Parliament (1999-2007); July 16, 2012.

Official Documents

European Union

European Union. 2016a. The Lisbon Strategy in Short. Available from: https://portal.cor.europa.eu/europe2020/Profiles/Pages/The LisbonStrategyinshort.aspx

European Union. 2016b. Treaty of Lisbon: Taking Europe into the 2st Century." Available from: http://europa.eu/european-union/eu-law/decision-making/treaties_en

European Union. 2014. "Highlights: Multiannual Financial Framework 2014-2020." Available from: http://europa.eu/newsroom/highlights/multiannual-financial-framework-2014-2020/index_en.htm & http://ec.europa.eu/budget/mff/index_en.cfm

European Union: High Level Group on the Modernisation of Higher Education. 2013. *Report to the European Commission: Improving the quality of teaching and learning in Europe's higher education institutions.* Luxembourg: Publications Office of the European Union.

European Stability Mechanism. 2012. European Stability Mechanism (ESM) issues bonds for the recapitalisation of the Spanish banking sector. Press Release No. 03/2012. December 5, 2012.

European Union. 2012. "Research and Innovation." Available from: http://europa.eu/pol/rd/

European Union. 2011a. "The Bologna Process –Towards the European Higher Education Area." Available from: http://ec.europa.eu/education/higher-education/doc1290_en.htm

European Union. 2008. Treaty on the Functioning of the European Union (TFEU), Treaty of Lisbon. *Official Journal of the European Union.* May 9, 2008, C 115.

European Union. 1992. Treaty on European Union (TEU), Treaty of Maastricht.

European Union. 1957. Treaty Establishing the European Economic Community (EEC), Treaty of Rome.

Council of Ministers:
European Council. 2013. "Recommendation for a COUNCIL RECOMMENDATION on Spain's 2013 national reform programme and delivering a Council opinion on Spain's stability programme for 2012-2016" 10656/1/13 19 June 2013.

European Council. 2009. "Council conclusions of 12 May 2009 on a strategic framework for European cooperation in education and training ('ET 2020')" *Official Journal of the European Union*, (2009/C 119/02).

Commission of the European Communities official documents:
European Commission. 2016a. Directorate General for Education and Culture. Available from: http://ec.europa.eu/dgs/education_culture/index_en.htm

European Commission. 2016b. "European Commission: Europe 2020." Available from: http://ec.europa.eu/europe2020/index_en.htm

European Commission. 2016c. Strategic Framework—Education & Training. Available from: http://ec.europa.eu/education/policy/strategic-framework_en

European Commission. 2016d. "Supporting the prevention of radicalisation leading to violent extremism." Communication from the Commission to the European Parliament, the European Council, the European Economic and Social Committee and the Committee of the Regions. COM(2016) 379 final. June 14, 2016.

European Commission. 2016e. Directorate-General for Education and Culture. *Education and Training Monitor.*

European Commission. 2015a. "The Bologna Process—Towards the European Higher Education Area." Updated July 23, 2015. Available from: http://europa.eu/legislation_summaries/education_training_youth/lifelong_learning/c11088_en.htm

European Commission. 2015b. European Semester Thematic Fiche: Tertiary Education Attainment. November 26, 2015.

European Commission. 2014. "Preventing Radicalisation to Terrorism and Violent Extremism: Strengthening the EU's Response." Communication from the Commission to the European Parliament, the European Council, the European Economic and Social Committee and the Committee of the Regions. COM(2013) 941 final. January 15, 2014.

European Commission. 2013a. "European Higher Education in the World." Communication from the Commission to the European Parliament, the European Council, the European Economic and Social

Committee and the Committee of the Regions. COM(2013) 499 final. July 11, 2013.

European Commission. 2013b. "Erasmus+ is the new EU programme for education, training, youth and sport for 2014-2020, starting in January 2014." Available from: http://ec.europa.eu/education/erasmus-plus/index_en.htm

European Commission. 2013c. "History of European co-operation in education" Education and Training. Updated 7 February 2013. Available from: http://ec.europa.eu/education/more-information/former-programmes_en.htm

European Commission. 2013d. Memo: Erasmus Programme in 2011-2012: The Figures Explained. July 8, 2013.

European Commission. 2013e. "Spring 2013 Eurobarometer: A greater dose of optimism." Press Release 23 July 2013. Available from: http://ec.europa.eu/public_opinion/archives/eb/eb79/eb79_en.htm

European Commission. 2013f. "Working together for Europe's young people: A call to action on youth unemployment." Communication from the Commission to the European Parliament, the European Council, the European Economic and Social Committee and the Committee of the Regions. COM(2013) 447 final. June 19, 2013.

European Commission Erasmus Statistics. 2013a. Erasmus+ 2014: Portugal Report. Erasmus+ Country Fact Sheets. Available from: http://ec.europa.eu/education/resources/statistics_en

European Commission Erasmus Statistics. 2013b. Erasmus+ 2014: Spain Report. Erasmus+ Country Fact Sheets. Available from: http://ec.europa.eu/education/resources/statistics_en

European Commission. 2012a. "Erasmus hits new record with 8.5% increase in student exchanges." Press Release IP-12-454_EN. August 5, 2012.

European Commission. 2012b. "Europe 2020 Targets." Available from: http://ec.europa.eu/europe2020/targets/eu-targets/index_en.htm

European Commission. 2012c. FAQ on Erasmus and its budget. Memo 12-906. November 27, 2012.

European Commission. 2012d. "Innovation Union." Available from: http://ec.europa.eu/research/innovation-union/index_en.cfm

European Commission. 2012e. "Investing in European Research: The 3% Objective," European Research Area. Available from: http://ec.europa.eu/research/era/areas/investing/investing_research_en.htm

European Commission. 2012f. "Learning from Each Other to Improve R&I Policies: The Open Method of Coordination." Available from: http://ec.europa.eu/research/era/partnership/coordination/method_of_coordination_en.htm

European Commission. 2012g. Staff Working Document SWD(2012) 373 final. Communication from the Commission. Rethinking education: investing in skills for better socio-economic outcomes. 20 November 2012.

European Commission. 2012h. "The EU averts funding crisis for Erasmus." Press Release. December 12, 2012. Available from: http://ec.europa.eu/education/news/20121212_en.htm

European Commission. 2011. "Supporting growth and jobs—an agenda for the modernisation of Europe's higher education systems." Communication from the Commission to the European Parliament, the Council, the European Economic and Social Committee and the Committee of the Regions. COM 2011 (567) Final. September 20, 2011.

European Commission. 2010a. Investing in Europe's Future: Fifth Report on Economic, Social, and Territorial Cohesion. Report from the Commission.

European Commission. 2010b. "Final Report: For the ExPost Evaluation of the European Social Fund (2000–2006)," Directorate General for Regional Policy, Contract Reference VC/2008/0693, 10 December 2010.

European Commission. 2009. *Report on Progress in Quality Assurance in Higher Education.* Brussels, September 21, 2009, COM(2009) 487 final.

European Commission. 2008. 2008/111/EC, Euratom: Commission Decision of 7 December 2007 establishing the European Research Area Board.

European Commission. 2007a. Green Paper. The European Research Area: New Perspectives {SEC(2007) 412} Brussels, 4 April 2007 COM(2007) 161 final.

European Commission. 2007b. COMMISSION DECISION of 7 December 2007 establishing the European Research Area Board. (2008/111/EC, Euratom).

European Commission. 2000. "Towards a European research area." COM(2000) 6 final. Communication from the Commission to the

Council, the European Parliament, the Economic and Social Committee and the Committee of the Regions. January 18, 2000.

European Commission. 1997. "Towards a Europe of Knowledge." COM (97) 563 final. Communication from the Commission to the Council, the European Parliament, the Economic and Social Committee and the Committee of the Regions. November 12, 1997.

European Parliament:

The Bologna Process: Stocking and Prospects. 2011. Policy Department Structural and Cohesion Policies, Directorate General for Internal Policies. Requested by the European Parliament's Committee on Culture and Education. IP/B/CULT/FWC/2010-001/Lot1/C1/SC1, January 2011.

Brown, Jacqueline and Victoria Joukovskaia. 2008. *The Bologna Process: Member States' Achievements to Date.* Policy Department Structural and Cohesion Policies. European Parliament, April 2008.

Katsavova, Ivana. 2015. European Parliamentary Research Services. *Higher Education in the EU: Approaches, Issues, Trends.* March 2015 - PE 554.169.

Portugal

Portugal: Main Legislation:

Decree-Law 369/2014 of March 18, 2014 (to establish technical degrees)

Ordinance 782/2009 of July 23, 2009 (content of national qualifications framework)

Ministerial Order 29-2008 (for registration of foreign diplomas)

Decree-Law 396/2007 of December 31, 2007 (NQF legal framework)

Decree-Law 369/2007 of November 5, 2007

Decree-Law 341/2007 of October 12, 2007 (recognition of foreign diplomas)

Decree-Law No. 62/2007 of September 10, 2007 (juridical framework)

Decree-Law 276-C/2007 of July 31, 2007 (to establish A3ES quality assurance agency)

Decree-Law 74/2006 of March 24, 2006 (academic degree structure)

Decree-Law 49/2005 of August 30, 2005 (amended the Education System Act of 1986)
Decree-Law 42/2005 (to establish the ECTS)
University Autonomy Act 1988
Decree-Law 46/86 of October 14, 1986 (The Education System Act)
Decree-Law 397/77 of September 17, 1977
Decree-Law 363/75 of July 11, 1975
Decree-Law 61/75 of February 18, 1975
Decree-Law 830/74 of December 31, 1974
Reform Act of July 25, 1973 "Act 5/73" to establish a Binary System of Higher Education

Portuguese Higher Education Resources and Official Publications:
APESP: Associação Portuguesa do Ensino Superior Privada. 2013. Available from: http://www.apesp.pt/
DGES. 2013. Director General for Higher Education (Direção-Geral do Ensino Superior). "FHEQ-Framework for Higher Education Qualification." Ministry of Education of Portugal. Available from: http://www.dges.mctes.pt/DGES/pt/AssuntosDiversos/FHEQ/
Ministry of Science, Technology, and Higher Education. 2010. Report: The Framework for Higher Education Qualifications in Portugal (FHEQ-Portugal). November 2010.
Strategy for Growth, Employment, and Industrial Development 2013-2020. 2013. Governo de Portugal. April 23, 2013. Lisbon, Portugal. Available from: http://www.portugal.gov.pt/media/1056912/20130424%20ECEFI%20apres%20Ing.pdf
Portas, Paulo. 2012. Foreign Minister of Portugal, Speech at Rice University, Houston, Texas. Hosted by Baker Institute for Public Policy; June 7, 2012.

Spain

Spain: Main Legislation:
Real Decreto 1112/2015, de 11 de diciembre, por el que se aprueba el Estatuto del Organismo Autónomo Agencia Nacional de Evaluación de la Calidad y Acreditación (to approve the organizational autonomy of accreditation agency ANECA).

Orden ECD/2654/2015, de 3 de diciembre, por la que se dictan normas de desarrollo y aplicación del Real Decreto 967/2014, de 21 de noviembre, en lo que respecta a los procedimientos para la homologación y declaración de equivalencia de títulos extranjeros de educación superior (to assimilate the equivalencies of foreign degrees in higher education.

Real Decreto 43/2015 de 2 de febrero 2015 por el que se modifica el Real Decreto 1391/2007, de 29 de octubre,por el que se establece la ordenación sobres de las enseñanzas universitarias oficiales, y el Real Decreto 99/2011, de 28 de enero, por el que se regulan las enseñanzas oficiales de doctorado (to modify previous decrees on degree structure).

Ley Orgánica para la Mejora de la Calidad Educativa (LOMCE) (Organic Law for the Improvement of Educational Quality), 2013.

Real Decreto 14/2012, de 20 de abril, de medidas urgentes de racionalización del gasto público en el ámbito educativo (of urgent measures to rationalize public spending in education).

Real Decreto 1027/2011, de 15 de julio, por el que se establece el Marco Español de Cualificaciones para la Educación Superior (to establish the MECES).

Real Decreto 900/2007 de 6 de julio, por el que se crea el Comité para la definición del Marco Español de Cualificaciones para la Educación (to establish the definition of the MECES Spanish and MECU EHEA National Qualifications Frameworks).

LOMLOU: Ley Orgánica de Universidades 4/2007, de 12 de abril, por la que se modifica la Ley Orgánica 6/2001, de 21 de diciembre

Ley Orgánica 2/2006, de 3 de mayo, de Educación.

Real Decreto RD 55/2005 de 21 de enero, por el que se establece la estructura de las enseñanzas universitarias y se regulan los estudios universitarios oficiales de Grado.

Real Decreto1125/2003, de 5 de septiembre, por el que se establece el sistema europea de créditos el sistema de calificaciones en las titulaciones universitarias de carácter oficial y validez en todo el territorio nacional (to establish the ECTS and official university academic degrees valid throughout the country).

Ley Orgánica 5/2002, de 19 de junio, de las Cualificaciones y de la Formación Profesional

LOU: Ley de Ordenación Universitaria (2001), Ley Orgánica 6/2001, de 21 de diciembre, de Universidades. The University Act in Spain.

LRU: Ley de Reforma Universitaria (1983).University Reform Law in Spain.

Spanish Higher Education Resources and Official Publications:
Buisán, Mario. 2013. Trade Commissioner, Embassy of Spain, Consulate in Coral Gables, Florida, USA. Miami-Florida European Union Center of Excellence Conference: Comparative Regional Perspectives on Innovation in Common/Single Markets. Presentation at Florida International University, March 22, 2013.

Calvo-Sotelo and Pablo Campos. 2010. *España, campus de excelencia internacional (Spain: Campus of International Excellence).* Government of Spain, Ministry of Education, Secretary General of Universities.

Conference of Advisors on Social Issues for Spanish Public Universities:
La Conferencia de Consejos Sociales de las Universidades Públicas Españolas. Available from: http://www.ccsup.es/www/

Fundación CYD (Fundación Conocimiento y Desarrollo). 2012. "Resume Ejecutivo." *Informe CYD 2012.* Barcelona, Spain.

LOU Key Reforms
Available from: http://noticias.universia.es/vida-universitaria/reportaje/2007/04/27/651107/claves-reforma-lou.pdf

Ministry of Economy and Competition. 2013. *Spanish Strategy of Science, Technology and Innovation 2013-2020.*

Ministry of Education, Culture, and Sport (*Ministerio de Educación, Cultura, y Deporte*). 2016. *Marco Europeo de Cualificaciones (MECU).* Available from: http://www.mecd.gob.es/educacion-mecd/mc/mecu/mecu.html

Ministry of Education, Culture, and Sport. 2015. *Datos y Cifras del Sistema Universitaria Español, Curso 2015-2016.* Data and Figures of the Spanish University System, School Year 2015-2016.

Ministry of Education, Culture, and Sport. 2014. *Strategy for the Internationalization of Spanish Universities 2015-2020.* Ministry of Education, Internationalisation Working Group. Secretary General of Universities. October 2014.

Ministry of Education, Culture, and Sport. 2013. Conference of Advisors and Commission of Experts. Proposal for the Reform and Improvement of the Spanish University System. February 2013.

Ministry of Education, Culture, and Sport. 2010. *Estrategia Universidad 2015 (University Strategy 2015): The Contribution of Spanish Universities to Socio-Economic Progress* 2010=2015. Ministry of Education: Secretary General of Universities. October 2010. Available from: http://www.educacion.gob.es/docroot/universidad2015/flash/eu2015-ingles/index.html

Spanish Professors' Associations

Available from: http://profesores.universia.es/asociaciones-docentes/asociaciones-docentes/

Spanish Students' Associations

http://universitarios.universia.es/asociaciones-representatividad/asociaciones-estudiantes-universitarios/ Available from: http://faaaa.universia.es/listadoasociaciones.aspx?seccion=Asociaciones#

University Networks and Associations

Available from: http://universidades.universia.es/agrupaciones/redes-y-asociaciones-universitarias/

APPENDIX H:
QUANTITATIVE DATA SOURCES

Tertiary Education Attainment

Eurostat. 2016. Tertiary educational attainment by sex, age group 30-34; Tertiary educational attainment—total. Available from:

http://epp.eurostat.ec.europa.eu/tgm/table.do?tab=table&init=1 &plugin=0&language=en&pcode=t2020_41 Short Description: "The share of the population aged 30-34 years who have successfully completed university or university-like (tertiary-level) education with an education level ISCED 1997 (International Standard Classification of Education) of 5-6. This indicator measures the Europe 2020 strategy's headline target to increase the share of the 30-34 years old having completed tertiary or equivalent education to at least 40% in 2020."

For Austria years 2000-2003, OECD. Education: Key tables from OECD - ISSN 2075-5120 - © OECD. 2010. Tertiary education graduation rates; Percentage of graduates to the population at the typical age of graduation.

Educational Spending as percentage of GDP

Eurostat. 2012. Expenditure on education as % of GDP or public expenditure [educ_figdp]. INDIC_ED. Total public expenditure on education as % of GDP, for all levels of education combined. Available from:

http://epp.eurostat.ec.europa.eu/statistics_explained/index.php/ Educational_expenditure_statistics

Missing data note: All countries for 2010 and 2011 take the previous value for 2009 and 2010. Belgium and Slovenia 2000 take next value for 2001. Malta 2000 and 2001 take the next value for 2002. Romania 2006 takes the value for 2005, and 2008 takes the value for 2007.

R&D as percentage of GDP

Eurostat. 2016. The indicator provided is GERD (Gross domestic expenditure on R&D) as a percentage of GDP. "Research and experimental development (R&D) comprise creative work undertaken on a systematic basis in order to increase the stock of knowledge, including knowledge of man, culture and society and the use of this stock of knowledge to devise new applications" (Frascati Manual, 2002 edition, § 63). Available from:

http://epp.eurostat.ec.europa.eu/tgm/table.do?tab=table&init=1& plugin=0&language=en&pcode=t2020_20

Missing data note: Greece 2000 takes the value for 2001; Greece 2002 takes the average value for 2001 and 2003. Sweden 2000 takes the value for 2001; Sweden 2002 takes the average value for 2001 and 2003.

Trade as percentage of GDP

World Bank. 2016. Trade is the sum of exports and imports of goods and services measured as a share of gross domestic product. Code: NE.TRD.GNFS.ZS. Source: World Bank national accounts data, and OECD National Accounts data files.

Available   from: http://data.worldbank.org/indicator/NE.EXP. GNFS.ZS

Missing data note: For Malta missing the years 2012, 2013, and 2014 take 2011 value.

Employment as percentage of population

World Bank. 2016 Employment to population ratio, 15+, total (%) (modeled ILO estimate). International Labour Organization, Key Indicators of the Labour Market database. Available from: http://data. worldbank.org/indicator/SL.EMP.TOTL.SP.ZS

GDP per capita

World Bank. 2016. GDP per capita, PPP (constant 2011 international $).

GDP per capita based on purchasing power parity (PPP). PPP GDP is gross domestic product converted to international dollars using purchasing power parity rates. An international dollar has the same purchasing power over GDP as the U.S. dollar has in the United States. GDP at purchaser's prices is the sum of gross value added by all resident producers in the economy plus any product taxes and minus any subsidies not included in the value of the products. It is calculated without making deductions for depreciation of fabricated assets or for depletion and degradation of natural resources. Code: NY.GDP.PCAP.PP.KD.

Missing data note: Malta has same values for 2013, 2014, and 2015 (2013 value for missing 2014 and 2015).

Source: World Bank, International Comparison Program database.

Available   from: http://data.worldbank.org/indicator/NY.GDP.
PCAP.PP.KD

Population

World Bank. 2016. Population, total refers to the total population.

(1) United Nations Population Division. World Population Prospects, (2) United Nations Statistical Division. Population and Vital Statistics Report (various years), (3) Census reports and other statistical publications from national statistical offices, (4) Eurostat: Demographic Statistics, (5) Secretariat of the Pacific Community: Statistics and Demography Programme, and (6) U.S. Census Bureau: International Database. Catalog Sources World Development Indicators. Available from: http://data.worldbank.org/indicator/SP.POP.TOTL

REFERENCES

Adelman, C. (2009). *The bologna process for U.S. eyes: Re-learning higher education in the age of convergence* (Institute for Higher Education Policy Report, April 2009). Retrieved from http://files.eric.ed.gov/fulltext/ED504904.pdf.

Adler, E. (1997). Seizing the middle ground: Constructivism in world politics. *European Journal of International Relations, 3,* 319–363.

Adler, E. (2002). Constructivism in international relations. In W. Carlsnaes, T. Risse, & B. A. Simmons (Eds.), *Handbook of international relations* (pp. 95–118). London: Sage.

Allmendinger, J., & Leibfried, S. (2003). Education and the welfare state: The four worlds of competence production. *Journal of European Social Policy, 13*(1), 63–81.

Almunia, J. (2010). *How competitive is the European Union?* (The Global Competitiveness Report). Cologny: World Economic Forum.

Álvarez, P. (2013, April 30). Movilidad sin barreras. *El País.*

Amaral, A., & Neave, G. (2008). On process, progress, success and methodology or the unfolding of the Bologna Process as it appears to two reasonably benign observers. *Higher Education Quarterly, 62*(1/2), 40–62.

Amaro de Matos, João. (2012). Associate Dean for International Affairs. NOVA University School of Business. Lisboa, Portugal. July 24, 2012.

Amaral, A., Tavares, O., & Santos, Cristina. (2013). Higher education reform in Portugal: A historical and comparative perspective of the new legal framework for public universities. *Higher Education Policy, 26,* 5–24.

ANECA. (2013). Fact Sheet. National Agency for Quality Assessment and Accreditation of Spain (ANECA). Madrid.

Anderson, B. (1983). *Imagined communities: Reflections on the origins and spread of nationalism.* London: Verso.

© The Editor(s) (if applicable) and The Author(s) 2017
B. Barrett, *Globalization and Change in Higher Education,*
DOI 10.1007/978-3-319-52368-2

Anderson, K. H., Heyneman, S. P., & Nuraliyeva, N. (2008). The cost of corruption in higher education. *Comparative Education Review, 52*(1), 1–24.

Ardovino, M. (2009). Imagined communities in an integrated Baltic region. *Demokratizatsiya: The Journal of Post-Soviet Democratization* 17(1) (Winter), 5–18.

Artal, P. (2013, July 3). El fin de la investigación en la universidad española. *El País.*

ASEAN. (2013). ASEAN Education Ministers Meeting (ASED). Retrieved from http://www.asean.org/communities/asean-socio-cultural-community/category/asean-education-ministers-meeting-ased.

Athanassopoulou, E. (2007). *United in diversity: European integration and political cultures.* London: I.B. Tauris.

Aunión, J. A. (2010, April 26). Los fallos no están en la reforma de Bolonia, sino en su aplicación. Entrevista: Androulla Vassilliou, Comisaria Europea de Educación. *El País.* Retrieved from http://www.elpais.com/articulo/educacion/fallos/estan/reforma/Bolonia/aplicacion/elpepusocedu/20100426elpepiedu_1/Tes.

Aunión, J. A. (2012, August 22). Tanto Bolonia para esto. *El País.*

Aunión, J. A. (2013, October 8). El PISA de adultos también deja a España a la cola de la OCDE. *El País.* Retrieved from http://sociedad.elpais.com/sociedad/2013/10/07/actualidad/1381178933_752744.html.

Bache, I. (2006). The europeanization of higher education: Markets, politics or learning? *Journal of Common Market Studies, 44*(2), 231–248.

Barcevičius, E., Weishaupt, J., & Zeitlin, J. (2014). *Assessing the Open Method Coordination: Institutional Design and NationalInfluence on EU Social Policy Coordination.* London: Palgrave Macmillan.

Barr, N. (1998). *Economics of the welfare state.* Oxford: Oxford University Press.

Barro, R., & Lee, J.-W. (2001). International data on educational attainment: Updates and implications. *Oxford Economic Papers, 3,* 541–563.

Barro, R., & Lee, J.-W. (2010). International database on human capital.

Berglund, S. (2003). Prospects for the consolidation of democracy in East Central Europe. *Japanese Journal of Political Science, 4*(2), 191–213.

Bhandari, R., & Blumenthal, P. (Eds.). (2010). *International students and global mobility in higher education: National trends and new directions.* New York: Palgrave Macmillan.

Bilefsky, D. (2012, April 28–29). Austerity backlash shakes Europe: Romanian government is latest to fall as anger rises over unpopular cuts. *International Herald Tribune*, p. 3.

Birchfield, V. (2008). *Income inequality in capitalist democracies: The interplay of values and institutions.* University Park: Pennsylvania State University Press.

Blyth, M. (2009). An approach to comparative analysis or a subfield within a subfield: Political economy. In M. Lichbach & A. Zuckerman (Eds.),

Comparative politics: Rationality, culture, and structure (2nd ed.). Cambridge: Cambridge University Press.

Bohle, D., & Greskovits, B. (2007). Neoliberalism, embedded neoliberalism and neocorporatism: Towards transnational capitalism in Central-Eastern Europe. *West European Politics, 30*(3), 443–466.

Boix, C. (2010). Origins and persistence of economic inequality. *Annual Review of Political Science, 13*(1), 489–516.

Bologna Process: Theoretical Considerations on National Conditions for International Policy Convergence. *Higher Education,* 56, 493–510.

Bologna Process. (1998). The Sorbonne Joint Declaration of 25 May 1998: "Joint declaration on harmonization of the architecture of the European higher education system." Ministers of Education of Italy, France, Germany, and the United Kingdom.

Bologna Process Stocktaking. (2005). *Report from a working group appointed by the Bologna Follow-up Group to the Conference of European Ministers Responsible for Higher Education, Bergen, 19–20 May 2005.*

Bologna Process Stocktaking. (2007). *Report from a working group appointed by the Bologna Follow-up Group to the Ministerial Conference in London, May 2007.*

Bologna Process Stocktaking. (2009). See Rauhvargers, Andres, Cynthia Deane, and Wilfried Pauwels.

Bologna Process Independent Assessment. (2010). The First Decade of Working on the European Higher Education Area. Volume 1: Detailed Assessment Report. Retrieved from http://www.ond.vlaanderen.be/hogeronder-wijs/bologna/2010_conference/documents/IndependentAssessment_1_DetailedRept.pdf.

Bologna Process Secretariat. (2016). European Higher Education Area. Retrieved from http://www.ehea.info/.

Bourdieu, P., & Passeron, J.-C. (1977). *Reproduction in education, society, and culture.* London: Sage.

Bridges, D., Jucevičenė, P., Jucevičius, R., McLaughlin, T., & Stankevičiūtė, J. (2007). *Higher education and national development: Universities and societies in transition.* London: Routledge.

Brown, J., & Joukovskaia, V. (2008). *The Bologna Process: Member states' achievements to date.* Policy Department Structural and Cohesion Policies. European Parliament, April.

Byeongju, J., Kejak, M., & Vinogradov, V. (2008). Changing composition of human capital: The Czech Republic, Hungary, and Poland. *Economics of Transition, 16*(2), 247–271.

Cappano, G., & Piattoni, S. (2009). Building up the European higher education area: The struggle between common problems, 'shared' goals and national trajectories. In European Consortium for Political Research Joint Sessions of

Workshops: The Politics of Governance Architectures: Institutions, Power, and Public Policy in the EU Lisbon Treaty.

Carvajal, D. (2004). Socialists gain amid massive rejection of Aznar's party : Voters reshape Spanish politics after terror strikes. *The New York Times*, March. Retrieved from http://www.nytimes.com/2004/03/15/news/15iht-spain_ed3__1.html.

Cerych, L. (1990). Renewal of Central European higher education: Issues and challenges. *European Journal of Education, 25*(4), 351–359.

Charlier, J.-E., & Croché, S. (2008). The Bologna Process: The outcome of competition between Europe and the United States and a stimulus to this competition. *European Education, 39*(4), 10–26.

Checkel, J. T., & Katzenstein, P. J. (Eds.). (2009). *European identity*. Cambridge: Cambridge University Press.

Chislett, W. (2016). *A new course for Spain: Beyond the crisis*. Madrid: El Real Instituto Elcano.

Chizhov, V. (2009). Russia and the European Union: Forming a strategic partnership. *International Affairs (Moscow), 55*(6), 47–52.

Chou, M.-H., & Ravinet, P. (2015). The rise of 'higher education regionalism': An agenda for higher education research. In J. Huisman, H. de Boer, D. Dill, & M. Souto-Otero (Eds.), *Handbook of higher education policy and governance* (pp. 361–378). Houndmills: Palgrave Macmillan.

Cini, M., & Borragán, N. P.-S. (2010). *"Europeanization". Un European Union politics* (3rd ed.). Oxford: Oxford University Press.

Coase, R. H. (1960). The problem of social cost. *The Journal of Law and Economics* 3, 1–44.

Cohen, D., & Soto, M. (2007). Growth and human capital: Good data good results. *Journal of Economic Growth, 12*, 51–76.

Council of Europe. (1954). *European cultural convention. Cunha, Alice. 2012. The European Economic Community's Third Enlargement*. Miami: European Union Center of Excellence EUMA Paper Series.

Curaj, A., Scott, P., Vlasceanu, L., & Wilson, L. (Eds.). (2012). *European higher education at the crossroad: Between the Bologna Process and national reforms. Parts 1 and 2*. Dordrecht: Springer Science+Business Media.

Cyert, R. M., & March, J. G. (1963). *A behavioral theory of the firm*. Englewood Cliffs, NJ: Prentice Hall. Retrieved from http://conventions.coe.int/Treaty/en/Treaties/html/018.htm.

Dahl, R. (1971). *Polyarchy: Participation and opposition*. New Haven, CT: Yale University Press.

Dale, R., & Robertson, S. (2009). Capitalism, modernity and the future of education the new social contract. In T. S. Popkewitz & F. A. Rizvi (Eds.), *Globalization and the study of education*. Chicago: National Society for the Study of Education Yearbook, *108*(2), 111–129.

Dalton, M., & Quinn, E. (2013). Portugal, Ireland get more time to repay. *Wall Street Journal*, Saturday/Sunday, April 13–14, A11.

Darden, K. A. (2009). *Economic liberalism and its rivals: The formation of international institutions among the Post-Soviet states.* Cambridge: Cambridge University Press.

Day, R. (2012). Erasmus future under threat after budget warnings. *Glasgow Journal*, November 7. Retrieved from http://www.journal-online.co.uk/article/9493-erasmus-future-under-threat-after-budget-warnings.

DeBardeleben, J. (Ed). (2008). *The boundaries of EU enlargement: Finding a place for neighbors.* Studies in Central and Eastern Europe, Series Editor: Roger E. Kanet. New York: Palgrave Macmillan.

Delgado, M. S., Henderson, D. J., & Parmeter, C. F. (2011). *Does education matter for economic growth?.* Binghamton: State University of New at Binghamton.

Della Porta, D., & Keating, M. (2008). *Approaches and methodologies in the social sciences: A pluralist perspective.* Cambridge: Cambridge University Press.

Demossier, M. (Ed.). (2007). *The European puzzle: The political structuring of cultural identities at a time of transition.* New York: Berghahn Books.

der Hoek, V. P. (Ed.). (2005). *Handbook of public administration and policy in the European Union.* Boca Raton: Taylor & Francis Group.

DGES. (2013). Director General for Higher Education (Direção-Geral do Ensino Superior). "FHEQ-Framework for Higher Education Qualification." Ministry of Education of Portugal. Retrieved from http://www.dges.mctes.pt/DGES/pt/AssuntosDiversos/FHEQ/.

Diener, E., Helliwell, J. F., & Kahneman, D. (2010). *International differences in well-being.* Oxford: Oxford University Press.

Diário Notícias. (2013). Manifestações: Um milhão e meio protestou contra Governo. March 2, 2013. Retrieved from http://www.dn.pt/inicio/portugal/interior.aspx?content_id=3084470.

Dobbins, Michael, & Knill, Christoph. (2014). *Higher Education Governance and Policy Change in Western Europe.* London: Palgrave Macmillan.

Dorado, A. C. (2012, November 4). En defensa de las universidades públicas. *El País.*

Dullen, S. (2012). Why the Euro crisis threatens the European single market. European Council on Foreign Relations. London: ECFR/64 October 2012.

The Economist. (2013, October 12). The Gated Globe: Special Report World Economy, pp. 1–20.

EHEA Ministerial Conference. (2012). Statement on the Bologna policy forum: Beyond the Bologna Process: Creating and connecting regional and global higher education areas. Retrieved from http://www.ehea.info/Uploads/(1)/Bucharest%20BPF%20Statement.pdf.

Eichengreen, B. (2012). When Currencies Collapse. *Foreign Affairs* Special 90th Anniversary Issue *91*(1), 117–134.

Engel, Steven T. (2005). Rousseau and imagined communities. *Review of Politics, 67*(3), 515–537.

Ertl, H. (2006). "European Union policies in education and training: The Lisbon agenda as a turning point?" *Comparative Education 42*(1), 5–27.

ESIB. 2003. The National Unions of Students in Europe (ESIB) Policy Paper. "*ESIB* and the Bologna Process—*Creating* a European *Higher Education Area for and with students.*" Retrieved from http://www.gencat.cat/diue/doc/doc_33201644_1.pdf.

EU Focus. (2012). The EU's single market at 20: A catalyst for jobs and growth. EU Focus, July 2012. Washington, DC: Delegation of the European Union to the United States.

European Commission. (1997). Towards a Europe of Knowledge. Communication from the Commission tothe Council, the European Parliament, the Economic and Social Committee and the Committee of the Regions. 12 November 1997. COM(97) 563 final.

European Commission. (2007a). Green paper. The European research area: New perspectives {SEC(2007) 412} Brussels, 4 April 2007 COM(2007) 161 final.

European Commission. (2007b). Commission Decision of 7 December 2007 establishing the European Research Area Board. (2008/111/EC, Euratom).

European Commission. (2008). 2008/111/EC, Euratom: Commission decision of 7 December 2007 establishing the European Research Area Board.

European Commission. (2010a). Investing in Europe's future: Fifth report on economic, social, and territorial cohesion. Report from the commission.

European Commission. (2010b). Final report: For the ExPost evaluation of the European social fund (2000–2006). Directorate General for Regional Policy, Contract Reference VC/2008/0693, 10 December.

European Commission. (2012a). Erasmus hits new record with 8.5% increase in student exchanges. Press Release IP-12-454_EN. August 5.

European Commission. (2012b). Europe 2020 Targets. Retrieved from http://ec.europa.eu/europe2020/targets/eu-targets/index_en.htm.

European Commission. (2012c). FAQ on erasmus and its budget. Memo 12-906. November 27.

European Commission. (2012d). Innovation union. Retrieved from http://ec.europa.eu/research/innovation-union/index_en.cfm.

European Commission. (2012e). Investing in European research: The 3% objective. European Research Area. Retrieved from http://ec.europa.eu/research/era/areas/investing/investing_research_en.htm.

European Commission. (2012f). Learning from each other to improve R&I policies: The open method of coordination. Retrieved from http://ec.europa.eu/research/era/partnership/coordination/method_of_coordination_en.htm.

European Commission. (2012g). Staff working document SWD (2012) 373 final. Communication from the commission. Rethinking education: Investing in skills for better socio-economic outcomes. 20 November.

European Commission. (2012h). The EU averts funding crisis for Erasmus. Press Release. December 12. Retrieved from http://ec.europa.eu/education/news/20121212_en.htm.

European Commission. (2013). Working together for Europe's young people: A call to action on youth unemployment. Communication from the Commission to the European Parliament, the European Council, the European Economic and Social Committee and the Committee of the Regions. COM(2013) 447 final. June 19.

European Commission. (2015a). The Bologna Process—towards the European higher education area. Updated July 23, 2015. Retrieved from http://europa.eu/legislation_summaries/education_training_youth/lifelong_learning/c11088_en.htm.

European Commission. (2015b). European Semester Thematic Fiche: Tertiary Education Attainment. November 26, 2015.

European Commission. (2016a). European Commission: Europe 2020. Retrieved from http://ec.europa.eu/europe2020/index_en.htm.

European Commission. (2016b). Strategic framework—education & training. Retrieved from http://ec.europa.eu/education/policy/strategic-framework_en.

European Council. (2009). Council conclusions of 12 May 2009 on a strategic framework for European cooperation in education and training ('ET 2020') *Official Journal of the European Union*, (2009/C 119/02).

European Council. (2013). Recommendation for a Council Recommendation on Spain's 2013 national reform programme and delivering a Council opinion on Spain's stability programme for 2012-2016" 10656/1/13 19 June.

European Journal of Education. (2010). Special issue: Ten years of the Bologna Process." 45(4).

European Stability Mechanism. (2012). European stability mechanism (ESM) issues bonds for the recapitalisation of the Spanish banking sector. Press Release No. 03/2012. December 5.

European Union. (2008). Treaty on the functioning of the European Union (TFEU), Treaty of Lisbon. *Official Journal of the European Union*. May 9, C 115.

European Union. (2011). The Bologna Process—Towards the European higher education area. Retrieved from http://ec.europa.eu/education/higher-education/doc1290_en.htm.

European Union. (2012). Research and innovation. Retrieved from http://europa.eu/pol/rd/.

European Union. (2014). Highlights: Multiannual financial framework 2014–2020. Retrieved from http://europa.eu/newsroom/highlights/multiannual-financial-framework-2014-2020/index_en.htm & http://ec.europa.eu/budget/mff/index_en.cfm.

European Union. (2016). Treaty of Lisbon: Taking Europe into the 21st century." Retrieved from http://europa.eu/european-union/eu-law/decision-making/treaties_en.

Eurostat. (2009). *The Bologna Process in higher education in Europe: Key indicators on social dimension and mobility.* eurostudent.eu.

Eurostat. (2012). European Commission statistics historical database.

Eurostat. (2016). European Commission statistics historical database.

Eurydice: Education, audiovisual and culture executive agency. (2011). Modernisation of higher education in Europe 2011: Funding and the social dimension. Retrieved from http://eacea.ec.europa.eu/education/eurydice/thematic_studies_en.php.

Fargues, P., Demetrios, G. P., Giambattista, S., & Madeleine, S. (2011). Shared challenges and opportunities for EU and US immigration policymakers. European University Institute and Migration Policy Institute Report.

Fishman, R. (2013). How Civil Society Matters in Democratization: Theorizing Iberian Divergence. *Paper prepared forpresentation at the 20th International Conference of Europeanists.*

Friedman, R., & Thiel, M. (Eds.). (2012). *European identity and culture: Narratives of transnational belonging.* London: Ashgate Press.

Fuentes, A. (2009). Raising education outcomes in Spain. *OECD Economics Department Working Papers,* No. 666, OECD Publishing.

Fulge, T., & Vögtle, E. M. (2014). Sweeping change—but does it matter? The Bologna Process and determinants of student mobility. In K. Martens, P. Knodel, & M. Windzio (Eds.), *InternaKtionalization of education policy: A new constellation of statehood in education?.* London: Palgrave Macmillan.

Galder, G., Etxebarrieta, O., & Zulaika, I. (2012, May 18). Bologna: Nunca quisimos tener Razón. *El País.*

Gänzle, S., Meister, S., & King, C. The Bologna process and its impact on higher education at Russia's margins: The case of Kaliningrad. *Higher Education, 57,* 533–547.

García de Cortázar, F. (2013). La destrucción de la enseñanza. Director, Fundación Dos de Mayo, Nación y Libertad, ABC. May 19, 2013.

Gardner, D. (2012, August 15). Spain: Autonomy under fire. Tensions between indebted regions and central government are growing amid the euro crisis. *Financial Times.*

Garrett, G. (1998). Global markets and national politics: Collision course or virtuous cycle? *International Organization, 52(4),* 787–824.

Geertz, C. (1973). *The interpretation of cultures.* New York: Basic Books.

Gellner, E. (1983). *Nations and nationalism*. Ithaca: Cornell University Press.

Gérard, M. (2007). Financing Bologna: Which country will pay for foreign students? *Education Economics, 15*(4), 441–454.

Gerber, A. S., Huber, G. A., Doherty, D., Dowling, C. M., & Ha, S. E. (2010). Personality and political attitudes: Relationships across issue domains and political contexts. *American Political Science Review, 104*(1), 111–133.

Germany, Federal Republic of. (1949). Basic Law for the Federal Republic of Germany. Constitution of the Federal Republic of Germany. Approved on May 8, 1949.

Globalisation, Societies and Education. 2010. Editorial, 8(1), 1–6.

Goedegebuure, L., Kaiser, F., Maassen, P., Meek, L., Van Vught, F., & De Weert, E. (Eds.). (1994). *Higher education policy: An international comparative perspective*. Oxford: Pergamon Press.

Goetz, K., & Wollmann, H. (2001). Governmentalizing central executives in post-communist Europe: A four-country comparison. *Journal of European Public Policy*, 8(6), 864–887.

Gornitzka, Å., & Maassen, P. (2000). Analyzing organizational change in higher education. *Comparative Social Research, 19*, 83–99.

Gornitzka, Å., Kogan, M., & Amaral, A. (Eds.). (2005). *Reform and change in higher education: Analysing policy implementation*. Dordrecht: Springer.

Gornitzka, Å., Kyvik, S., & Stensaker, B. (2005). Implementation analysis in higher education. In Å. Gornitzka, M. Kogan, & A. Amaral (Eds.), *Reform and change in higher education: Analysing policy implementation*. Dordrecht: Springer.

Greif, A. (1998). Historical and comparative institutional analysis. *The New Institutional Economics, 88*(2), 80–84.

Grek, S., & Law, Martin. (2009). A short history of europeanizing education: The new political work of calculating the future. *European Education, 41*(1), 32–54.

Gürüz, K. (2008). *Higher education and international student mobility in the global knowledge economy*. Albany: State University of New York.

Haas, E. B. (1958). *The uniting of Europe: Political, economic, and social forces*. Stanford: Stanford University Press.

Haas, P. M. (1992). Introduction: Epistemic communities and international policy coordination. *International Organization*, 46(1) (Winter), 1–35.

Hall, P. A. (1989). *The political power of economic ideas: Keynesianism across nations*. Princeton: Princeton University Press.

Hamilton, D. S. (2011). *Europe 2020: Competitive or complacent?*. Washington, DC: Center for Transatlantic Relations.

Hatakenaka, S. (2004). *University-industry partnerships in MIT, Cambridge, and Tokyo: Storytelling across boundaries*. New York: RoutledgeFalmer.

Haug, G., & Tauch, C. (2001a). Trends II: Towards the European higher education area: Survey of main reforms from Bologna to Prague. Summary and conclusions: Review of structures and trends in the countries not covered in 1999 in the Trends 1 Report. European Universities Association.

Haug, G., & Tauch, C. (2001b). Trends in learning structures and higher education (II). Follow-up Report prepared for the Salamanca and Prague Conferences of March/May 2001. April 2001.

Helmke, G., & Levitsky, S. (2004). Informal institutions and comparative politics: A research agenda. *Perspectives on Politics*, 2(4), 725–740.

Hervás, M. (2012). La marcha de parados llega a Madrid. ("The march of unemployed arrives to Madrid."). *El País*. July 21.

Heydemann, S. P. (2008). Institutions and economic performance: The use and abuse of culture in new institutional economics. *Studies in Comparative International Development, 43*, 27–52.

Heyneman, S. P. (2009). What is appropriate role for government in education? *Journal of Higher Education Policy, 3*, 135–157.

Heyneman, S. P. (2010). A comment on the changes in higher education in the Post–Soviet union. *European Education*, 42(1) (Spring), 76–87.

Heyneman, S. P. (2011). International trade in education and its discontents: Threats or benefit? *Lifelong Learning in Europe*, XVI(1), 14–18.

Hoareau, C., Ritzen, J., & Marconi, G. (2012). The of university policy for progress in Europe: Policy report. United Nations University UNU–MERIT. December.

Hollis, M., & Smith, S. (1990). *Explaining and understanding international relations*. Oxford: Clarendon Press.

Horvat, P., & Evans, G. (2010). Age, inequality, and reactions to marketization in post-communist Central and Eastern Europe. *European Sociological Review*, first published online July 9. doi:10.1093/esr/jcq033.

Hroch, M. (2007). *Comparative studies in modern European history: Nation, nationalism, social change*. Cambridge: Cambridge University Press.

Huntington, S. P. (1968). *Political order in changing societies*. New Haven: Yale University Press.

International Monetary Fund. (2012a). Fiscal policy and employment in advanced and emerging economies. Report Prepared by the Fiscal Affairs Department. June 15.

International Monetary Fund. (2012b). IMF Country Report No. 12/77. Portugal: Third Review Under the Extended Arrangement and Request for Waiver of Applicability of End-March Performance Criteria—Staff Report; Staff Statement; Press Release on the Executive Board Discussion; and Statement by the Executive Director for Portugal. April.

Iversen, T. (2005). *Capitalism, democracy, and welfare*. Cambridge: Cambridge University Press.

Jablecka, J. (2007). Legitimation of nonpublic higher education in Poland. In S. Slantcheva & D. C. Levy (Eds.), *Private higher education in post-communist Europe*. New York: Palgrave Macmillan.

Jensen, N. (2003). Democratic governance and multinational corporations: Political regimes and inflows of foreign direct investment. *International Organization, 57*(3), 587–616.

Jongbloed, B., Maassen, P., & Neave, G. (Eds.). (2000). *From the eye of the storm: Higher education's changing institutions*. Klewer Academic Publishers.

Joshua, C., Fontanella-Khan, J., & Parker, G. (2012). Growth funds likely target of EU cuts. *Financial Times*, November 22.

Kanet, R. E. (Ed.). (2008). *Identities, nations and politics after communism*. London: Routledge.

Katsavova, I. (2015). European parliamentary research services. *Higher education in the EU: Approaches, issues, trends*. March 2015—PE 554.169.

Kaufmann, D., Kraay, A., & Mastruzzi, M. (2010). The worldwide governance indicators: Methodology and analytical issues (World Bank Policy Research Working Paper No. 5430).

Kirschbaum, S. J. (Ed.). (2007). *Central European history and the European Union: The meaning of Europe*. Studies in Central and Eastern Europe. Series Editors: Roger E. Kanet. New York: Palgrave Macmillan.

Kitschelt, H., Lange, P., Marks, G., & Stephens, J. D. (Eds.). (1999). *Continuity and change in contemporary capitalism*. Cambridge: Cambridge University Press.

Kitschelt, H, Lange, P., Marks, G., & Stephens, J. D. (2001). An asset theory of social policy preferences. *American Political Science Review, 95*(4), 875–893.

Krasner, S. D. (1988). Sovereignty: An institutional perspective. *Comparative Political Studies, 21*, 66–94.

Kwiek, M. (2004). The emergent European educational policies under scrutiny: The Bologna process from a Central European perspective. *European Educational Research Journal, 3*(4), 759–776.

Lake, D. A., & Powell, R. (Eds.). (1999). *Strategic choice and international relations*. Princeton: Princeton University Press.

Laursen, F. (Ed.). (2011). *The making of the EU's Lisbon treaty: The role of member states*. Bruxelles: P.I.E. Peter Lang International Academic Publishers.

Leonard, M. (2011). Four scenarios for the reinvention of Europe. European Council on Foreign Relations. London: ECFR/43 November.

Lichbach, M. I., & Zukerman, A. S. (Eds.). (2009). *Comparative politics: Rationality, culture, and structure* (2nd ed.). Cambridge: Cambridge University Press.

Loomis, S., & Rodriguez, J. (2009). Institutional change and higher education. *Higher Education, 58*(4), 475–489.

Lorca-Susino, M. (2011). Spain and the brain drain in the 21st century. In J. Roy & M. Lorca-Susino (Eds.), *Spain in the European Union the First twenty five years (1986–2011)* (pp. 211–228). Miami: Miami-Florida European Union Center of Excellence.

Maassen, P., & Stensaker, B. (2011). The knowledge triangle, european higher education policy logics and policy implications. *Higher Education, 61*, 757–769.

Macedo, G. (1999). *The European heritage label.* Cambridge: Cambridge University Press.

Magalhães, A. (2013). TRUE policy template. Matosinhos: CIPES Centre for Research on Higher Education Policies (CIPES).

Mankiw, N. G., Romer, D., & Weil, D. N. (2010). A contribution to the empirics of economic growth. *The Quarterly Journal of Economics, 107*(2), 407–437.

Mares, I. (2009). The comparative political economy of the welfare state. In Irving, M. L., & Zuckerman, A. (Eds.). *Comparative politics: Rationality, culture, and structure* (2nd ed). Cambridge: Cambridge University Press.

Marko, J., & Unger, H. (2010). *Research and tertiary education in Central and South-East Europe: Developments, structures and perspectives in the light of EU integration.* Bolzano: European Academy.

Matei, Liviu. (2012a). Chief Operating Officer and Professor of Public Policy, Central European University, Budapest, Hungary. July 18, 2012.

Matei, L. (2012b). "A policy gap" financing in the European higher education area. In Curaj, A., Scott, P., Vlasceanu, L., & Wilson, L. (Eds.), *European higher education at the crossroad: Between the bologna process and national reforms. Parts 1 and 2.* Dordrecht: Springer Science+Business Media.

McCormick, J. (2008). *Understanding the European Union* (4th ed.). New York: Palgrave Macmillan.

McCormick, J. (2012). What has the European Union ever done for us? In J. Roy (Ed.), *The state of the union(s): The Eurozone crisis, comparative regional integration and the EU model* (pp. 35–44). Miami: Miami-Florida European Union Center of Excellence.

McDonnell, L. M., MT, P., & Benjamin, Roger (Eds.). (1992). *Rediscovering the democratic purposes of education.* Lawrence: University Press of Kansas.

McGrath, S. (2000). Education and development: Thirty years of continuity and change. *International Journal of Educational Development, 30*(6), 537–543.

McNamara, K. R. (2005). Constructing Europe: Insights from historical sociology. *Comparative European Politics, 8*(1), 127–142.

McNamara, K. (2015). *The politics of everyday Europe.* Oxford: Oxford University Press.

Ministry of Economy and Competition. (2013). *Spanish strategy of science, technology and innovation 2013–2020.*

Ministry of Education, Culture, and Sport. (2013). Conference of Advisors and Commission of Experts. Proposal for the Reform and Improvement of the Spanish University System. February 2013.

Ministry of Education, Culture, and Sport (*Ministerio de Educación, Cultura, y Deporte*). (2016). *Marco Europeo de Cualificaciones (MECU)*. Government of Spain. Retrieved from http://www.mecd.gob.es/educacion-mecd/mc/mecu/mecu.html.

Ministry of Education, Culture, and Sport. (2010). *Estrategia Universidad 2015 (University Strategy 2015): The Contribution of Spanish Universities to Socio-Economic Progress* 2010–2015. Ministry of Education: Secretary General of Universities. October 2010. Available from: http://www.educacion.gob.es/docroot/universidad2015/flash/eu2015-ingles/index.html

Ministry of Science, Technology, and Higher Education. (2010). Report: The framework for higher education qualifications in Portugal (FHEQ-Portugal).

Molina, I. (2007). Hacia un Espacio Europeo de Educación Superior. Fundación Alternativas: Seminarios y Jornadas 40/2007. Murcia, 5 Febrero.

Montavlo, G. J. (2013). *Formación y empleo de los graduados de enseñanza superior en España y en Europa*. Valencia: Instituto Valenciano de Investigaciones Económicas (IVIE).

Mora, J.-G., & Vidal, J. (2005). Two Decades of Change in Spanish Universities: Learning the Hard Way. In Åse Gornitzka etal. (Eds.), *Reform and Change in Higher Education* (pp. 135–152). Dordrecht: Springer.

Mora, J.-G., (2013, June 14). Universidades y empleo. *El País*.

Moravcsik, A. (1994). Why the European Union strengthens the state: Domestic politics and international policy cooperation. Center for European Studies Working Paper Series #52, Harvard University School of Government.

Moravcsik, A. (1997). Taking preferences seriously: A liberal theory of international politics. *International Organization, 54*(4), 513–553.

Moravcsik, A. (2005). The European constitutional compromise and the neo-functionalist legacy. *Journal of European Public Policy, 12*, 349–389.

Mundell, I. (2013, January 24). EU rolls out university ranking. *European Voice*. Retrieved from http://www.europeanvoice.com/article/imported/eu-rolls-out-university-ranking/76231.aspx.

Neave, G. (2012). Scientific Director, centre for research in higher education policies (CIPES), Matosinhos (Porto), Portugal; July 23.

Neave, G., & Veiga, A. (2012). The Bologna Process: Inception, 'take up' and familiarity. *Higher Education*.

Neave, G., Blückert, K., & Nybom, T. (2006). *The European research university: An historical parenthesis?*. New York: Palgrave Macmillan.

Nye, J. S. (2004). *Soft power: The means to success in world politics*. New York: PublicAffairs.

Odell, J. (2001). Case study methods in international political economy. *International Studies Perspectives, 2,* 161–176.

Olsen, J. P. (2007). The institutional dynamics of the European university. In P. Maassen & J. P. Olsen (Eds.), *University dynamics and European integration.* Dordrecht: Springer.

Olsen, J. (2009a). "Change and continuity: an institutional approach to institutions of democratic government." *European Political Science Review, 1*(1), 3–32.

Olsen, J. (2009b). "Democratic Government, Institutional Autonomy and the Dynamics of Change," *Working Paper No. 01,* January 2009 ARENA Working Paper. Available from: http://www.sv.uio.no/arena/english/research/publications/arena-publications/workingpapers/.

Olsen, J. P., & Guy Peters, B. (1996). Introduction: Learning from experience? In J. P. Olsen & B. G. Peters (Eds.), *Lessons from experience: Experiential learning from administrative reform in eight democracies.* Oslo: Scandinavian University Press.

Orenstein, M. A. (2015). Reassessing the neo-liberal development model in Central and Eastern Europe. In V. A. Schmidt & M. Thatcher (Eds.), *Resilient liberalism in Europe's political economy.* Cambridge: Cambridge University Press.

Organization for Economic Cooperation and Development (OECD). (2008). *Tertiary education for the knowledge society.* OECD Report.

Organization for Economic Cooperation and Development (OECD). (2010a). *Education at a glance.* OECD Report.

Organization for Economic Cooperation and Development (OECD). (2010b). *Employment outlook.* OECD Report.

Organization for Economic Cooperation and Development (OECD). (2011a). *Divided we stand: Why inequality keeps rising.* OECD Report.

Organization for Economic Cooperation and Development (OECD). (2011b). *Tackling the challenges of migration: Regulation, integration, and development.* OECD Report.

Organization for Economic Cooperation and Development (OECD). (2012). Education indicators in focus—2012/05 (May).

Ortega y Gasset, J. (1910). La pedagogía social como programa político. *Lecture given to the 'El Sitio' Society in Bilbao,* (1), 503–521 on March 12.

Ostrom, E. (1986). An agenda for the study of institution. *Public Choice, 48,* 3–25.

Ostrom, E. (1990). Governing the Commons: The Evolution of Institutions for Collective Action. New York: Cambridge University Press.

Ostrom, E. (2005). *Understanding institutional diversity.* Princeton: Princeton University Press.

Ostrom, E. (2007). Institutional rational choice: An assessment of the institutional analysis and development framework. In P. A. Sabatier (Ed.), *Theories of the policy process* (pp. 21–64). Cambridge: Westview Press.

Papatsiba, V. (2006). Making higher education more European though student mobility? Revisiting EU initiatives in the context of the Bologna Process. *Comparative Education, 42*(1), 93–111.

Pastor, R. (2011). *The North American idea: A vision of a continental future.* Oxford: Oxford University Press.

Peet, R., & Hartwick, E. (2009). *Theories of development: Contentions, arguments, alternatives* (2nd ed.). New York: Guilford Press.

Peña, P. S., & Sole-Olle, A. (2009). *Evaluating of the effects of decentralization on educational outcomes in Spain.* Institut d'Economia d'Barcelona: Universitat de Barcelona.

Pereira, Á.S., & Lains, P. (2012). From an Agrarian Society to a Knowledge Economy?: The Rising Importance of Educationto the Portuguese Economy, 1950-2009. In Neave, Guy and Alberto Amaral (Eds.). 2012. *Higher Education in Portugal 1974–2009: A Nation, a Generation* (pp. 109–134). Dordrecht: Springer.

Peters, B. G. (1999). *Institutional theory in political science: The new institutionalism.* London: Pinter.

Pierson, P. (Ed.). (2001). *The new politics of the welfare state.* Oxford: Oxford University Press.

Pierson, P. (2005). The study of policy development. *Journal of Policy History, 17*(1), 34–51.

Pollack, M. A. (2009). The new institutionalism and European integration. In A. Wiener & T. Diez (Eds.), *European integration theory* (2nd ed., pp. 125–143). Oxford: Oxford University Press.

Porteiro, C. (2012). Interview with Xavier Prats, Director General of Education and Culture at the European Commission in Brussels, Belgium. "La crisis exacerba problemas que ya estaban presentes en el sistema educativo." September 11, 2012.

Portela, M., Sa, C., Alexandre, F., & Cardoso, A. R. (2009). Perceptions of the Bologna Process: What do students' choices reveal? *Higher Education, 58,* 465–474.

Portugal, Government of. (2010). Ministry of Science, Technology, and Education. The Framework for Higher Education Qualifications in Portugal (FHEQ-Portugal). November 2010.

Powell, W. W., & DiMaggio, P. J. (2001). *The new institutionalism in organizational analysis.* Chicago: University of Chicago Press.

Prügl, E., & Thiel, M. (2009). *Diversity in the European Union.* New York: Palgrave Macmillan.

Putnam, R. D. (1988). Diplomacy and domestic politics: The logic of two-level games. *International Organization,* 42(3) (Summer), 427–460.

Rachman, G. (2012, April 9). Europe has yet to make Europeans. *Financial Times.*

Radaelli, C. M., & Schmidt, V. A. (2005). *Discourse and policy change in Europe.* New York: Routledge.

Raivio, K. (2008). University reform—A prerequisite for success of knowledge-based economy? In Mazza, C., Quattrone, P., & Riccaboni, A. (Eds.), *European Universities in transition: Issues, models, and cases.* Northampton: Edward Elgar Publishing Limited, viii–xviii.

Raunio, T. (2011). The changing world of EU governance. *International Studies Review, 13,* 314–317.

Ravinet, P. (2006). When constraining links emerge from loose cooperation: Mechanisms of involvement and building of a follow up structure in the Bologna Process. Report for the third international conference *Euredocs,* University of Kassel.

Rehn, O. (2012, August 13). How we'll build European Monetary Union 2.0. *Wall Street Journal.*

Reichert, S., & Haug, G. (2003). Trends 2003: Progress towards the European higher education area. Bologna four years after: Steps toward sustainable reform of higher education in Europe. European Universities Association and European Commission.

Rodin, S. (2009). Higher education reform in search of Bologna. *Politička misao, 46*(5), 21–38.

Rodríguez-Pose, A., & Tselios, V. (2009). Education and income inequality in the regions of the European Union. *Journal of Regional Science, 49*(3), 411–437.

Rodrik, D. (2007). *One economics, many recipes: Globalization, institutions, and economic growth.* Princeton: Princeton University Press.

Rosamond, B. (2000). *Theories of European integration.* New York: St. Martin's Press.

Roy, J. (2006). The challenge of EU enlargement. In J. Roy & R. Domínguez (Eds.), *Towards the completion of Europe: Analysis and perspectives of the New European enlargement.* Miami: Miami-Florida European Union Center of Excellence.

Roy, J. (Ed.). (2012). *The state of the Union(s): The Eurozone crisis, comparative regional integration and the EU model.* Miami: Miami-Florida European Union Center of Excellence.

Roy, J., & Domínguez, R. (Eds.). (2009). *Lisbon fado: The European Union under reform.* Miami: Miami-Florida European Union Center of Excellence.

Roy, J., & Lorca-Susino, M. (Eds.). (2011). *Spain in the European Union: The first twenty-five years (1986–2011).* Miami: Miami-Florida European Union Center of Excellence.

Royo, S. (2011). Lessons from Portugal and Spain in the EU after 25 Years: The challenges of economic reforms. In J. Roy & M. Lorca-Susino (Eds.), *Spain in the European Union: The first twenty-five years* (pp. 1986–2011). Miami: Miami-Florida International European Union Center.

Russett, B. (1993). *Grasping the democratic peace: Principle for a post-cold war world.* Princeton: Princeton University Press.

Sabatier, P. A. (2005). Policy implementation to policy change: A personal odyssey. In Å. Gornitzka, M. Kogan, & A. Amaral (Eds.), *Reform and change in higher education: Analysing policy implementation* (pp. 17–34). Dordrecht: Springer.

Sabatier, P. A., & Weible, C.M. (2007). The advocacy coalition framework. In P. A. Sabatier (Ed.), *Theories of the policy process* (pp. 189–220). Cambridge: Westview Press.

Sáinz González, J. (2016). Secretarío General de Universidades. Ministerio de Educaciön, Cultura, y Deporte (MECD). Government of Spain. May 30, 2016.

Sandholtz, W., & Sweet, A. S. (1998). *European integration and supranational governance.* Oxford: Oxford University Press.

Sassatelli, M. (2002). Imagined Europe: The shaping of a European cultural identity through EU cultural policy. *European Journal of Social Theory, 5*(4), 435–451.

Schmidt, V. A. (2005). Democracy in Europe: The impact of European integration. *Perspectives on Politics, 3*(4), 761–779.

Schmidt, V. A. (2006). *Democracy in Europe: The EU and national polities.* Oxford: Oxford University Press.

Schmidt, V. A. (2008). Discursive institutionalism: The explanatory power of ideas and discourse. *Annual Review of Political Science, 11*, 303–326.

Schmidt, V. A. (2009a). Re-Envisioning the European Union: Identity, democracy, economy. *Journal of Common Market Studies, 47*, 17–42.

Schmidt, V. (2009b). The EU and its Member States: From Bottom Up to Top Down. In David Phinnemore & Alex Warleigh-Lack (Eds.). *Reflections on European Integration: 50 Years of the Treaty of Rome.* (pp. 194–211). London: Palgrave Macmillan.

Selznick, P. (1996). Institutionalism 'old' and 'new'. *Administrative Science Quarterly, 41*, 270–277.

Sevillano, E. (2013,September 16). Titulaciones novedosas: diferenciarse o morir. *El País.*

Sil, R., & Katzenstein, P. (2010). *Beyond paradigms: Analytic eclecticism in the study of world politics.* New York: Palgrave Macmillan.

Simmons, B., & Elkins, Z. (2004). The Globalization of Liberalization: Policy Diffusion in the International Political Economy. *American Political Science Review*, *98*(1), 171–189.

Sin, C. (2012). Academic understandings of and responses to Bologna: A three-country perspective. *European Journal of Education*, *47*(3), 392–404.

Sin, C., Veiga, A., & Amaral, A. (2016). *European Policy implementation and higher education analyzing the Bologna Process*. London: Palgrave Macmillan.

Skidelsky, R. (2012). The future of globalisation in the light of the economic collapse of 2008 for *A New Era of Geo-economics: Assessing the Interplay of Economic and Political Risk*. IISS Seminar, March, 23–25.

Slantcheva, S., & Levy, D. C. (Eds.). (2007). *Private higher education in post-communist Europe*. New York: Palgrave Macmillan.

Smith, D. G. (2012). German universities 'share blame' for problems, *Speigel Online, International*: The World from Berlin. August 15, 2012. Retrieved from http://www.spiegel.de/international/germany/press-review-on-bologna-process-education-reforms-a-850185.html.

Sørensen, M. P., Carter B., & Mitchell Y. (2016). Excellence in the knowledge-based economy: From scientific to research excellence. *European Journal of Higher Education*, *6* (3), 217–236.

Steiner-Khamsi, G. (2010). The politics and economics of comparison. *Comparative Education Review*, 54(3), 323–342.

Stensaker, B., Välimaa, J., & Sarrico, C. (Eds.). (2011). *Managing reform in universities. The dynamics of culture, identity and organizational change*. New York: Palgrave Macmillan.

Streeck, W., & Thelen, K. (2005). *Beyond continuity: Institutional change in advanced political economies*. Oxford: Oxford University Press.

Streitwieser, B. (Ed.). (2014). *Internationalisation of higher education and global mobility*. Oxford: Syposium Books.

Teague, P. (2001). Deliberative Governance and EU Social Policy. *European Journal of Industrial Relations*, *7*(1), 7–26.

Thiel, M. (2011). *The limits of transnationalism: Collective identities and EU integration*. New York: Palgrave Macmillan.

Thiel, M. (2012). 'European identity' in the 21st century: Moving from external marker to internalized practice. In J. Roy (Ed.), *The state of the union(s): The Eurozone crisis, comparative regional integration and the EU model* (pp. 23–44). Miami: Miami-Florida European Union Center of Excellence.

Tilak, J. B. G. (2008). Higher education: A public good or a commodity for trade? *Prospects*, *38*, 449–466.

Triadó, I., Xavier, M., Meritxell Estebanell Minguell, M., Dolors Márquez Cebrián, & Ignacio del Corrall Manuel de Villena. (2013). Identificación del perfil competencial docente en educación superior. Barcelona: Universitat de Barcelona, Institut de Ciències de l'Educació.

Tyson, A. (2016). Acting Director for Strategy, Directorate-General Education, Youth, Sport and Culture. European Commission; April 25, 2012; September 6, 2016.

Ulnicane, I. (2016). Research and innovation as sources of renewed growth? EU policy responses to the crisis. *Journal of European Integration, 38*(3), 327–341.

U-Multirank. (2013). The multidimensional ranking of higher education institutions. Retrieved from http://www.u-multirank.eu/.

UNCTAD. (2013). *World investment report 2013.* Geneva: United Nations Conference on Trade and Development.

UNESCO. (2016). *Evaluation of UNESCO's regional conventions on the recognition of qualifications in higher education.* Internal Oversight Service IOS/ EVS/PI/149. Evaluation Office, June.

Universia Portugal. (2011). Comissão Europeia elogia Portugal como bom aluno. July 14.

U.S. Chamber of Commerce. (2013). Issues: Postsecondary education policy. Retrieved from http://www.uschamber.com/issues/education/postsecondaryed.

Vallespín, I. (2013, July 15). Especializado sí, pero con bagaje. *El País.*

Vázquez, R. M. (2013). University Student, Governing Council Member. Universidad de Salamanca, Spain. Correspondence July 2013.

Vegas, E., & Coffin, C. (2015). When education expenditures matter: An empirical analysis of recent international data. *Comparative Education Review, 59*(2), 289–304.

Veiga, A. (2012). Bologna and globalisation: Drivers of reforms on European higher education. In J. Ruiz Flores, Sergio, L., Sandoval, A., José Antonio Ramírez Díaz (Eds.), *Región y Globalización. Articulación social de los mercados laborales* (pp. 138–160). Editorial Académica Española.

Veiga, A., & Neave, G. (2015). Managing the dynamics of the Bologna reforms: How institutional actors re-construct the policy framework. *Education Policy Analysis Archives, 23*(59).

Veugelers, R. (2011). A policy agenda for improving access to higher education in the EU. European Expert Network on Economics of Education (EENEE) Analytical Report No. 9 Prepared for the European Commission, March 2011.

Vögtle, E. M., Knill, C., & Dobbins, M. (2010). To what extent does transnational communication drive cross-national policy convergence? The impact of the Bologna Process on domestic higher education policies. *Higher Education, 61,* 77–94.

Vught, V., & Frans, A. (1989). *Governmental strategies and innovation in higher education.*, Higher Education Policy Series London: Jessica Kingsley Publishers.

Wall, D. (2012, August 21). Finland calls for deeper EU integration. *Wall Street Journal.*

Wise, P. (2007, July 2). Lisbon leads the union while lagging in performance leagues. *Financial Times.*

Wise, P. (2013, April 5). Portugal court rules against austerity. *Financial Times.*

World Economic Forum. (2015). *The Global Competitiveness Report 2015–2016.* Cologny: World Economic Forum Center for Global Competitiveness and Performance.

World Economic Forum. (2016). *The Future of Jobs: Employment, Skills and Workforce Strategy for the Fourth Industrial Revolution.* Cologny: World Economic Forum.

About the Author

Sarah Austin @ Magnolia Portraits

Beverly Barrett, Ph.D. is an international policy specialist, educator, and researcher. With a focus on institutional change and public policy, she researches regional integration through higher education reform as well as international trade and governance. Dr. Barrett earned her doctorate in International Studies at the University of Miami in Florida while serving in a fellowship with the European Union Center of Excellence. She completed her B.S. (cum laude) in Human and Organizational Development at Vanderbilt University. Proficient in Spanish, Italian, and French, she studied at the Universidad Complutense in Madrid, Spain, while at Vanderbilt. In the M.A. program at Johns Hopkins University School of Advanced International Studies (SAIS) in Bologna, Italy, and Washington, D.C., she specialized in International Economics and Foreign Policy. Dr. Barrett's background includes service in public affairs with the U.S. House of Representatives, the White House Office of Cabinet Affairs, and the U.S. Department of State in Helsinki, Finland. Additionally, she served as Program Director with Literacy Texas and as Public Affairs Representative with the Houston Branch of the Federal Reserve Bank of Dallas. Presently, she is a lecturer in Global Studies at the Bauer College of Business and at the Hobby School of Public Affairs at the University of Houston.

© The Editor(s) (if applicable) and The Author(s) 2017
B. Barrett, *Globalization and Change in Higher Education*,
DOI 10.1007/978-3-319-52368-2

INDEX

© The Editor(s) (if applicable) and The Author(s) 2017   305
B. Barrett, *Globalization and Change in Higher Education*,
DOI 10.1007/978-3-319-52368-2

CPSIA information can be obtained
at www.ICGtesting.com
Printed in the USA
LVHW081631150522
718813LV00006B/398